63- 2385

THE NOBLER PLEASURE

Dryden's Comedy in Theory and Practice

By

FRANK HARPER MOORE

Chapel Hill

THE UNIVERSITY OF NORTH CAROLINA PRESS

To Dougald MacMillan

I am grateful to the committee of the Faculty Research and Professional Development Fund of North Carolina State College for a grant to aid in the publication of this book. I should also like to thank the Ford Foundation for a grant extended through its program for assisting American university presses in the publication of works in the humanities and the social sciences.

CONTENTS

THE NOBLER PLEASURE

Dryden's Comedy in Theory and Practice

I. INTRODUCTION

WHEN THE Restoration of King Charles II in 1660 brought about the restoration of public theaters, which had been proscribed under the Commonwealth, two companies of actors were chartered, the King's Company and the Duke of York's Company. In February, 1663, the King's Company performed a comedy, *The Wild Gallant*, written by John Dryden, then a young man of thirty-two who was probably best known as the author of a poem in praise of Oliver Cromwell and two in praise of Charles II. Thirty-one years later, in January, 1694, the United Company of actors (the King's Company, after a period of hard times, had in 1682 merged with the Duke's Company) produced Dryden's last play, *Love Triumphant*, a tragicomedy. By then Dryden had become famous as poet, dramatist, and critic. He died in 1700.

Dryden wrote or helped write twenty-seven plays. Of these, thirteen are comedies or tragicomedies, and some of the others contain comic episodes. Many of the critical works which have earned him his reputation as the first great English critic are concerned with drama, and much of the dramatic criticism has to do with comedy.

The professional writer in Dryden's time found the writing of plays a far better means of making money and building a reputation than the writing of dramatic criticism. No doubt Dryden's critical writing was partly motivated by a genuine interest in drama; no doubt he hoped to gain some reputation and profit by publishing it; but his main concern as a dramatic critic was his own work as playwright. He wished to work out a theoretical basis for the writing of successful plays; and he wished to justify those plays to the public. Nearly all of his important pieces of dramatic criticism were first published along with one or another of his plays, and in his criticism he repeatedly refers to his plays.

Although Dryden's theory and practice of comedy would seem to be a promising subject for investigation, very little has hitherto been done with it. Indeed, Dryden's work as a comic dramatist has in general been disparaged and neglected. Nearly all of the critical discussions of his comedies, favorable as well as unfavorable, are brief and incidental to treatments of other subjects—usually Dryden's life and works, or Restoration drama. And although some authorities have praised Dryden's comedies,[1] and some have seen his work as an important factor in the shaping of Restoration comedy,[2] still widely current is the traditional view that as a writer of comedy he was a hack who catered ignobly to the low and capricious tastes of his audience.

Eighteenth-century critics showed moderation in condemning him. The *Biographia Dramatica,* for example, admitted the indecency of his plays, but excused Dryden on the grounds that his necessities obliged him to cater to the depraved town, and added that Dryden's "fair confession . . . of his unfitness for the writing of comedy (and his comic pieces it is that have been the most severely handled by the critics) would, one might imagine, have been sufficient to silence the clamour of that snarling band."[3] *The Dramatic Censor* assumed a similar position, but used stronger terms: "Notwithstanding there are some well imagined whimsical characters in his comic writings, the detestable licentiousness with which they are loaded renders them obnoxious . . . it seems Dryden's peculiar misfortune to have written in a reign when vice was patronized by the highest authority."[4]

Dr. Johnson's judgment, more thoughtful and original than those of other eighteenth-century critics, was on the whole derogatory: "In comedy, for which he professes himself not naturally qualified, the mirth which he excites will perhaps not be found so much to arise from any original humour or peculiarity of character nicely distinguished and diligently pursued, as from incidents and circumstances, artifices and surprises; from jests of action rather than of sentiment. What he had of humourous or passionate, he seems to have had not from nature, but from other poets; if not always as a plagiary, at least as an imitator."[5]

Nineteenth-century critics expressed themselves much more forcibly. Hazlitt said, "Dryden's comedies have all the point that there is in ribaldry, and all the humour that there is in extravagance. I am sorry I can say nothing better of them. He was not at home in this kind of writing, of which he was himself conscious."[6] An anonymous reviewer succinctly observed, "Of the comedies of Dryden we have said nothing, and all we shall say is this, that they are forced and exaggerated exhibitions of an attempt at comic wit, wrung from a brain which, being ill adapted for a successful effort, took refuge in obscenity."[7]

According to Macaulay, Dryden "was utterly destitute of the power of exhibiting real human beings." His "comic characters are without mixture, loathsome and despicable." His tragicomedies are particularly absurd, because in them "the angels and the baboons" are juxtaposed. Since he could not create character, "in his comedies he supplied its place, sometimes by wit, but more frequently by intrigue. . . . He thus succeeded at least in making these pieces very amusing."[8] W. D. Christie charged that Dryden, not only in his comedies but in his other works, "pandered to low tastes by coarse language and indecent ideas . . . showing . . . a prurient love of the indecent,

which is a blot on his character."[9] J. C. Collins said that
Dryden, unfitted for the composition of comedy, had no
eye for its subtleties, but provided "bustle," "intrigue,"
"piquant wit," and "obscenity" for "a profligate court" and
a "debased and licentious mob."[10]

The trend of unfavorable criticism continued in the
present century, and Dryden's criticism as well as his comedies came in for abuse. Dryden's "dicta on dramatic
theory" were charged with "hopeless shallowness and inconsistency," and it was held that his plays manifest "the
same lack of depth and insight."[11] It was said that Dryden
"was not dowered with a true sense of comedy, more than
once expressing his contempt for it," but was guided by "an
unerring sense for changes in public taste."[12] Dryden wrote
plays to make money, it was said, and "this was unfortu-
nate, as he knew himself, for he had hardly any real
dramatic power. . . . Furthermore, the coarseness of the
stage encouraged Dryden's worst tendency."[13] Dryden's
own remarks were quoted as proof that he had no talent
for comedy, and he was said to be "the least original"
comic dramatist of his period. His critical prefaces and
dedications were described as "occasional pieces in support of whatever their author might be doing at the moment."[14]

The current of adverse criticism weakened somewhat
in subsequent decades; yet we find that an otherwise excellent critical study of Dryden, published in 1950, contains
only one paragraph on Dryden's comedies, a paragraph
beginning, "I do not propose to speak of his Comedies as
he thought little of them."[15]

Partly responsible for this current of adverse criticism
are two of Dryden's contemporaries. In 1691 Gerard
Langbaine accused him of wholesale plagiarism; in 1698
Jeremy Collier accused him of immorality and profaneness.
But, curiously enough, Dryden himself is probably chiefly

responsible. He often made unflattering comments on his work as comic dramatist. He once said that he wrote comedies only to please the public, not to enhance his literary reputation. Several times he wrote of comedy as a "low" genre. He said that he lacked aptitude for the writing of comedy and that the "discouragements" of writing for the stage gave him a "loathing" for the task. And more than once he acknowledged and apologized for the indecency of his writings. As may be seen in the material quoted above, many of the critics who deplore Dryden's comedies reinforce their judgment by citing his own poor opinion of them. Of course Dryden's writings also include other passages in which he defends, and even praises, his comedies; but usually the critics either dismiss these passages as insincere or fail to mention them at all. In still other passages Dryden discusses comedy without alluding to his own works. These passages are held to be inconsistent with his practice. Moreover, it is sometimes charged that his dramatic criticism is inconsistent within itself.

All of this seems a little hard on Dryden. Certainly there is good reason for taking a much kinder view of his activities as a writer and critic of comedy. The charge that he wrote his comedies to make money by pleasing the audience is after all not a very grave one. The doctrine of pleasure as an end of literature has a highly respectable ancestry, and even dramatists must live. Dryden's view of comedy as a "low" genre is not peculiar to him; it is a conventional dogma stemming from Aristotle.

His attitude towards comedy was not always disapproving. In the *Essay of Dramatic Poesy,* his most famous piece of dramatic criticism, he analyzed not a tragedy but a comedy, Jonson's *Epicoene,* as "the pattern of a perfect play." His statement that in writing his comedies he aimed solely at profit and cared nothing for reputation is counter-

balanced by a subsequent statement, made in the dedication of his tragicomedy *The Spanish Friar*. Having called
attention to the "care and pains" he has bestowed on the
play, he continues: "Few good pictures have been finished
at one sitting; neither can a true just play, which is to bear
the test of ages, be produced at a heat. . . . For my own
part . . . I dare venture nothing without a strict examination; and am as much ashamed to put a loose indigested
play upon the public, as I should be to offer brass money
in a payment; for though it should be taken (as it is too
often on the stage) . . . a judicious reader will discover,
in his closet, that trashy stuff, whose glittering deceived
him in the action."

The celebrated passage in the preface to *Don Sebastian*
in which Dryden expresses loathing for the discouraging
task of writing for the stage needs to be seen in the light of
his circumstances at the time. When he wrote it, early in
1690, he was an old man in a precarious financial condition. The Revolution of 1688 had cost him his pension;
his despised adversary Shadwell had supplanted him as
Poet Laureate; though he still had a few influential friends,
he had lost most of his standing at Court; and, just at this
time when circumstances forced him to rely heavily on income from his plays, mismanagement and dissension in the
United Company (for which he was then writing) reduced
his chances of success.[16] The most striking feature of the
preface to *Don Sebastian* is not the statement of Dryden's
discouragement; it is the subsequent indication that Dryden took pains with and was proud of the play he wrote
under such depressing conditions.

The charge that Dryden plagiarized is unwarranted.
Dryden, like Shakespeare, often used borrowed material
in his plays, but his handling of his sources is sufficiently
original to exempt him from the charge of plagiarism or
slavish imitation. Ned Bliss Allen, after a careful study

of the sources and the alleged sources of Dryden's comedies (including those cited by Langbaine), concludes that although Dryden indeed borrowed widely, he extensively altered what he borrowed, so that "his comedies . . . are still his own."[17]

Jeremy Collier, in censuring the immorality and profaneness of the English stage, attacked not only Dryden but several other dramatists, Congreve among them. He was a clergyman, and his discussion of Dryden shows that he was chiefly upset by Dryden's numerous satirical references to priestcraft. Dryden's comedies (with the exception of *Limberham,* for which there are extenuating circumstances) are no more indecent than are those of most of his contemporaries. What is extraordinary is not the depravity of his comedies but his admission of guilt. If like his fellow dramatists he had boldy defended himself against Collier's attack, subsequent critics would probably have been a good deal more circumspect in their accusations.

Dryden's admission that he lacked aptitude for writing comedy is no proof that his comedies are inferior or that he took no pains with them. He tried, with considerable success, to compensate for his lack of natural ability by hard work. Since he was neither a slavish imitator nor a comic genius, he must have worked from a theory of comedy. For surely it is unreasonable to suppose that the first great English dramatic critic had no theory of comedy, or that he had one but expunged it from his mind whenever he wrote a comedy; and the charge that his critical prefaces are designed to justify the plays to which they are prefixed seems a rather uncharitable way of acknowledging that his theory corresponds to his practice.

During the thirty-one years of his activity as a comic dramatist, Dryden's critical opinions changed; consequently he has been charged with inconsistency and insincerity. Actually these changes constitute a reasoned development of his theory; they are the products not of inconsistency and insincerity but of openmindedness and continued interest. There would be far better cause for condemning Dryden if his theory had remained fixed, if he had formulated a complete and ironclad theory at the outset of his career and had obdurately stuck to it in the teeth of his further experience and maturer thought.

No separate, comprehensive study of Dryden's theory and practice of comedy has been published.[18] A few studies of his dramatic theory and practice have appeared. These are brief and general, and their authors slight the comedies in favor of the serious plays. The two most important ones are Margaret Sherwood's *Dryden's Dramatic Theory and Practice* (1899) and G. R. Noyes' Introduction to his edition of *Selected Dramas of Dryden with The Rehearsal* (1910).

Sherwood contends that Dryden's work as a comic dramatist is not in accord with his dramatic theory, but she does not support this contention by providing a detailed chronological comparison of the critical documents and the comedies. Her view is that Dryden, anxious to please and astute enough to know what would please, imitated other dramatists. However, she points out that his imitations were not slavish. Essentially, she thinks, he borrowed from other dramatists what he himself lacked: a comic sense, or comic spirit.[19]

But a comic sense is so nebulous a concept that we cannot say with any certainty what one is, much less where it came from. And even if Dryden in writing a comedy did borrow some other man's comic sense, how did he get from the borrowed comic sense to the finished play? Sherwood does not answer this question satisfactorily. Now and then she mentions, more or less in passing, a practical principle of composition, but on the whole she is concerned with spirit, not form. She finds fault with Dryden's theory because she considers it practical and shallow rather than philosophical and profound.[20] But a professional dramatist cannot afford to neglect the practical. When Dryden undertook the writing of a comedy, he needed principles more exact than the hazy idea of borrowing the comic sense of other men without slavishly imitating them. Furthermore, Dryden, who did not have the opportunity to read Meredith's *Essay on Comedy,* probably thought just as highly of his practical approach as Sherwood does of her philosophical one, and considered his conception of comedy (which, as Sherwood points out, is based in part on Aristotle) as profound as anyone else's. Sherwood's study is valuable for its perceptive comments, made from the post-Meredith point of view, on Dryden's comedies and criticism; but it is inadequate as a study of the relation of the comedies to the criticism.

Noyes is more matter-of-fact in his approach. He divides Dryden's career as dramatist into three periods, 1663-1670, 1670-1678, and 1678-1693. In the first period, he says, Dryden's position was a compromise between French regard for the rules of drama and English regard for variety, with some leaning towards the English. In the second, Dryden leaned more to the French and their rules, but based his principles of characterization on the practice of Elizabethan dramatists. In the third, he firmly allied himself with the French, though his allegiance was still somewhat qualified by his regard for the Elizabethans, Shakespeare in particular. Noyes applies this developing theory to Dryden's practice, finding some correspondence but concluding that Dryden as dramatist was essentially an opportunist.[21]

Because Noyes pays serious attention to Dryden's theory, regarding it as developing rather than inconsistent, and because he is interested in considering Dryden's theory from Dryden's point of view, I believe that his approach to the problem is sounder than Sherwood's. But Noyes' study is too brief and general to be conclusive. Probably because the space at his disposal was limited, he devotes only thirty-four pages to outlining the development of Dryden's dramatic theory and applying the theory to Dryden's practice. The comedies in particular are neglected. He disposes of *Secret Love, Sir Martin Mar-All,* and *An Evening's Love* in one short paragraph,[22] condemns *The Assignation* without discussing it,[23] and does not even mention *Amphitryon.*

Ned Bliss Allen took the unprecedented step of devoting an entire book to Dryden's comedies: *The Sources of Dryden's Comedies* (1935). I am considerably indebted to his thorough examination of Dryden's sources. But I cannot accept the view of Dryden as comic dramatist at which Allen arrives. His view is very much like Sherwood's. Paradoxically, he holds that Dryden was both original and servile: original in handling his sources, servile in following the oscillations of public tastes by imitating whatever kind of comedy happened to be popular at the moment in the theater for which he was writing.[24]

The first half of this judgment is well founded on comparison of Dryden's comedies and their sources. But the second half is founded only on the possibility of certain influences on Dryden. The influences on an author, unless the author himself admits them, are very difficult to detect. And it is doubtful that any modern critic, however learned and perspicacious, can determine the oscillations in the tastes of London playgoers nearly three hundred years before his own time with sufficient accuracy to demonstrate that Dryden was following them. Experienced Broadway producers often go badly astray in attempting to calculate the tastes of audiences today. If we wish to determine the influence on Dryden of audience tastes and the work of other dramatists, our best course is to find out what Dryden himself said about it. As a matter of fact, Dryden in his critical writings has a good deal to say about it. But in Allen's book Dryden's dramatic criticism is hardly ever considered.

Although Dryden as comic dramatist and critic of comedy was not a degraded opportunist, the circumstances of his life did have a bearing on his plays and on his criticism. Dryden made his living by writing, at a time when the author's position was far more precarious than it is in our own age. He wrote for a cynical and obstreperous audience. The money he earned from books published and plays performed was not enough; he also depended on the patronage of government officials and the rich, who had to be repaid with political support and with flattery. He was repeatedly involved in violent political, religious, and literary controversies. Such circumstances must be taken into account in the study of his theory and practice of comedy.

Since Dryden's theory changed, the comparison of theory and practice must be made chronologically. This chronological approach is troublesome because Dryden did not at all times discuss all aspects of comedy. For example, his first play was staged in 1663, but he did not discuss the morality of comedy until 1671. I have therefore had to postpone my discussion of morality until I reached 1671, and to assume that Dryden's views on morality underwent no important change between 1663 and 1671.

Upon comparing Dryden's theory of comedy with his practice, in the light of the relevant circumstances of his life, I found that his career as comic dramatist falls into the following six periods (the dates are those of the first performances of the plays):

Period 1. *The Wild Gallant*. February, 1663.
The Rival Ladies. *c*. May, 1664.

(An interval of nearly three years.)

Period 2. *Secret Love*. March, 1667.

(An interval of five months.)

Period 3. *Sir Martin Mar-All*. August, 1667.
The Wild Gallant (revised). 1667.
The Tempest. November, 1667.
An Evening's Love. June, 1668.

(An interval of more than three years.)

Period 4. *Marriage à la Mode*. late in 1671.
The Assignation. October or November, 1672.

(An interval of more than five years.)

Period 5. *Limberham*. March, 1678.
The Spanish Friar. March, 1680.

(An interval of nearly ten years.)

Period 6a. *Don Sebastian*. December, 1689.
Amphitryon. October, 1690.

(An interval of more than three years.)

Period 6b. *Love Triumphant*. *c*. January, 1694.

The development of Dryden's theory of comedy falls into two major phases, the first including periods 1 through 4, the second including periods 5 and 6.

In the following chapters I shall discuss each of these periods in detail, with the hope of thereby illuminating Dryden's theory of comedy, his comedies and tragicomedies, and his career as a comic dramatist.

II. 1663-1664: APPRENTICESHIP

1.

DRYDEN'S COMEDY *The Wild Gallant,* the first of his plays to be performed, was produced by the King's Company in February, 1663. It was not a success. It was revived in 1667, and it was first published in 1669. The prologue to the 1667 production tells us that Dryden, when he first wrote the play, lacked sophistication, considering its hero, the wild gallant, "monstrous leud" because he is "suspected with his Landlords Wife"; but that now, having acquired "knowledge of the Town," he thinks the hero

a very civil man;
And, much asham'd of what he was before,
Has fairly play'd him at three Wenches more.

Apparently Dryden revised the play at some time between its two appearances in order to make the wild gallant wilder. The line about the three wenches probably refers to an episode in Act IV in which three prostitutes are displayed. Presumably it was the revised version that was printed; and in the printed version the wild gallant, Loveby, is still not very wild, as Restoration gallants go. It is impossible more exactly to determine the extent and nature of Dryden's revisions, and the printed version of the play is the only one available. The subsequent discussion rests on the assumption that the printed version is not essentially different from the version that was performed in 1663.

In the prologue to the original version, a character identified as "Prologue" consults two astrologers to learn the fate of the play. One of the astrologers ends the consultation by saying,

it is your Authors lot,
To be indanger'd by a Spanish Plot.

"Prologue" thereupon addresses the audience as follows:

Our Poet yet protection hopes from you,
But bribes you not with any thing that's new.
Nature is old, which Poets imitate,
And for Wit, those that boast their own estate,
Forget *Fletcher* and *Ben* before them went,
Their Elder Brothers, and that vastly spent:
So much 'twill hardly be repair'd again,
Not, though supply'd with all the wealth of *Spain;*
This play is *English,* and the growth your own;
As such it yields to *English* Plays alone.

The prologue and Dryden's statement in the preface that "the Plot was not Originally my own" have been widely taken as evidence that *The Wild Gallant* is a play of the "Spanish intrigue" type, based on some Spanish source— even though "Prologue" categorically says that the play is English. But Allison Gaw has convincingly demonstrated that the prologue's "Spanish Plot" and "wealth of Spain" lines are allusions not to Dryden's play but to a rival play, Tuke's *Adventures of Five Hours,* a close adaptation of a Spanish play, which had been presented with great success by the Duke's Company shortly before the appearance of *The Wild Gallant.*[1] There have been other attempts to determine the source of the plot that Dryden says he borrowed,[2] but none has been conclusive, and Dryden tells us in the preface that the borrowed plot was "so alter'd, by me . . . that, whoever the Author was, he

could not have challeng'd a Scene of it." We may therefore assume that *The Wild Gallant* is not a close adaptation of some other play.

However, it is reasonable to suppose that Dryden, a
beginner, would imitate the work of playwrights of proven
ability. Whom would he be likely to choose as model?
At that time Shakespeare, Beaumont and Fletcher, and
Ben Jonson seem to have been generally regarded as the
greatest English dramatists. It is they whose works Dryden was to analyze and praise two or three years later
when he wrote his *Essay of Dramatic Poesy*. From 1660
on, their plays were often successfully revived. The two
companies relied on them especially during the months
immediately following the Restoration, when few new plays
were available.[3] We can imagine Dryden attending some
of these early revivals, noting the response of the audience
to various scenes and meditating a play of his own.

As Dryden points out in the *Essay of Dramatic Poesy,*
Beaumont and Fletcher specialized in the portrayal of
love and wit as practiced by gentlefolk, while Jonson had
little to do with love, wit, or gentlefolk, but specialized in
the portrayal of the humours, or extravagant follies, of
members of the lower classes. It is very likely that Dryden
would get the idea of combining both sorts of comedy in
one play. I believe that he attempted such a combination
in *The Wild Gallant*.

The 1663 prologue seems to hint at this combination:
nature, which dramatists imitate, is old, says "Prologue,"
and wit has been "vastly spent" by Fletcher and Jonson—
in other words, these earlier English dramatists have already discovered the best ways of imitating nature. He
then says that the play is English and that there is nothing
new in it. The implication is that Dryden in writing *The
Wild Gallant* adopted the methods of imitating nature used
by Fletcher (and, presumably, Beaumont) and Jonson.

The play itself fits this conception admirably. It contains genteel and witty lovers like those in the comedies of Beaumont and Fletcher; it also contains humours characters like those in Jonson's comedies. Constance, witty daughter of the wealthy Lord Nonsuch, loves the wild gallant, Loveby, a witty young gentleman who has squandered his inheritance. Nonsuch wants his daughter to marry Sir Timorous, a rich fool. By deceiving her father, Constance succeeds in marrying Loveby, while Isabel, her witty and impoverished cousin, manages to marry Sir Timorous. Several of the characters have "humours" that they frequently display. Sir Timorous has the humour of excessive timidity; Will Bibber, a tailor, is so infatuated with wit that he trades clothing for bad jokes; and Justice Trice is an epicure so fond of entertaining that when no real guests are available he entertains imaginary ones, gambling with them and accusing them of cheating.

There are in the play traces of Jonsonian influence other than the employment of humours characters. Dryden in the *Essay of Dramatic Poesy* notes with approval Jonson's device of preparing the audience to appreciate a character by having another person give a preliminary character sketch of him. Dryden himself uses this device four times in the opening scene of *The Wild Gallant*. Jonson often brings together contrasting characters in order comically to accentuate outstanding traits of each. For example, in *Every Man in His Humour* the braggart Bobadil is exposed as a coward when he becomes involved in a quarrel with the irascible Downright. In *The Wild Gallant* Sir Timorous and Lord Nonsuch are thus set off against each other. Sir Timorous has been negotiating with Nonsuch for the hand of Constance; but when Nonsuch introduces him to Constance, he infuriates the testy old man by bashfully denying that he loves the girl. Jonson, unlike most of his contemporaries, usually conformed to the

unities of time and place. Dryden, in making *The Wild
Gallant* conform approximately (the place is London, the
time two days) may have been imitating Jonson.

The wit, the sophistication, the cynicism, and the
emancipated behavior of Constance, Isabel, and Loveby
all have general parallels in the plays of Beaumont and
Fletcher. Dryden, I think, imitated them selectively, not
indiscriminately. In the *Essay of Dramatic Poesy* he
praises the comedies of Beaumont and Fletcher for their
"gaiety" and for their representation of the "wild debaucheries, and quickness of wit in repartees" of gentlemen. But the persons of quality in the comedies of Beaumont and Fletcher are not always gay, debauched, and
witty; they often lapse into romatic sentimentality. Of all
the plays of Beaumont and Fletcher, *The Wild-Goose
Chase* is most like a Restoration comedy of manners; but
even in this play there are such lapses. The hero, Mirabel,
is described in the dramatis personae as "a great defier of
all Ladies in the way of Marriage, otherwise their much
loose Servant."⁴ But when Oriana, who is in love with
him, pretends that she has been driven mad by his scornful treatment of her, the great defier of all ladies abjectly
and tearfully begs her pardon. Oriana is described as a
"witty follower of the Chase"—that is, pursuer of Mirabel,
the Wild Goose. But unlike a witty Restoration heroine
she blushes when she is accused of being in love with
Mirabel, and she manifests a most unsophisticated concern for her virtue. In *The Wild Gallant,* however, the
sophisticated, offhand manner of the witty characters is
maintained throughout the play. Again, in the *Essay* Dryden objects to mute and passive heroines. In the comedies
of Beaumont and Fletcher the heroines are often fairly
active, but sometimes they subside into the weaker sex.
In *The Wild-Goose Chase* three women engage in divers
schemes designed to discomfit or ensnare their respective

gallants; but the schemes are engineered by a man. And when Oriana's pretended madness fails to catch the Wild Goose, she blushes and is weakly ashamed. In *The Wild Gallant* Constance and Isabel do their own scheming, and they are never daunted by any male.

Probably because of Dryden's lack of experience, the play has some notable defects. The plot is weak and straggling. It consists not of one main strand, but of several lesser strands loosely woven together. During the first three acts Constance amuses herself by stealing money from her father and conveying it mysteriously to Loveby; not until Act IV does she take steps to marry him. Isabel's efforts to marry Sir Timorous are opposed by two parasites, Burr and Failer, who also attempt to double-cross each other. Loveby's dealings with his landlord, Bibber, provide still another meager strand. Loveby is at first dunned by Bibber and later gets money from him on the pretext of buying a place at Court for his wife Frances, who has extravagant social ambitions. The development of these various actions is slowed and sometimes stopped by exhibitions of humour on the part of the characters involved. For example, in Act III Loveby, at the instigation of Failer, is arrested by bailiffs, but this development is neutralized immediately when Bibber, in exchange for a couple of bad jokes, pays for his release. Justice Trice's displays of humour have no valid connection with any of the actions. In its structure the play resembles Jonson's two early humours comedies, *Every Man in His Humour* and *Every Man Out of His Humour,* whose actions are also multiple, straggling, and slowed by displays of humour. In the *Essay* Dryden notes with approval the presence in Jonson's *Epicoene* of underplots that are adequately linked to the main plot and subservient to the main plot. But *Epicoene* is much more tightly constructed than the two humours comedies or *The Wild Gallant.* Possibly Dryden

was aware of its superior construction when he wrote
The Wild Gallant, but despaired of equaling it.

An inexperienced dramatist, not trusting his ability to
write subtle comedy or the ability of the audience to com-
prehend it, is apt to rely heavily on obvious effects. It is
at least partly for this reason, I believe, that Dryden has
made the humours of *The Wild Gallant* what he later
called "mechanic" humours—that is, the crude humours
of persons of low manners and breeding (Nonsuch is a
lord in name only). Dryden could cite Jonson's comedies
as precedents; in the *Essay* he points out that mechanic
humours were Jonson's favorites. But in the *Essay* Dryden
showed disapproval of such humours, and he may have
disapproved of them when he wrote *The Wild Gallant,* including them for the sake of their obviousness. For the
same reason, apparently, he has generously seasoned the
play with crudely extravagant and spectacular scenes,
some involving these mechanic humours, some not. The
most notable of these is in Act IV, where the gullible
Nonsuch is convinced that the devil has got him pregnant.
In Act II is another such scene. Loveby, who believes that
the devil is supplying him with money, arranges to meet
the devil at night. In pitch darkness, with his sword
drawn, he encounters Failer and mistakes him for the
devil. Failer runs off, screaming for help. Roused by the
uproar, Trice, Burr, and Sir Timorous enter "undress'd."
The last act affords a whole spate of spectacular incidents,
featuring a minor character "antickly habited; with a torch
in one hand, and a wand in the other"; Constance disguised as the goddess Fortune; secret marriages, surprisals,
mistaken identities, plots, counterplots, counter-counter-
plots, music, and dancing.

A bad side-effect of Dryden's reliance on extravagance
is an inconsistency in Loveby. He is supposed to be a
wit, and in his dialogues with Constance he is witty,

though he generally comes off second-best; but in order to provide spectacular scenes Dryden makes him appear almost as gullible as Nonsuch, for he believes that the devil is keeping him in funds and that he can improve his financial situation by literally marrying the goddess Fortune.

Because of these extravagant episodes, the modern reader sees the play as a farce, not a comedy. But what seems preposterous to us may have seemed sufficiently believable to Dryden. We find many of Jonson's humours characters incredible, but Dryden in the *Essay* calls humours characterization "the imitation of what is natural," and praises Jonson not only as the outstanding creator of humours characters but as "the most . . . judicious writer which any theatre ever had." The humour of Justice Trice, one of the most extravagant features of *The Wild Gallant,* is adapted from the humour of Carlo Buffone, a character in *Every Man Out of His Humour.*[5] The most extravagant episode in the play is that of Nonsuch's fancied pregnancy; but there is evidence that not long before the production of the play an elderly gentleman attracted attention in London by manifesting the same delusion.[6] Dryden might have justified Loveby's credulity on the ground that Loveby is so anxious to get money that he is not disposed to inquire too curiously into the source of supply.

The Wild Gallant is certainly not a good play, and the 1663 prologue is far from adequate as a statement of Dryden's contemporary theory of comedy. However, if we consider the evidence of the prologue and the nature of the play itself, we can see *The Wild Gallant* as a sincere attempt by Dryden to combine in one play of his own the characteristic excellences of Jonsonian and Fletcherian comedy.

2.

In the 1663 prologue to *The Wild Gallant,* Dryden set
up his "old" and English play against Tuke's new and
foreign play, *The Adventures of Five Hours* (foreign since
it is an adaptation from the Spanish, and new according
to its prologue: "The English Stage ne'er had so New a
Play").[7] Tuke's play had been very successful; Dryden's
failed. What was Dryden to do? Two consecutive fail-
ures at the outset of his career might have finished him as
a dramatist. It is not surprising that he temporarily
shelved his theory and made his second play, *The Rival
Ladies* (*c.* May, 1664), a close imitation of Tuke's hit.

It is interesting to compare the prologues to *The Wild
Gallant* and *The Rival Ladies* as indications of Dryden's
attitude towards the two plays. *The Wild Gallant* was
written in accord with his theory; consequently, in the prologue he defends the conception of the play (it is old and
English, an imitation of nature in the manner of Fletcher
and Jonson) but apologizes for his execution of it ("He
could have wish'd it better for your [the audience's]
sakes"). But in the prologue to *The Rival Ladies* he
adopts the opposite point of view: he is contemptuous of
the conception of the play, but says that he has made it a
good specimen of its kind. The prologue begins by stating
that modern plays are totally deficient in wit and then goes
on to list some absurd features of these witless modern
plays. (Dryden's use of the plural may mean that other
Spanish-intrigue plays had appeared; or he might have
been thinly disguising his attack on Tuke's play. Some of
his allusions make it clear that he had Tuke's play in
mind.) The prologue continues,

Such deep Intrigues you'r welcome to this Day:
But blame your Selves, not him who Writ the Play;

Though his Plot's Dull, as can be well desir'd,
Wit stiff as any you have e'r admir'd:
He's bound to please, not to Write well; and knows
There is a Mode in Plays as well as Cloaths.

Dryden's critical standards have not changed; in both prologues he is in favor of the old English fashion in drama,
opposed to the new, foreign fashion of Tuke's play. (His
opposition to the new fashion refers only to the undesirable
features of Tuke's play and others like it: dullness, stiff wit,
absurd intrigues. Dryden was not opposed to novelty itself. Though *The Wild Gallant* is old as an imitation of
Jonson and Fletcher, it is new as a combination of Jonsonian and Fletcherian comedy.)

The resemblance of *The Rival Ladies* to *The Adventures of Five Hours* is unmistakable. Dryden later specialized in tragicomedies with two plots, one serious and one
comic; but *The Rival Ladies,* like Tuke's play, is a one-
plot tragicomedy in which a potentially tragic situation
comes to a happy ending. Both plays are set in Spain,
both are founded on the enormously complicated amours
of a set of lovers. Both contain two Spanish nobles, each
of them the guardian of a sister whom he orders to marry
against her inclinations. In both, the resulting conflicts
produce a rapid succession of vicissitudes involving disguises, swordfights, nocturnal prowlings, mistaken identities, and discussions of love and honor, and end with the
pairing off of the gentlemen and ladies to the satisfaction
of all concerned (one of Dryden's ladies is at the end of
the play still unable to accept the man who wants her;
but she expects a change of heart). In both plays comic
relief is provided by servants. Both are written in blank
verse interspersed with passages in rhyme.

However, the two plays differ in some respects. The
action of Tuke's play lasts five hours and is confined to

three or four streets and houses in the city of Seville. Dryden tells us in the *Essay of Dramatic Poesy* that because of its short time of action the play was regarded with "much wonder"; he also says that such strict attention to the unity of time is a "beauty," and he speaks approvingly of Jonson's equally strict attention to the unity of place in *Epicoene*. But he has not imitated Tuke in either respect. The action of *The Rival Ladies* lasts two days, and although it is confined to the city of Alicant and its environs, the setting shifts, in a manner abhorrent to the unity of place, from forest to town house to seacoast to shipboard. The greater disunity of Dryden's play is probably the result of its greater complexity; where Tuke provides four lovers, Dryden provides six, and correspondingly increases the number and intricacy of the complications. Probably Dryden thought that the chief appeal of Tuke's play lay in its elaborate plot (as is indicated by his reference in the prologue to "deep Intrigues"), and in order to beat Tuke at his own game sacrificed strict adherence to the unities of time and place. In the *Essay* Dryden commends abundance of characters and elaborateness of plot as productive of a pleasing variety, "if . . . the parts are managed so regularly, that the beauty of the whole be kept entire, and that the variety become not a confused and perplexed mass of accidents." Probably he objected to Tuke's plot not because of its elaborateness but because of its absurdity, as the prologue indicates; and, as the prologue also shows, he was willing to admit that his own plot was just as absurd.

In Tuke's play two principal servants, Diego and Flora, afford most of the comedy. Dryden in the *Essay* says that most of the new French plays "are, like some of ours, derived from the Spanish novels. There is scarce one of them without a veil, and a trusty Diego, who drolls much after the rate of the *Adventures*." Shortly thereafter he says, "I grant the French have performed what was possible on the ground-work of the Spanish plays; what was pleasant before, they have made regular: but there is not above one good play to be writ on all those plots; they are too much alike to please often; which we need not the experience of our own stage to justify." These two passages are a little confusing, since Dryden first speaks of the French as working from Spanish novels, and then of their working on the "ground-work" of Spanish plays. But it is clear enough that both the French and the English adaptations from the Spanish are undesirable because of their sameness and that "a trusty Diego" is a stock figure in such adaptations. Accordingly, he has made *The Rival Ladies* a little different. In his play there are no characters corresponding to Diego and Flora, and there is much less servants' comedy than there is in Tuke's. Instead, there is a sort of comedy not found in Tuke's. It involves two of the serious characters, Honoria and Angellina. Suffering from unrequited love for the same man, they disguise themselves as boys and follow him about. In Act I the two "boys" are asked to sleep together. Each thinking that the other is a genuine male, they violently object. In Act IV these "rival ladies" engage in a comical sword-fight with one another—an improvement on the duel in *Twelfth Night* (so Dryden may have thought) because that affords only *one* lady disguised as a boy.

Another difference between Dryden's play and Tuke's is that Dryden's ladies, especially the two rival ladies, take an active part in the promotion of their affairs, while Tuke's do little but lament their lots. The superior initiative of Dryden's heroines is consistent with his disapproval of mute and passive heroines.

Both plays have a prominent heroic element, but Dryden's is considerably more heroic than Tuke's. In Dryden's, conflicts between love and honor occur more fre-

quently and explicitly than they do in Tuke's, and Dryden's
Gonsalvo is in speech and swordsmanship more nearly
akin to the transcendent worthies of the heroic plays than
are any of Tuke's characters. Dryden subsequently became the foremost writer of heroic plays in England. *The
Indian Queen,* a heroic play that he wrote in collaboration with Sir Robert Howard, was produced early in 1664,
a few months before *The Rival Ladies.* However, it is
likely that *The Rival Ladies* was written before *The Indian
Queen.*[8] For Dryden, the heroic element of *The Rival
Ladies* seems to have been its chief point of interest. He
dedicated the play to the Earl of Orrery, an author of
plays in the heroic vein. In the dedicatory epistle his discussion of the play consists mainly of a defense of his use
of rhyme in some of the heroic episodes.[9] His defense of
this "new way" of writing, as he calls it, is additional evidence that he was no literary reactionary.[10]

On the whole *The Rival Ladies* is inconsistent with
Dryden's theory of comedy. Indeed, in no other comedy
or tragicomedy, with the possible exception of *Limberham,*
did he imitate the work of another dramatist as closely as
he did in this one. Yet even in *The Rival Ladies* there
are clear signs of an independent critical intelligence.
Realizing that the essential appeal of Tuke's play resided
in its elaborate and absurd love-intrigue, he made his own
plot no less absurd and even more elaborate. Recognizing
the danger of too much sameness, he eliminated the stock
figures of trusty Diego and his female counterpart and re-
placed them with the transvestite ladies. And when Tuke's
heroic element gave him an opportunity to pursue a genuine interest of his own, he made the most of it.

III. 1665-1667: THE THEORY FORMULATED AND APPLIED

1.

The Indian Queen was followed by Dryden's heroic play *The Indian Emperour* in the spring of 1665. In June of that year the theaters were closed because of an outbreak of plague. Dryden went to the country home of the Earl of Berkshire at Charlton, Wiltshire, and during his stay there wrote *An Essay of Dramatic Poesy*. It was probably during the same period that he wrote his next play, *Secret Love, or, The Maiden Queen,* a tragicomedy, which was successfully performed in March, 1667, soon after the theaters reopened.

The *Essay*[1] consists of a series of three debates conducted by four polite disputants. After a play has been defined to the satisfaction of all, Crites argues that the drama of the Ancients was superior to that of the Moderns. Eugenius defends the opposite view. Then Lisideius argues that modern French drama is better than modern English drama, and Neander argues the superiority of English drama. Finally Crites argues against, and Neander for, the use of rhyme in plays. Dryden both in his dedication and in the *Essay* itself refrains from identifying himself with any of the disputants or their views. However, since Eugenius and Neander clearly have the better of the arguments, and since they are in fundamental agreement with one another, it is reasonable to suppose that their opinions are Dryden's. Significantly, they do most of the talking. Together they are given nearly two-thirds of the total wordage of the four debates. Neander alone is given nearly half.

All four agree that a play should be "A just and lively image of human nature, representing its passions and humours, and the changes of fortune to which it is subject, for the delight and instruction of mankind." By "just" is meant "exact"; the image must be true to life. By "lively" is meant "animated." In terms of a figure that Neander later uses, a play that is just but not lively is like a statue, while a play that is both just and lively is like a living man. In this definition the emphasis is on character, not plot. Later Neander says that "the soul of Poesy . . . is imitation of humour and passions."

Dryden accepted Aristotle's idea that men are naturally delighted by imitations of nature. Dryden also believed that a play can delight mankind (or Englishmen, at least) by its variety. He apparently conceived of two sorts of variety. One is that which is afforded by the presence of diverse elements in a play: defending the multiple plots of English plays, Neander says that "our variety" will please an audience more than do the single actions of French plays. The other is that which is afforded by novelty: Eugenius, complaining of the repeated use of familiar stories in Greek tragedy, says, "the novelty being gone, the pleasure vanished."

The other function of a play, the instruction of mankind, is sadly neglected in the *Essay*. The four debaters nearly always defend or attack on the basis of the play's ability or inability to please; they never defend a play by contending that, although boring, it is very instructive, nor do they ever attack one by contending that, though pleasing, it is not instructive. Besides the definition of a play, the only explicit reference to instruction is made by Eugenius, when he accuses the Greek and Roman dramatists of erring "in the instructive part" by violating the principle

of poetic justice. The examples cited by Eugenius are all
tragic; it is not clear that Dryden intended the same conception of instruction to be applied to comedy. It is clear,
though, that Dryden at this stage of his career was far
more interested in pleasing than in instructing.

But it is also evident that in his desire to please the
public he was not slavish or indiscriminate. Arguing
against rhymed plays, Crites says that the people are prejudiced in favor of unrhymed plays and that it is futile to
go against the stream of public opinion. Neander replies
by representing the opposition of the people to rhymed
plays not as a permanent and insurmountable obstacle but
as a temporary "difficulty." He then differentiates between
two kinds of people, the "populace," whose opinion does
not matter, and the "noblesse," whose opinion, Dryden
definitely implies, does matter. In other words, the dramatist should not aim to please everyone, but should aim
to please the discriminating; and he should not be a slave
to present tastes, not even those of the discriminating, but
should, if he thinks it desirable, introduce new fashions in
plays. The context of these remarks has to do with serious
drama, but there is no good reason to suppose that Dryden's conception of the dramatist's relation to public opinion did not include the comic dramatist. Earlier in the
Essay, it is true, Neander says that since comedy has to do
with ordinary persons and events, "every one is a proper
judge" of comedy—a statement that seems to qualify the
populace along with the noblesse as competent judges of
comedy. But it qualifies them only as judges of the naturalness of the persons and events represented. Furthermore, elsewhere in the *Essay* Neander includes ladies and
gentlemen and their amours in the province of comedy.
Of these the noblesse, not the populace, would be qualified as judges by their experience. As I shall subsequently
show, Dryden seems to have preferred ladies and gentle-

men in love as the material for comedy. This preference is consistent with his aiming to please the noblesse rather than the populace. "Gentlemen will now be entertained with the follies of each other," he remarked a few years later, in the course of demonstrating the inappropriateness in his own age of Jonson's low comedy.[2]

Dryden's notion of laughter also seems to be Aristotelian. According to Aristotle's *Poetics,* the ludicrous "consists in some defect or ugliness which is not painful or destructive. To take an obvious example, the comic mask is ugly and distorted, but does not imply pain."[3] Dryden too thought that the perception of abnormality produces laughter. In the preface to *Annus Mirabilis* (1667) he distinguishes thus between Heroic Poetry and Burlesque: "the one shows nature beautified, as in the picture of a fair woman, which we all admire; the other shows her deformed, as in that of a Lazar, or of a fool with distorted face and antic gestures, at which we cannot forbear to laugh, because it is a deviation from Nature." And in the *Essay,* discussing humours, Neander says that "deviations from common customs" are the likeliest producers of "that malicious pleasure in the audience which is testified by laughter."

Dryden has a good deal to say about humours in the *Essay.* From the time of Ben Jonson, who was the most celebrated exponent of humours characterization, until the present day, there has been considerable disagreement on the subject of humours. Dryden must have been aware of confusion or difference of opinion in his own time, for he goes to considerable trouble to clarify humours theory. Neander elaborately defines a humour as

some extravagant habit, passion, or affection, particular . . . to some one person, by the oddness of which, he is immediately distinguished from the rest of men; which being lively and naturally represented, most frequently begets that malicious pleasure in the audience which is testified by laughter; as all things which are deviations from common customs are ever the aptest to produce it: though by the way this laughter is only accidental, as the person represented is fantastic or bizarre; but pleasure is essential to it, as the imitation of what is natural.

This definition includes extravagance, or deviation from the norm, in degree as well as in kind; that is, the humour need not be a new passion: it can be a commonplace passion exaggerated. Most men have some sensitivity to noise; they will jump if a gun unexpectedly goes off behind them. But Jonson's Morose, whom Neander justifies as a humours character, has an abnormal sensitivity to noise; he is agitated by any sound, however slight. Furthermore, the definition requires that the humour be natural; it is an abnormality, but it must be a plausible abnormality; mere freakish behavior will not do. Neander demonstrates that Morose's humour is plausible, crediting it to a combination of "delicate hearing" and the peevishness of a domineering old man.

It is this requirement of naturalness which leads Dryden to regard the laughter that greets a humours character as accidental rather than as an essential part of the pleasure to be derived from "the imitation of what is natural." Men will laugh as readily at the unnatural extravagance of farce as at the natural extravagance of humours comedy. Neander makes this clear in discussing "the *ridiculum* . . . which stirred up laughter in the Old Comedy." This *ridiculum* consists in extravagance without naturalness. Thus Aristophanes makes Socrates ridiculous, says Neander, not by justly imitating his actions, but by making him behave childishly and absurdly. Since laughter is provoked as readily by bad art as by good, it is not a praiseworthy reaction. But in Dryden's theory, disparagement of laughter does not necessarily mean disparagement of comedy and should not be cited as evidence that Dryden did not take his own comedies seriously. Ben Jonson, whose seriousness as a comic dramatist is not often questioned, expresses in a passage of his *Timber: or Discoveries* the same low opinion of laughter. In the same passage Jonson objects to Aristophanes' treatment of Socrates.[4] Elsewhere in the *Essay* Neander commends Jonson for "the precepts which he has laid down in his *Discoveries.*"

Having distinguished between humours and the Old Comedy, in which there is singularity but no naturalness, Neander proceeds to distinguish between humours and the "New Comedy" of Terence and Plautus, in which, he contends, there is naturalness but no singularity, "only the general characters of men and manners; as old men, lovers, serving-men, courtezans, parasites." These two distinctions point to humours comedy as the best passage between the farcical absurdities of the Old Comedy and the monotonous type characters of the New.

Despite its insistence on idiosyncrasy, Dryden's concept of a humour is not in conflict with the concept of comedy as a vehicle for the ridicule of fashionable follies. With its requirement of naturalness and its inclusion of deviations in degree as well as in kind, his definition admits the possibility of a humour that is the exaggeration of some fashionable folly. Ben Jonson, in the prologue to *Every Man Out of His Humour*—the very place where he defines a humour—promises to "strip the ragged follies of the time."[5] For Jonson the "follies of the time" were what he calls "false humours"—that is, affected humours, inconsistent with one's true character: the bravado of a coward, for example. Dryden does not distinguish between true and false humours. Perhaps he thought that although the coward's swaggering is a pretense, his passion for setting himself up as a bravo is a true humour, and that a distinction between true and false humours is there-

fore superfluous. Anyway, he must have been aware of
Jonson's equation of humours and the follies of the times.

In the course of his explanation of humours, Neander
says that Falstaff is not a humours character because
"there are many men resembling him; old, fat, merry,
cowardly, drunken, amorous, vain, and lying. . . . Falstaff . . . is not properly one humour, but a miscellany of
humours or images, drawn from so many several men: that
wherein he is singular is his wit . . . his quick evasions."
This passage is puzzling. Does Dryden mean that Falstaff
is disqualified as a humours character because singularity
of wit can never be a humour? Or does he mean that Falstaff's singularity of wit is disqualified as a humour (*one*
extravagant habit) by the presence of his other qualities,
so that the total effect is that of a "miscellany of humours"?
I incline to the latter interpretation; Dryden, I think, conceived of a humours character as a kind of monomaniac,
as Morose is. But if Falstaff is a "miscellany of humours,"
his characteristics other than his wit must also be potential
humours, each disqualified as a humour only by the presence of the others. Then why does Neander say that Falstaff is singular only in his wit? In calling Falstaff's other
characteristics "humours or images" Neander seems to be
equivocating; possibly Dryden himself was a little un-
certain.[6] Some years later, in the second phase of his theory, he changed his mind about Falstaff.

Neander thus appraises the work of Beaumont and
Fletcher: "they understood and imitated the conversation of
gentlemen . . . whose wild debaucheries, and quickness of
wit in repartees, no poet can ever paint as they have done.
Humour, which Ben Johnson derived from particular persons, they made it not their business to describe: they represented all the passions very lively, but above all, love."[7]
Here Neander is merely saying that Beaumont and Fletcher
did not choose to write humours comedy. He does not

mean that witty, profligate gentlemen, and love, are by their nature unfit for humours comedy. His definition of a humour excludes neither gentlemen nor love. When elsewhere in the *Essay* he says of Jonson, "Humour was his proper sphere; and in that he delighted most to represent mechanic people," he clearly implies that Jonson had a choice and could, if he had wished, have taken his humours from a higher social level.

Dryden himself seems to have preferred gentlemen and ladies as comic characters. Besides praising Beaumont and Fletcher for their imitation of the "conversation of gentlemen," Neander praises *Epicoene* because in it Jonson, despite his predilection for "mechanic people," has "described the conversation of gentlemen . . . with more gaiety, air, and freedom, than in the rest of his comedies." Such a preference is consistent with the disapproval of "lowness" which is manifest in much of Dryden's criticism. Comedy is by its nature ("the imitation of common persons and ordinary speaking") lower than the serious play ("nature wrought up to an higher pitch"). In Dryden's heroic plays nature is wrought up to a very high pitch indeed, and he was probably in favor of anything that could be done within the confines of the genre to elevate comedy. Neander commends Jonson for elevating the action of *Epicoene* by having it take place on an extraordinary occasion, a "signal and long-expected day." A dramatist might also elevate a comedy by making his "common persons" gentlemen instead of "mechanic people."

The wit[8] of mechanic people is low, is apt to consist largely of crude "clenches" (puns) and low whimsies, to which Neander objects strenuously, citing as one cause of flatness and insipidity in Shakespeare the frequent degeneration of his "comic wit" into "clenches." (Dryden himself had used such low forms of comic wit in *The Wild Gallant,* but he did so in order to ridicule the low tastes of the tradesman Bibber.) The conversation of gentlemen, on the other hand, consists largely of elegant repartee, by which Neander sets great store: "As for Comedy, repartee is one of its chiefest graces; the greatest pleasure of the audience is a chace of wit, kept up on both sides, and swiftly managed."

If the opponents in such a chase of wit are a man and a woman, and the contest is to be kept up on both sides, the lady must be as articulate as the gentleman. Hence we find Eugenius making the following objection to Roman comedy: "As for the poor honest maid, whom all the story is built upon, and who ought to be one of the principal actors in the play, she is commonly a mute in it: she has the breeding of the old Elizabeth way, for maids to be seen and not to be heard; and it is enough you know she is willing to be married, when the fifth act requires it." Later Eugenius complains that in Roman comedy when lovers are brought together the gentleman is as mute as the lady.

Dryden apparently thought well of the use of love in drama. Eugenius advocates its employment in serious plays on the ground that it is "the most frequent of all the passions, and . . . being the private concernment of every person, is soothed by viewing its own image in a public entertainment"—a curious extension of Aristotle's theory of purgation which Dryden may have intended to apply to comedy as well. However, given his preference for gentlemen and ladies as comic characters, the popularity of love as a fashionable recreation is sufficient warrant for its employment in comedy.

In regard to tone, Dryden seems to have preferred "gay" comedy. Neander commends the gaiety of Jonson's imitation of gentlefolk in *Epicoene,* and also says that "a certain gaiety" in the comedies of Beaumont and Fletcher is responsible for their great popularity at that time.

Dryden's idea of variety as a source of pleasure lies behind Lisideius' and Neander's debate concerning French and English plots. The chief argument of Lisideius in favor of the comedies of the French is their regularity: their adherence to the unities of time, place, and action, and to the principle of decorum. By adhering to these rules the dramatist makes his play more natural. Neander's main counter-argument is that the French plays, though regular, are barren, lacking the pleasurable variety of the English. He admits that poorly integrated subplots are reprehensible, but contends that a play is sufficiently unified if the subplots "are conducing to the main design." He defends tragicomedy on the grounds that "contraries, when placed near, set off each other," and that "a continued gravity keeps the spirit too much bent; we must refresh it sometimes."

However, Neander confesses that the infractions of the "laws of Comedy" in English plays are "errors." Rather than imitate the barrenness of French plots, one should sacrifice a little naturalness for the sake of variety; but the best plays afford a maximum of naturalness as well as of variety. Consequently, when Neander comes to the selection of a model of perfection in drama, he takes it from the works not of Shakespeare, who "did not perfectly observe the laws of Comedy," or of Fletcher, who "through carelessness made many faults," but of Jonson, "who was a careful and learned observer of the dramatic laws." The play he chooses is *Epicoene*. He praises the play for its fidelity to the unities; for the variety it affords by its "many persons of various characters and humours" and by under-plots well integrated with the main plot; and for its wit and its representation of the conversation of gentlemen, wherein it excels all the rest of Jonson's comedies.

A very peculiar feature of the *Essay* is this: although Neander in his debate with Lisideius is supposed to be proving that contemporary English drama is better than contemporary French drama, he does not cite any contemporary English dramatist or English play (twice he refers to *The Adventures of Five Hours,* but he regards it, not with approval, as a "Spanish translation"). Instead, he repeatedly cites the works of Shakespeare, Beaumont and Fletcher, and Jonson as proof of the superiority of the English. But at the beginning of the debate Lisideius had admitted the superiority of English drama in the days of Beaumont and Fletcher and Jonson. His basic contention is that since then the English drama has deteriorated and the French drama has improved. Neander replies pretty effectively to the second half of this contention, and in so doing cites several French dramatists and French plays. But he fails miserably to reply to the first half. Near the end of the debate he makes excuse for this weakness in argument: "if I do not venture upon any particular judgment of our late plays, 'tis out of the consideration [that] . . . betwixt the extremes of admiration and malice, 'tis hard to judge uprightly of the living." But if he cannot uprightly judge particular contemporary English plays, how can he uprightly judge contemporary English drama, or convince an intelligent opponent that his judgment is well founded? Dryden was ordinarily very good at dialectic; how are we to account for the feebleness of his defense of contemporary English drama?

The answer is, I think, that Dryden was not seriously interested in defending contemporary English drama against contemporary French drama; or, for that matter, in defending modern drama against the drama of the ancients. The debates, like the debaters, and like the situation of the debaters (they are supposed to be boating on the Thames) are merely devices used to add interest to the discussion and to avoid the imputation of vanity, presumption, and dogmatism. Dryden's anxiety to avoid such an imputation is manifest in his "Advertisement to the Reader": "The drift of the ensuing Discourse was chiefly to vindicate the honour of our English writers, from the censure of those who unjustly prefer the French before them. This I intimate, lest any should think me so exceeding vain, as to teach others an art which they understand much better than myself."

Dryden's fears were well founded: when Sir Robert Howard attacked the *Essay*, in his preface to *The Duke of Lerma* (1668), he did accuse Dryden of being arrogant and magisterial. Replying to this accusation, Dryden in his "Defence of an Essay of Dramatic Poesy" quotes the above passage from the "Advertisement" and then continues: "I am very confident that there is scarce any man who has lost so much time as to read that trifle [the *Essay*], but will be my compurgator as to that arrogance whereof I am accused. The truth is, if I had been naturally guilty of so much vanity as to dictate my opinions; yet I do not find that the character of a positive or self-conceited person is of such an advantage to any in this age, that I should labor to be publicly admitted of that order." This statement is an effective retort to Sir Robert, who was widely regarded as a positive, conceited person and had recently been successfully caricatured as Sir Positive At-All in Shadwell's comedy *The Sullen Lovers*;[9] but the statement also reflects Dryden's desire to stay on the good side of the public, on whom his professional success largely depended.

When he patriotically announces that his purpose in the *Essay* was chiefly to vindicate the English writers, he is not to be taken any more seriously than he is when he says that "others" understand the art of writing plays much better than he does, or that it is a waste of time to read "that trifle" the *Essay*. Actually, his purpose in the *Essay* is to explain tactfully to the English audience what makes a good English play—that is, a play which will please the English audience, a play of the sort he himself was attempting to write.

In fulfilling his purpose he evaluates the principal bodies of dramatic literature, as he knew them: the drama of the Greeks and Romans, the English drama of the "last age," and the contemporary French drama. He finds no characteristics of the Greek and Roman drama worthy of imitation. The regularity of the French drama is worthy of imitation, but the dramatist must not through inordinate attention to regularity deprive the play of pleasurable variety. The greatest dramatists are Shakespeare, Beaumont and Fletcher, and Jonson. Shakespeare is represented by Neander as an uneven genius, writing from instinct, "not laboriously, but luckily"; inimitable at his best, unworthy of imitation at his worst. Beaumont and Fletcher and Jonson are not only imitable but complementary. Beaumont and Fletcher excel in the portrayal of gay, witty, and amorous gentlefolk, but they do not concern themselves with humours characters, and through carelessness they make many faults. Jonson, on the other hand, is the most judicious of dramatists, in characterization as well as in plot construction; he specializes in humours characters; but he has a predilection for "mechanic" persons and does not excel in the portrayal of love and gentlefolk. A good comedy, then, will have as much regularity as is consistent with variety; it will have amorous gentlefolk, like Fletcher's; and it will follow Jonson in judicious plotting and characterization, particularly in "humours" characterization.

Neander's defense of rhyme is manifestly a justification of Dryden's own practice in *The Indian Queen* and

The Indian Emperour—both of which Neander mentions, along with Davenant's *The Siege of Rhodes* and Orrery's *Mustapha*. Neander mentions no good contemporary English comedy or tragicomedy because there was none. Besides Dryden, the only major Restoration dramatist who had produced a comedy before Dryden wrote the *Essay* was Etherege, whose first play, *Love in a Tub,* appeared in 1664. And this is not a play on which Dryden could rest the defense of contemporary comedy. It is a tragicomedy, whose comic plot is a loosely constructed mixture of low foolishness and profligate wit, very like *The Wild Gallant* and possibly influenced by it. Dryden's own previous work in comedy was no better that Etherege's. *The Wild Gallant* was an unsuccessful embodiment of a theory that had not yet been adequately worked out; *The Rival Ladies* was a concession to the sometimes erring tastes that Dryden in the *Essay* was trying to educate. *Secret Love,* the play Dryden wrote at about the same time he wrote the *Essay,* had not yet appeared on the stage or in print.

Though written in 1665, the *Essay* was not published until 1668. We do not know why it was not published sooner. Perhaps Dryden felt that despite the debate disguise the *Essay* might be attacked, and that if it were attacked the forthcoming *Secret Love* might be hurt rather than helped.

Of Dryden's major works of dramatic criticism, the *Essay* is the only one that he published separately; each of the others was attached to one or another of his plays. And the *Essay* is not as separate as it seems to be. Having called attention to the correspondence between the *Essay* and the prologue to *Secret Love,* W. P. Ker remarks that the prologue to *Secret Love* is the epilogue to the *Essay of Dramatic Poesy.*[10] He might better have said that the *Essay of Dramatic Poesy* is the preface to *Secret Love.*

2.

The prologue to *Secret Love* begins:

I.

He who writ this, not without pains and thought,
From *French* and *English* Theatres has brought,
Th' exactest Rules by which a Play is wrought.

II.

The Unities of Action, Place, and Time;
The Scenes unbroken; and a mingled chime
Of *Johnson's* Humour, with *Corneilles* rhyme.

Having analyzed the four principal bodies of dramatic literature, Dryden had found that the two worthy of imitation were the French and the English. The characteristic excellence of the French, he had decided, was the justness (that is, the fidelity to nature, the verisimilitude) it achieved through its regularity (its adherence to the unities and to the principle of decorum). The characteristic excellences of English drama were the liveliness and variety of its characterization and plotting. Now, having found out the ingredients of a good play, he has written one, providing in it both the justness of the French and the liveliness and variety of the English.

The play is a two-plot tragicomedy. The heroic serious plot concerns itself with several love-honor conflicts, the most notable one occurring in the bosom of the Maiden Queen of Sicily, whose love for her favorite Philocles is opposed by her honorable obligation not to marry beneath herself. The comic plot deals with the amours of a cheerful pair of young lovers, Celadon and Florimel, with Florimel, the lady, busily and successfully engaged in thwarting Celadon's repeated attempts to be unfaithful.

In making the play a two-plot tragicomedy, Dryden
has conformed to the doctrines of the *Essay,* in which
such tragicomedies are commended for the variety they
afford. Still in conformity with the *Essay,* Dryden has also
tried to provide justness by adherence to the unities and
to the principle of decorum. Now Dryden's previous tragicomedy, *The Rival Ladies,* in which he widely deviated
from his theory, is a one-plot tragicomedy. According to
Dryden's theory, one-plot tragicomedies are weakened by
their violation of the principle of decorum. Dryden in the
Essay shows his awareness of this principle when he says
that comic episodes might "allay or divert" the "concernments" of a serious play. He also shows it in the preface
to *Secret Love.* Comparing *The Indian Emperour* and
Secret Love, he says, "the Argument of that [the *Emperour*] was much more noble, not having the allay of
Comedy to depress it." Later in the preface he shows his
awareness more specifically. Answering criticisms of *Secret Love,* he says, "That which with more reason was objected as an indecorum, is the management of the last
Scene of the Play, where *Celadon* and *Florimell* are treat-
ing too lightly of their marriage in the presence of the
Queen, who likewise seems to stand idle while the great
action of the *Drama* is still depending. This I cannot otherwise defend, than by telling you I so design'd it on purpose to make my Play go off more smartly."

There is likely to be more indecorum in one-plot tragicomedy than in two-plot tragicomedy. Comic episodes in
a one-plot tragicomedy must be a part of the serious action, and as often as not they involve one or more of the
serious characters. In *The Rival Ladies* we see the heroines at one time participating in deadly serious rhymed
love-debates, at another engaging in a comical duel. In
a two-plot tragicomedy, on the other hand, one set of

events and characters is consistently serious, the other consistently comic. There must be some interaction of characters and events, of course, or the play will be disunified; consequently, there must be some indecorum, but not so much as in the one-plot tragicomedy, where the same plot and the same characters are alternately frivolous and solemn.[11]

Seemingly unaware of the conflicting requirements of unity and decorum, critics have accused Dryden of making only futile and perfunctory attempts to link the two actions of his tragicomedies, as though he had only to interweave them as tightly as possible.[12] Actually he had to maintain a difficult balance, linking the two actions enough to avoid excessive disunity, but keeping them separate enough to avoid excessive indecorum. In *Secret Love* he links the two plots by using the following devices. He makes all the characters members of the Sicilian court, and thus makes it probable that they are mutually acquainted and even related by blood or marriage. He makes Celadon, the comic hero, a cousin and friend of Philocles, the serious hero. He also makes Celadon a capable soldier—an attribute not inconsistent with Celadon's addiction to amours. Hence we are not surprised when Celadon at the head of a bunch of rowdies saves Philocles from being murdered by the villain Lysimantes. Dryden employs as intermediaries two minor characters, Asteria, the Queen's confidante, and Flavia, a Maid of Honour. Asteria is Celadon's sister. Flavia is the cousin of Florimel, the comic heroine, and she spies for Lysimantes. As minor characters, Asteria and Flavia can move freely in both plots without causing any serious breaches of decorum. Florimel as the Queen's ward is linked to the serious plot. By using these devices Dryden is able to adhere pretty well to the unities and to keep his scenes unbroken (except for one lapse, between the first two scenes of Act IV) and at the same time to keep indecorum at a reasonable level.

In the *Essay* tragicomedy is commended for its contrast as well as for its variety. Dryden's use of contrast in *Secret Love* is marked and effective. The heroic love in the serious plot is diametrically opposed to the unheroic love in the comic plot. Philocles, everlastingly faithful to his Candiope, alternates with the fantastically promiscuous Celadon; and the Queen, who is horrified at the mere thought of so much as revealing her love for Philocles, alternates with Florimel, who, when her gallant strays, brazenly goes out and fetches him back.

In the prologue Dryden not only acknowledges his general indebtedness to the *"French* and *English* Theatres,"* but, more specifically, announces that the play contains

<blockquote>
a mingled chime
Of *Johnson's* Humour, with *Corneilles* rhyme.
</blockquote>

"Corneilles rhyme" undoubtedly refers to the serious plot, which has heroics like Corneille's and is in part written in rhyme. *"Johnson's* Humour" must refer to the comic plot. But the sprightly and amorous gentlefolk of the comic plot seem Fletcherian rather than Jonsonian. Why, then, does Dryden intimate that they are Jonsonian? It is true that Jonson was well thought of and that his name might serve to recommend a play; but, according to Neander's statement in the *Essay,* Beaumont and Fletcher were then twice as popular on the stage as Jonson was, so that their names would have been even more likely to recommend the play.

The reasonable assumption is that Dryden meant what he said, and that the comic plot features his version of the Jonsonian humours that he had discussed, very approvingly and at considerable length, in the *Essay.*

In the comic plot Celadon and Florimel get not merely most but nearly all of the attention, and Dryden in claiming *"Johnson's* humour" must be referring to them. They are both courtiers and are therefore consistent with Dryden's preference for gentlefolk as comic characters. But Dryden's definition of a humour does not exclude gentlefolk; Celadon and Florimel can be courtiers and still be humours characters.

According to Dryden's theory, the dramatist who tries to create a humours character has the difficult task of making extreme eccentricity seem plausible. Celadon's and Florimel's single-minded pursuit of the pleasures of promiscuity, with its corollary disparagement of chastity and marriage, would have been readily accepted as natural by the cynical noblesse whom Dryden aimed to please. The humour of both is a wild gaiety that leads them to extremes of speech and behavior as they set about following their natural inclinations. That both have the same humour is inconsistent with Neander's stipulation that a humour must be "particular . . . to some one person," but by making the humours the same except for the difference in sex Dryden was able to show the lady successfully competing with the gentleman in his own specialty—a situation of obvious dramatic value, and one consistent with Dryden's disapproval of mute and passive heroines.

A modern reader, with preconceived notions of the wildness of Restoration rakes, might think that the Restoration audience would look upon the behavior of Celadon and Florimel as natural but not extravagant. However, it is likely that their behavior was considered out of the ordinary in degree, and perhaps also in kind, by Dryden's contemporaries. Some of the desirable Restoration ladies must have taken themselves and their amours very seriously, and accordingly must have insisted on being

wooed not flippantly, as Celadon woos Florimel, but in
the elevated language of the French romances, with repeated protestations of ardent and eternal passion. This
idealized kind of love, customarily described as "platonic,"
was highly fashionable in court circles during the reign of
Charles I.[13] It survived in the Restoration as a literary
fashion, not only in the French romances but in the heroic
plays, and it may have influenced the behavior of some
lovers in real life. If the Restoration had no ladies vain
enough to enjoy being idolized, it must have been a rare
age indeed. John Harrington Smith finds in several plays
of the period certain allusions that suggest some currency
in real life of the platonic mode.[14] In Dryden's next comedy, *Sir Martin Mar-All,* Lord Dartmouth, a roué, woos
Mrs. Christian, whom he intends to seduce, in highly romantic terms. Significantly, such romantic requirements
are burlesqued by Florimel in Act II. When Celadon becomes importunate, she asks for "proofs of love":

I would have a Lover, that if need be, should hang himself,
drown himself, break his neck, or poyson himself, for very
despair: he that will scruple this, is an impudent fellow if he
sayes he is in love. . . . However you will grant it is but decent
you should be pale, and lean, and melancholick, to shew you
are in love: and that I shall require of you when I see you
next. . . . Shall I make a proposition to you? I will give you
a whole year of probation to love me in; to grow reserv'd,
discreet, sober and faithful; and to pay me all the services of
a Lover.

Even if the lady did allow herself to be wooed with
flippant wit, she would certainly insist on having a monopoly of her lover, and he would therefore take great pains
to persuade her that she was the sole object of his attentions. He might conceivably woo two women at the same
time, if they were strangers to each other, but he would
hardly go so far as Celadon in undertaking three and woo-

ing two of them, sisters, in the same place and at the same time. A spirited mistress, when threatened with losing her lover to another woman, would certainly take action to keep him; but few would resort to Florimel's extreme measure of disguising herself as a gallant and setting herself up as her lover's rival. Florimel at one point refers to Celadon as "a pretty odd kind of fellow." It is unlikely that she would call him odd if she, or Dryden, or the audience, considered his behavior commonplace.

In the *Essay* Neander notes as "almost . . . a rule" Jonson's practice of recommending to the audience a choice "character or humour" "by a pleasant description of it before the person first appears." Dryden uses this device, with modifications, in *Secret Love*. At the very beginning of the play Asteria says to Celadon, who has just returned from a trip abroad, "I hope . . . you have brought your good humour back again to Court." Celadon replies, "I never yet knew any Company I could not be merry in, except it were an old Womans." Here Celadon's character is described not before he appears but as soon as he appears, not by another person but by himself; and his remark is a succinct description of his humour. The subsequent dialogue elaborates on this description; Celadon is revealed as a wit and a spendthrift who is, he says, simultaneously in love with two sisters. In the same scene Dryden provides a preliminary description of Florimel. Asteria speaks of her as "the Queen's Ward, a new Beauty, as wilde as you, and a vast Fortune." "As wilde as you" is a brief but adequate description of Florimel's humour.

The word "humour" is used several times in the comic plot. In Dryden's day the word had meanings other than the Jonsonian one. When Celadon says of a hypothetical mistress, "I might go to her to be merry, and she, perhaps, be out of humour," "out of humour" obviously means noth-

ing more than "out of sorts." But when Asteria refers to
Celadon's "good humour" just before Celadon speaks a
line that succinctly describes his humour, it seems likely
that Dryden intended the Jonsonian meaning. So did he,
I think, in a line spoken by Florimel. Celadon has just
announced that he changes mistresses as often as he
changes linen. Florimel says to herself, "A pretty odd
kind of fellow this: he fits my humour rarely." Since
Celadon's humour is the same as hers, he of course fits
it rarely.

Neander says that Jonson derived his humours from
particular persons. It has often been noted that Celadon's
individualized description of Florimel in Act I is also a
description of Nell Gwyn, who played the part.[15] Nell
Gwyn's behavior was considered emancipated even in
those careless times. Possibly she was the particular person from whom Florimel's humour was derived.

The comic plot of *Secret Love* corresponds to Dryden's
theory in other ways. In the *Essay* he praises repartee as
one of the "chiefest graces" of comedy; Celadon and
Florimel never meet without repartee. In the *Essay* he
objects to the muteness and passiveness of the heroines in
Roman comedy; Florimel is as active and as talkative as
Celadon. In the *Essay* he regards character as the most
important element of drama, the "soul of poesy"; in *Secret Love* the comedy is founded much more on the characters of Celadon and Florimel than on what happens to
them.

Though Dryden relies mainly on witty dialogue as a
means of representing the comical extravagance of Celadon
and Florimel, he also makes use of comic situation, as
when Florimel surprises Celadon in the embraces of
Sabina. He uses a few spectacular scenes: Celadon has a
swordfight with two soldiers (in the *Essay* Neander de-

fends the representation of violence on the stage), and Celadon and Florimel engage in a dancing contest. Though Celadon and Florimel are more admirable for their wit than ridiculous because of their humour of wildness, the play has one episode in which contemporary folly is ridiculed. The setting is nominally Sicily, but clearly Sicily, as an island, stands for England, and Florimel's impersonation of a gallant mocks English fops. "If cloathes and a *bon meen* will take 'em, I shall do't," she says; ". . . I can manage the little Comb,—set my Hat, shake my Garniture, toss about my empty Noddle, walk with a courant slurr, and at every step peck down my Head." Dazzled by this glittering surface, Olinda and Sabina are enticed away from Celadon. A remark made by Sabina when Florimel's true sex is revealed is a comment on the fop appropriate to all disillusioned ladies: "Well if ever I believe a man to be a man for the sake of a Perruks and Feather again—." Possibly we have in this remark a slight bow to instruction as a function of drama; but in the play, as in the *Essay,* Dryden's main concern is with the other function, pleasure.

3.

Reviewing Dryden's career as a comic dramatist up to this point, we clearly see a pattern of development. From Dryden's earnest but clumsy attempt to combine Fletcherian and Jonsonian comedy in *The Wild Gallant* we move to his careful and extended evaluation of Beaumont and Fletcher and Jonson in the *Essay of Dramatic Poesy,* and thence to *Secret Love.* The superiority of *Secret Love* to *The Wild Gallant* is a measure of the development of Dryden's theory. In *The Wild Gallant* there are two sets of characters: the witty lovers and the foolish humours characters. As a result, the repartee often gives way to "low" displays of "mechanic" humour. In *Secret Love* Fletcherian wit and Jonsonian humour are fused in the same characters, Celadon and Florimel, who in displaying their humour also display their wit. The plot of *The Wild Gallant* is straggling and episodic; the two plots of *Secret Love* are carefully constructed to compromise between the conflicting requirements of unity and decorum. In *The Wild Gallant* character is sometimes sacrificed for the sake of spectacular incidents; in *Secret Love* incident is subordinate to character.

We see Dryden as imitative, yet original. Contemplating the works of his great predecessors, he sees the futility of attempts at complete originality. As he puts it in the prologue to *The Wild Gallant,*

> And for Wit, those that boast their own estate,
> Forget *Fletcher* and *Ben* before them went,
> Their Elder Brothers, and that vastly spent.

Yet even in his first play we find some originality: he tries to combine both sorts of comedy in one play, and he tries to avoid the inconsistent romanticism of Fletcher's young lovers. In the *Essay* we find the same outlook as that expressed in the prologue to *The Wild Gallant*; indeed, we find the same metaphor, except that the elder brothers have now become fathers. Speaking of Fletcher, Jonson, and Shakespeare, Neander says, "We acknowledge them our fathers in wit; but they have ruined their estates themselves, before they came to their children's hands." Therefore, Neander continues, dramatists of the present age should give up writing or try some new way of writing. New in treatment rather than new in essence, Dryden means. In this context he is defending the use of rhyme in plays; but his idea could equally well be applied to the comic plot of *Secret Love,* Jonsonian and Fletcherian in its derivation, yet not like any play that Beaumont and Fletcher or Jonson ever wrote.

We see Dryden bent on pleasing his audience, yet with his own ideas as to what should please, ready to try new ways of writing even if they ran counter to the audience tastes of the moment. His Fletcherian-Jonsonian *Wild Gallant,* written in accord with his theory, failed. His imitation of Tuke's Spanish-intrigue play, *The Rival Ladies,* which was not written in accord with his theory, succeeded. Yet in the *Essay of Dramatic Poesy* we find only a couple of half-contemptuous references to the Spanish drama, but pages of praise and analysis of Beaumont and Fletcher and Jonson. And it was on Beaumont and Fletcher and Jonson, not on the Spanish, that he relied in the comic plot of *Secret Love.*

IV. 1667-1668: THE PERILS
OF SUCCESS

1.

The Feign'd Innocence, or Sir Martin Mar-All first appeared in August, 1667, five months after *Secret Love*. It turned out to be one of the most popular plays of the Restoration period. The circumstances of its production and publication are peculiar. Dryden was at the time writing regularly for the King's Company, but *Sir Martin* was presented by their rivals, the Duke's Company. The Stationer's Register (24 June 1668) lists not Dryden but the Duke of Newcastle as author of the play. No author is given on the title pages of the first three quartos (two in 1668, the third in 1678). The next quarto (1691) lists Dryden as author. Pepys wrote that the play was "made by my Lord Duke of Newcastle, but, as every body says, corrected by Dryden."[1] Langbaine in 1691 listed the 1678 quarto among Dryden's works with the remark, "This Play is generally ascrib'd to Mr. *Dryden,* tho' his Name be not affix'd to it."[2] Another contemporary, John Downes, wrote, "Sir *Martin Marral,* The Duke of *Newcastle,* giving Mr. *Dryden* a bare Translation of it, out of a Comedy of the Famous *French* Poet *Monseur Moleiro:* He Adapted the Part purposely for the Mouth of Mr. *Nokes,* and curiously Polishing the whole."[3]

William Cavendish, First Duke of Newcastle,[4] was a person who might well have had a hand in *Sir Martin.* In the course of his long life he was patron to several professional dramatists, among them Ben Jonson and Thomas

Shadwell, who was the most celebrated Restoration imitator of Jonson's humours comedy. Furthermore, Newcastle was an amateur playwright who sometimes had re-
course to the anonymous assistance of his protégés. According to Anthony à Wood, James Shirley "did . . . much
assist his generous patron William duke of Newcastle in
the composure of certain plays, which the duke afterwards
published."[5] *The Country Captain,* a comedy attributed
to Newcastle, so strongly resembles Shirley's comedies
that when A. H. Bullen came upon an untitled manuscript
version of the play he confidently, and perhaps justly,
printed it as Shirley's.[6] Another comedy attributed to Newcastle, *The Triumphant Widow,* bears an equally marked
resemblance to the works of Shadwell. Indeed, large portions of the play reappeared, altered but clearly recog-
nizable, in Shadwell's *Bury Fair.*[7] Dryden too seems for
a time to have enjoyed, or at least hoped to enjoy, Newcastle's patronage, for he dedicated to Newcastle his next
comedy, *An Evening's Love,* performed in 1668 and
printed in 1671.

In view of Newcastle's habit of getting professional
assistance in his plays, one must be careful in arriving at
a judgment of his capacity as dramatist. A short dramatic
piece, entitled *A Pleasante & Merrye Humor off A Roge,*
may with some confidence be attributed to Newcastle
alone, since it exists in a manuscript in his handwriting in
the library at Welbeck Abbey, formerly his principal
country seat. The position of the *Roge* in the manuscript
indicates that it was written between 1655 and 1660, and
the manuscript is a fair copy;[8] we may therefore assume
that the *Roge* is neither a piece of juvenilia nor a rough
draft. It is decidedly amateurish in construction, characterization, and dialogue. Most of its episodes occur, revised, in *The Triumphant Widow.* "After reading New-

castle's draft," says Alfred Harbage, "one is inclined to give whatever credit is due for *The Triumphant Widow,* and indeed for Newcastle's other late comedy, *The Humourous Lovers, . . .* to Thomas Shadwell."[9] The evidence seems to indicate that Newcastle was an amateur with more enthusiasm than ability. I believe that Dryden deserves the credit for *Sir Martin* as a finished product, and that Newcastle was either directly or indirectly responsible for the raw material from which it was manufactured.[10]

Sir William Davenant, manager of the Duke's Company, was an old acquaintance of Newcastle, and it is easy to imagine how he would get hold of a play by the Duke. It is more difficult to see why Dryden, associated with a rival company, would be selected either by Davenant or by the Duke to adapt the play. Possibly he was selected because he was a rising young dramatist, with three consecutive successful plays to his credit.[11] The next question is why did Dryden agree to undertake the job? Not because he had any high hopes for the play, either as an aesthetic or as a financial success. Although his extensive alterations of Molière's play are often in line with his theory, he could not change the basic situation of *L'Étourdi,* and that situation is ill suited to his ideal of comedy. He preferred comedy of wit; Celadon and Florimel manifest their extravagant wildness chiefly in witty dialogue. But *L'Étourdi* is a comedy of folly. A young man, thwarted in love by the opposition of his elders, turns for assistance to his clever valet, but by his blundering spoils the fantastically ingenious schemes that the valet concocts. Obviously such a hero could not be made a Celadon.

Moreover, Dryden must have thought that adaptation of Molière was a risky business. Before 1667 only one English adaptation of Molière had been staged: Davenant's

Playhouse to be Let (1663) contains a loosely translated portion of *Sganarelle, ou le cocu imaginaire,* designed to satirize the performance of a troupe of French comedians. Its lack of success is manifest in the fact that between 1663 and 1667 no English dramatist adapted Molière. The great popularity of *Sir Martin* is probably responsible for the wide use of Molière in subsequent Restoration comedies.[12] Dryden's opinion on the use of French plays is probably reflected in Neander's disparagement of French drama in the *Essay,* particularly in Neander's statement, in a context including comedy as well as tragedy, that "no French plays, when translated, have, or ever can succeed on the English stage."[13] But it is not unlikely that Newcastle should attempt to import Molière. As a royalist in exile on the Continent, part of the time in Paris, he probably heard talk of the success of Molière's early comedies, among them *L'Étourdi,* and may even have seen them performed. Two of the early English adaptations of Molière—Flecknoe's *Demoiselles à la Mode* and Shadwell's *Sullen Lovers* —were dedicated to him.

Dryden's main inducement in undertaking the task was, I think, the favor of the Duke of Newcastle—perhaps the very "favours" for which he expresses thanks in dedicating to Newcastle his next comedy, *An Evening's Love.* Consequently, I believe that the play is best seen as a compromise between Dryden's desire to please the Duke and his desire to follow his own theory of comedy.

If Dryden had not aimed to please the Duke, he could have made the adaptation conform much more closely to his theory. Although he could not have made the blundering Sir Martin a wit, he could have reduced the emphasis on Sir Martin's folly by adding another plot, serious or witty, of equal or greater importance. But Newcastle would of course want the play to be primarily a comedy of folly, as Molière's is. Accordingly, Dryden, although he has drastically altered Molière's plot and has added a subplot for variety, has made the blundering Sir Martin his principal figure and has indeed made him a bigger fool than Molière's Lélie.

Like *Secret Love*, *Sir Martin* agrees with Dryden's theory in adhering approximately to the unities of action, place, and time. Since both of its plots are comic, Dryden in linking them was not troubled with the problem of indecorum.

In the subplot Mrs. Christian, a young fortune-hunter, coached by her aunt, the veteran Lady Dupe, sells herself to Lord Dartmouth and then, discovering that she is pregnant, induces him to provide a husband for her. Dryden links the plots by having Dartmouth hire Warner, Sir Martin's clever servant, to find the husband. Warner chooses as victim Sir Martin's rival, Sir John Swallow. Lady Dupe is another important link. She is Sir Martin's cousin, and she assists Sir Martin in his efforts to marry the heroine, Millisent, in despite of Millisent's father, Squire Moody. When Millisent and Moody come to town, Lady Dupe persuades them to stay at her house, where Mrs. Christian is also operating. Dryden is therefore able to adhere to the unity of place, and even to keep his "scenes unbroken" most of the time. The unity of time, curiously enough, is preserved in the main plot, but not in the subplot. The events of the main plot occupy only a day. At the beginning of the play Lord Dartmouth has not yet "enjoyed" Mrs. Christian. When, in Act III, she announces that she is pregnant by him, it is clear that not hours but days have elapsed in the subplot. In Act IV, Dartmouth clearly implies a lapse of days when he complains that "every night" he has to buy Mrs. Christian's favors anew.

It is unlikely that Dryden would have been guilty of

such a discrepancy if he had been free to invent a subplot. Significantly, the subplot is unlike any of Dryden's other comedies, but it resembles rather closely the subplot of *The Humorous Lovers,* a play attributed to Newcastle (there is no strong evidence of a ghostwriter's hand in this one, but, with Newcastle, we can never be sure) which was performed by the Duke's Company only about four and a half months before the first appearance of *Sir Martin.* In the *Humorous Lovers* subplot Mrs. Hood, a worldly and unscrupulous old matchmaker, teaches Dameris, an innocent country girl, how to turn her charms to profit. As is Mrs. Christian, Dameris is instructed to raise her price by playing hard to get; like Mrs. Christian, she proves to be an apt pupil and is ultimately married to a wealthy fool who is pleased by her seeming innocence. There are differences between the two subplots: greater stress is placed on Mrs. Christian's affectation of innocence than on Dameris'; Mrs. Christian is shown in lengthy scenes using her wiles, Dameris is not; and in the *Humorous Lovers* subplot there is no character corresponding to Lord Dartmouth. But the parallels seem too striking to be coincidental. It is not likely that Dryden of his own accord imitated the *Humorous Lovers* subplot; surely he could have found some way to please Newcastle without perpetrating a discrepancy in time. It is more likely that Newcastle specifically suggested the subplot, perhaps even wrote the original draft of it, and left it to poor Dryden to polish it and fit it into the play as well as he could.

L'Étourdi is not the only source of the main plot of *Sir Martin.* About half of it is taken from another French comedy, Quinault's *L'Amant indiscret.* However, Quinault's play is very like Molière's; indeed, they have a common source. Dryden's idea was probably to select the most effective episodes of both plays. In Quinault's the

heroine has a maid, Rosette. Dryden uses her in his denouement, and some of the episodes from Quinault he perhaps chose because she figures in them. His selection was
also influenced by his modifications of characters and situation. For example, the early episodes of *L'Étourdi* have
to do with Mascarille's efforts to get money so that Lélie
may buy his inamorata, who is a slave. Since Dryden's
Millisent is not a slave, he employs none of these episodes.

The episodes that Dryden has borrowed from Molière
and Quinault border on farce, and two that he has taken
from other sources go even further. In Act V, Sir Martin
attempts to prove himself a man of parts by pretending to
sing and play the lute while Warner, concealed nearby,
actually provides the music. The ruse is discovered when
Sir Martin grows so enthralled by his performance that he
continues to go through the motions after Warner stops
producing the sounds. The other episode, the last in the
play, is still more outlandish. Sir Martin, Warner, and
a confederate, disguised as mummers, crash a party cele-
brating Sir John Swallow's imminent marriage to Millisent.
On the pretext of playing a game called the "Frolick of the
Altitudes," they induce Moody and Sir John to stand on
tall stools. While the pair are thus marooned, Warner,
Sir Martin, Millisent, and the maid Rose sneak away and
marry.

In both French plays the blundering lover finally gets
his girl, through a rather improbable turn of events. In
Quinault's play the clever valet and the maid Rosette are
also to be married. Dryden provides a different denouement, which is just as improbable as the French ones.
Millisent, having discovered at last that Sir Martin is a
fool and Warner a wit, disguises herself and Rose and, in
the double wedding that follows, lets Rose marry Sir

Martin while she marries Warner. It then transpires that
Warner is a gentleman who has squandered his estate.

In accord with his theory, Dryden has made Sir Martin and Squire Moody humours characters; not in accord
with his theory, he has made them mechanic humours.
Sir Martin's humour is an extravagant self-conceit that
leads him to fancy himself a wit, particularly as a shrewd
concocter of schemes, when he is in fact an abysmal fool.
Dryden imitates Jonson's method by having another character (Warner) define Sir Martin as a "plotting Fool" before Sir Martin appears. Molière's Lélie once and Quinault's Cléandre twice plume themselves on schemes they
have devised, and these scenes may have given Dryden the
idea for Sir Martin's humour. But the conceit of Lélie and
Cléandre is transitory, while Sir Martin's is made the key-
stone of his character and is emphasized throughout the
play.

Squire Moody's humour is also introduced in the Jonsonian fashion before he appears. Lady Dupe says of him,

> the old Squire is humoursome;
> He's stout, and plain in speech and in behaviour;
> He loves none of the fine Town-tricks of breeding,
> But stands up for the old *Elizabeth* way in all things.

There is nothing like this idosyncrasy in the characters of
Moody's French counterparts, Trufaldin in *L'Étourdi* and
Lidame in *L'Amant indiscret.* Downright, in Jonson's
Every Man in His Humour, has the humour of irascible in-
sistence on plain speaking and may be the source of
Moody's humour. In trying to persuade Moody that Sir
Martin is "of his humour," other characters twice describe
him as "downright."

Squire Moody, like Sir Martin, displays his humour
throughout the play. At one point Dryden sets the two

humours against each other for comic effect. Sir Martin, a conceited fool and a gentleman by birth, is a fop. When brought into the presence of Squire Moody he attempts to impress the old man with his modish speech and behavior. Such affectation of course infuriates the downright Moody. As I have noted, Dryden similarly exploits two of the humours in *The Wild Gallant,* and in doing so may be imitating Jonson.

Warner and Millisent fit Dryden's theory. Warner is of Celadon's species, a witty, profligate gentleman, very different from the stock clever servant of the two French comedies. Because of his status as servant and because the foolish Sir Martin dominates the play, Warner's character as gallant is not well developed. There are no extended passages of repartee between him and Millisent or even between him and Rose. However, his wit is demonstrated by the intrigues he concocts and by the resourcefulness that he shows in saving himself when Sir Martin's folly has put him into an embarrassing situation. His "wildness" is frequently indicated by his cynical and indelicate manner of speaking; and in the concluding lines of the play, when Warner's status as gentleman has at last been revealed, Dryden is able to provide a very brief passage of amorous repartee between him and Millisent.

As Warner is of Celadon's species, so Millisent is of Florimel's. Her character, like Warner's, is developed only sketchily. However, her "wildness" is indicated by the escapade in which she marries Warner, who, as far as she knows, is only a servant; and her wit and admiration for wit are manifested at intervals throughout the play. She is attracted to Sir Martin because he has been represented to her as a wit. As soon as she learns the truth, she rejects him and chooses Warner, the true wit. Like Warner, she is very different from her counterparts in the two French plays. Molière's Célie and Quinault's Lucresse occasionally show cleverness in intriguing (Célie once, Lucresse twice), but neither of them ever evinces any admiration for wit, and both are on the whole mute and passive heroines of the sort that Dryden objects to in the *Essay*.

Millisent's maid Rose has as her counterpart Quinault's Rosette, the maid of Lucresse. Rose is wittier than Rosette, just as Millisent is wittier than Lucresse. It is pretty clear that in Warner, Millisent, and Rose, Dryden attempted to provide at least a flavoring of the gaiety, wit, and profligacy he praised in the *Essay* and used so extensively in *Secret Love*.

Though the resemblance is by no means as close as that of the subplots, the main plot of *Sir Martin,* with its mechanic humours, its extravagant farce, and its flavoring of profligate wit, is somewhat like Newcastle's *Humorous Lovers.* In Newcastle's play the flavoring of wit is afforded in two characters: Mrs. Pleasant, a witty and coquettish widow, and Colonel Boldman, a witty rake who scorns legitimate love in favor of the relationships that are to be had on a strictly commercial basis. In the course of their amorous skirmishing, Boldman pretends to go mad. Newcastle exploits this feigned madness in extravagantly farcical scenes. At one point Boldman enters, his face blackened with soot, and announces that he has just returned from a journey to hell, of which he gives an absurd and vulgar account in doggerel. Jonsonian humour is provided in two other characters, Furrs and Sir Anthony Altalk. Sir Anthony is a fop who has the humour, very feebly developed, of "affecting . . . general acquaintance."[14] As a humorous fop he is of course analogous to Sir Martin. Furrs is an old man whose humour is an extravagant fear of cold. His humour is the excuse for farcical scenes: dancers repre-

senting the four winds blow upon him with bellows, Boldman partially disrobes him and douses him with water.
Furrs as a humorous old man is analogous to Moody; and,
like Furrs, Moody is the victim (in the Frolick of the Altitudes) of a farcical practical joke.

The Boldman-Pleasant affair in *The Humorous Lovers*
indicates that Newcastle had some regard for amorous wit,
but the culminating farcical episodes of Boldman's feigned
madness, as well as the mechanic humours of Furrs and
Altalk and the nature of the subplot, indicate that his
regard for farce and folly was even greater. I believe that
Dryden, though he preferred comedy of love and wit,
made *Sir Martin* primarily a comedy of folly to please
Newcastle, conforming to his theory only when he could
do so without running counter to Newcastle's predilections.

2.

The revised *Wild Gallant* also appeared in 1667. Why
did Dryden, who only recently, in March, 1667, had succeeded with his comedy of love and wit in *Secret Love,*
endanger his hard-won reputation by resuscitating this
early failure, a play quite different from *Secret Love?*

It will be remembered that *Sir Martin* was presented
by the Duke's Company, although Dryden was at the time
writing regularly for the King's Company. Although it was
not until 1691 that Dryden was named in print as the
author of *Sir Martin,* Pepys's entry shows that in 1667 it
was widely known that Dryden had helped write the play.
It was probably not until early in 1668 that Dryden en-
tered into his agreement with the King's Company, whereby he was to provide them with three plays a year in return for a share and a quarter in the company.[15] But
even before this formal agreement the King's Company

must have felt that they had some moral claim on Dryden's output because he had been writing regularly for them; and certainly they would not have been pleased to learn that he had had a hand in the huge success of the rival company. Now *The Wild Gallant* is somewhat like the main plot of *Sir Martin*. Both are a mixture of Jonsonian humours, absurd intrigue, and amorous wit. There is even a correspondence between the two sets of characters: Lord Nonsuch and Squire Moody, the humorous old fathers; Sir Timorous and Sir Martin, the humorous fools who are unsuccessful suitors; Constance and Millisent, the witty daughters; Isabel and Rose, their witty companions; Loveby and Warner, the witty, impoverished gallants who are successful suitors. In both plays the unsuccessful suitor is punished for his folly by being tricked into marriage with the witty and impecunious companion of the heroine. Perhaps to soothe the members of the King's Company Dryden suggested the revival of *The Wild Gallant,* arguing that since it was the same sort of play as *Sir Martin* it should do pretty well.

In the epilogue to the revised version Dryden comments on the difficulty of writing comedy. Since comedy deals with common persons and events, he says, everyone is qualified as a critic, and "each defect may spye." And

> What's so common, to make pleasant too,
> Is more than any wit can always do.

Present English tastes make the task still more difficult. The audience insists on having a fool caricatured in each new comedy, and as a result the fools are growing wary. Furthermore, when with "much adoe" a fool is got on the stage,

> Your Poets make him such rare things to say,
> That he's more Wit than any Man i'th' Play.

> But of so ill a mingle with the rest,
> As when a Parrat's taught to break a jeast.

Under such conditions "our dull Poet" is "in despair to please." The prologue concludes,

> Would you but change for serious Plot and Verse
> This mottley garniture of Fool and Farce,
>
> .   .   .   .
>
> Our Poet yields you should this Play refuse:
> As Tradesmen, by the change of fashions, lose
> With some content their fripperies of *France,*
> In hope it may their staple Trade advance.

Dryden undoubtedly preferred "serious Plot and Verse" to any sort of comedy. Yet it should be noted that he is here objecting not to the best comedy but to the "mottley garniture of Fool and Farce" presently in fashion. His allusion to the "fripperies of *France*" apparently means that he considered farce to be a French fashion adopted in England. This interpretation is consistent with the *Essay,* in which Neander accuses French comedy of imitating the unnatural "ridiculum" of the "Old Comedy," and also with Dryden's preface to *An Evening's Love,* written four years later, in which he condemns farce as a French import. If the epilogue has this meaning, Dryden is implicitly condemning his own farcical and very popular adaptation from the French, *Sir Martin.* Indeed, it may even be that the great success of *Sir Martin* occasioned his complaint against the current fashion in comedy.

Dryden's willingness to let the audience "refuse" *The Wild Gallant* and his figurative association of the play with the "fripperies of *France*" indicate that at this time he had a low opinion of the play. I have suggested that upon maturer consideration he came to realize that this play, which in the 1663 prologue he had defended as old and English, resembled the Frenchified farce of *Sir Martin.* But if *The Wild Gallant* is farcical, it is not so by intention. When the play was published two years later, Dryden made this point clear in a passage of his preface: "It was the first attempt I made in *Dramatique Poetry;* and, I find since, a very bold one, to begin with *Comedy;* which is the most difficult part of it . . . I doubt not but you will see in it, the uncorrectness of a young Writer." In other words, the play is an attempt at true comedy, weakened by the blunders of a beginner.

Another feature of the epilogue to the revived *Wild Gallant* requires discussion. The epilogue begins,

> Of all Dramatique Writing, Comick Wit,
> As 'tis the best, so 'tis most hard to hit.

The statement that comedy is the best of all sorts of dramatic writing is quite at odds with Dryden's statement in the preface to *An Evening's Love,* four years later, that comedy is "inferior to all sorts of dramatic writing." It is this second view of comedy which is Dryden's true view. In the *Essay of Dramatic Poesy,* written in 1665, comedy is regarded as "low" because it deals with "common persons and ordinary speaking." And thirty years later, in "A Parallel of Poetry and Painting," Dryden expressed the same opinion of comedy.

Furthermore, the statement that comedy is the best sort of drama does not fit its context. Nowhere in the epilogue does Dryden explain why he thinks comedy the best, nor is his subsequent account of comedy very flattering. And his wish that the audience

> Would . . . change for serious Plot and Verse
> This mottley garniture of Fool and Farce

is inconsistent. If comedy is the best of all sorts of drama, why does he not wish that the audience would change farce for true comedy, instead of for serious plays?

There is a simple and plausible solution to the problems created by "As 'tis the best." Sargeaunt lists as one of Dryden's peculiar spellings "lest" for "least."[16] If Dryden had written "lest" in the second line of the epilogue, the printer could have changed it to "best" merely by mistaking the *l* for a *b*—a mistake not difficult to make, since the two letters look somewhat alike in script, and since "lest" is an unusual spelling. Once made, the mistake would probably have got by any proofreader but Dryden himself, for the word fits its immediate context well enough; only when it is considered in its relation to the epilogue as a whole does its inconsistency become apparent. Even Dryden might have failed to notice the mistake; neither the epilogue nor the play to which it is attached is a work to whose publication he would have given very careful attention.

What Dryden actually wrote, I believe, is that comedy is the *least* of all sorts of drama. The *Oxford English Dictionary* lists as an earlier meaning of "least" "Lowest in power or position; meanest," and quotes as an example a line of Dryden's translation of the *Aeneid*. Applying this meaning to the epilogue, we obtain, "comedy is the lowest, or meanest, of all sorts of drama." This statement is quite in accord with the *Essay,* the preface to *An Evening's Love,* and "A Parallel of Poetry and Painting." Furthermore, it fits its context very well. In lines 3-8 of the epilogue, Dryden calls attention to the "common" subject-matter of comedy; it is this common subject-matter which makes comedy the "most hard to hit" of all sorts of drama, and, according to Dryden's view, it is also this common subject-matter that makes comedy the least, or lowest, of all sorts of drama. Here are the first eight lines, with "lest" substituted for "best":

> Of all Dramatique Writing, Comick Wit,
> As 'tis the lest, so 'tis most hard to hit.
> For it lies all in level to the eye,
> Where all may judge, and each defect may spye.
> Humour is that which every day we meet,
> And therefore known as every publick street;
> In which, if e'r the Poet go astray,
> You all can point, 'twas there he lost his way.

In the *Essay* Neander makes precisely the same connection between the lowness and the difficulty of comedy, and makes it in similar terms: "this excellent contrivance [the plot of *Epicoene*] is still the more to be admired, because 'tis comedy, where the persons are only of common rank, and their business private, not elevated by passions or high concernments, as in serious plays. Here every one is a proper judge of all he sees, nothing is represented but that with which he daily converses: so that by consequence all faults lie open to discovery, and few are pardonable." Since comedy is the most difficult as well as the lowest of all sorts of drama, we can readily understand why Dryden ends the epilogue by wishing for a change to "serious Plot and Verse."

3.

In early November of 1667, some two and a half months after the appearance of *Sir Martin,* the Duke's Company staged an adaptation of Shakespeare's *Tempest* written by Dryden and Sir William Davenant. Perhaps it was Dryden's work on the very successful *Sir Martin* which gave him the opportunity to collaborate with Davenant. It is likely that he welcomed the opportunity; collaboration

with Davenant, who was probably the most prominent theatrical figure of that day, was something of an honor, as
well as potentially profitable.

In his preface Dryden gives an account of the collaboration which seems reliable. Davenant, he says, conceived
the idea of creating, as a counterpart of the woman who
has never seen a man, a man who has never seen a woman. "This excellent contrivance he was pleas'd to com-
municate to me, and to desire my assistance in it. I confess that from the very first moment it so pleas'd me, that
I never writ any thing with more delight. . . . my writing
received daily his amendments." The other major addition
to the play is an expansion of the low-comedy plot. This
Dryden attributes almost entirely to Davenant. I shall con-
fine my discussion to the portion of the play which Dryden
says that he wrote: that involving the male and female
innocents.

The man who has never seen a woman is a new character, Hippolito, brought as a child to the island by Prospero. Another new character, Dorinda, sister to Miranda,
is provided as Hippolito's mate. Prospero, having learned
by astrological prognostication that danger threatens Hippolito if he sees a woman, has kept his male and female
charges separated, telling Hippolito that women are the
natural enemies of men, the two girls that men are the
natural enemies of women. The three young people and
Ferdinand become involved in a quadrangular relationship
that produces jealousies and rivalry.

The portion of the play involving these four lovers has
been subjected to severe deprecation by modern critics.
The principal charges against it are indecency and absurdity: "The . . . scenes of suggestive innocence are . . .
obviously the result of the immoral, degenerate qualities
of the age. . . . It loved to hear the coarsest of sentiments
retailed by girls hardly out of their teens";[17] "one aim and

one alone animated its authors: to pander";[18] "the character of Hippolito . . . is almost the silliest in dramatic literature";[19] Dorinda is "really pathological," Miranda is "older but no wiser."[20] But Dryden's portion of the play is not so indecent or so absurd as it is made out to be. The indecency of Dryden's portion is founded almost wholly on double meanings spoken unintentionally by the three innocents and intentionally by the sophisticated persons who converse with them. Typical specimens of both kinds occur in the following passage from Act II:

PROSP. [Women] despise old age, and spare it for that reason:
It is below their conquest, their fury falls
Alone upon the young.

HIP. Why then the fury of the young shall fall on them again.
Pray turn me loose upon 'em . . .

PROSP. They'll haunt you in your very sleep.

HIP. Then I'le revenge it on them when I wake.

Such dialogue is not especially noxious. Like the similar dialogue in *Secret Love,* it is witty, and the Restoration audience probably considered it more witty than indecent. The charge that Dryden's indecency is aggravated by the supposed innocence of three of the characters seems unjust. The three innocents manifest nothing more than a strong attraction towards and curiosity about the opposite sex. Such an attitude is usually considered entirely normal and healthy. Nor do the experienced Ferdinand and Prospero attempt to debauch or disillusion these innocents; they are steered into marriage, and their embarrassing questions are answered or avoided with a reasonable degree of delicacy.

In justifying as normal the behavior of the three innocents I have answered in part the charge of absurdity.
Indeed, it is curious that the innocents should be branded
as both indecent and unnatural, since to young people in
their circumstances sexual exuberance would be quite natural. It is of course very unlikely that the three should
have been kept so innocent for so long, that Hippolito and
the girls should have been separated on a small island for
years, only to meet quite easily soon after the play begins.
But then it is also unlikely that Prospero should be able to
summon up spirits by waving a wand, and Shakespeare,
not Dryden, is responsible for that implausible circumstance. The basic situation of the play, like that of Shakespeare's, is intentionally fantastic, as is shown by its sub-
title, *The Enchanted Island*. If the situation is accepted,
the behavior of Dryden's persons becomes adequately natural. Later, in "The Grounds of Criticism in Tragedy,"
Dryden said that Shakespeare in Caliban "seems . . . to
have created a person which was not in Nature, a boldness
which, at first sight, would appear intolerable; for he
makes him a species of himself, begotten by an incubus
on a witch. . . . Whether or no his generation can be defended, I leave to philosophy; but of this I am certain,
that the poet has most judiciously furnished him with a
person, a language, and a character, which will suit him."
The same idea, I believe, is behind Dryden's own characterization of Hippolito, Dorinda, and Miranda. He left
it to philosophy to decide whether anyone could be kept so
innocent so long, and occupied himself with judiciously
conforming the behavior of the three to their hypothetical
innocence.

As a matter of fact, Dryden seems to have taken something of a philosophical interest in the nature of innocence.
When he later turned *Paradise Lost* into a play, he called
it *The State of Innocence*. Though the play is no master-

piece, Dryden took it seriously; and, in several ways, his Adam and Eve, in their attitudes and conduct, resemble the three innocents in *The Tempest*. Indeed, sometimes the conduct and attitudes of the three innocents also resemble those of Milton's Adam and Eve; and Milton is hardly ever charged with willful absurdity or indecency. *Paradise Lost* was first published in August, 1667. Dryden could have read it in time to be influenced by it in the characterization of his own innocents. The parallels I am about to cite are too general to stand as evidence of Milton's influence on Dryden (though I think that there is a possibility of some influence). I cite them to counter the charges of indecency and absurdity.

It seems natural the each of the three should take Prospero's word that the opposite sex is dangerous, since none of them has any knowledge to the contrary. It is also natural that the girls, despite Prospero's warning, should try to get a look at their "enemy." Milton's Eve is similarly rash and self-willed when, despite Adam's warning against the wiles of Satan, she insists on facing the danger alone. When Miranda and Dorinda see Hippolito, they are so strongly attracted by him that they vie with one another for the privilege of addressing him. Dorinda wins. Hippolito, obeying a mysterious impulse, takes her hand; the physical contact intensifies the mutual attraction that they experience. Milton's Adam is strongly drawn to Eve when first he sees her; he at once begins to persuade her to join him in the "Nuptial Bow'r," and as a result of the subsequent lovemaking, is "transported" and enslaved by her beauty and charm.[21] Indeed, his vulnerability to female charm is his sole weakness. Eve's behavior upon first seeing a man differs from Dorinda's (though I am not sure that it is much more natural): instinctively coy, she runs away. A little later she behaves more like Dorinda: Adam pursues, explaining, and when his "gentle hand" seizes hers, she yields.[22]

After the meeting Dorinda, realizing how "tame" Hippolito has been, is confident of her ability to handle him, and she subsequently develops into something of a coquette. Dryden's Eve is instinctively coquettish. Milton's Eve also seems to have a kind of innocent embryonic coquetry; Milton describes her as acknowledging her subjection to Adam with "coy submission," "sweet reluctant amorous delay."[23]

Later Hippolito refuses to believe that he and Dorinda will ever grow old; but this is a natural error, universal among the young. Hippolito then learns from Ferdinand that the mysterious longing he experiences is love. Practically all Restoration comedy (not to mention contemporary drama) depends upon the naturalness of Hippolito's next reaction. He resolves to increase his pleasure by loving not one woman, but all women. He asks Ferdinand and Dorinda to help him win the love of Miranda and is surprised when they refuse. But, humanly self-centered and unreasonable, he strenuously objects when Dorinda threatens to love Ferdinand.

Hippolito and Dorinda are ignorant of death. When he is bady wounded in a duel, they think he is falling into a "cold sleep," and Dorinda wishes to build a fire to warm him. Both Milton's Adam and Dryden's Eve are ignorant of death until it is explained to them.[24] Milton's Adam also confuses sleep with a permanent condition, though his confusion is the reverse of Hippolito's: about to fall asleep for the first time after his creation, he apprehends dissolution.[25]

After Ariel's magic has revived Hippolito, he and Dorinda speculate on the nature of the soul. They identify it as the breath—an error common among primitive peoples, and one of which Dryden must have been aware, for he was surely enough of a Latin scholar to be acquainted with the various meanings of the word *anima.*

Presently Hippolito resolves the romantic conflict by announcing that henceforth he will be constant to Dorinda, because his fear of losing her has taught him to appreciate her. In the closing scene Dryden capitalizes not too indelicately on the three innocents' embarrassing but natural ignorance of the reproductive process. Dryden's Adam and Eve are similarly ignorant.

Dryden sometimes goes a little too far. Hippolito's proposal that he and Ferdinand fight by taking turns with a single sword transcends the bounds of common sense. He goes too far also in what is perhaps the only portion of the play which would have suited a nineteenth-century moralist. Just after Miranda has seen Hippolito for the first time, Prospero asks her whether she loves the creature. She replies, "How is it likely that I should, except the thing had first lov'd me?" "Cherish those thoughts: you have a gen'rous soul," says Prospero. And Dryden's treatment of innocent love in *The Tempest* is on the whole far less elevated and refined than Milton's in *Paradise Lost,* even than Dryden's in *The State of Innocence.* But the general resemblances I have cited indicate that Dryden meant his portion of *The Tempest* to be comedy, not obscene farce. We can understand why Pepys found *The Tempest* not the most indecent, or the most absurd, but the "most innocent" play he ever saw.[26]

Ferdinand, like Miranda, has a generous soul; the two are perfectly constant to one another from the beginning and behave nobly throughout the play. They are akin to the serious lovers of Dryden's tragicomedies and heroic plays. Hippolito and Dorinda, on the other hand, are akin to the comic lovers of the tragicomedies. Like Celadon,

Hippolito is unaffectedly promiscuous. His promiscuity is constrasted with Ferdinand's constancy when the two debate at length the question whether it is advisable to love one or to love all. Dorinda, like Florimel, is a pushing young thing who is aware of the power of her charms and not averse to using it. Like Florimel, she is ready to take an active part in keeping her man. When Hippolito announces that he intends to love Miranda, too, she threatens in retaliation to take up with Ferdinand. Her behavior here constrasts with that of Miranda, who says that if Ferdinand proves false she will die. Clearly, in working out the characters of his four lovers Dryden has made use of the same contrast of serious and comic love which he employed in *Secret Love*.

4.

Dryden's next comedy, *An Evening's Love, or The Mock Astrologer,* was successfully staged by the King's Company in June, 1668. It was not published until 1671, when it appeared with a preface which is an important statement of Dryden's views concerning comedy. I shall discuss the preface as a whole in its chronological context in my next chapter, citing in the present discussion only passages which have to do specifically with the play.

This play is fuller of variety than any of Dryden's previous ones. It consists of two plots, both of them comic, in which nine lovers (including two servants) engage simultaneously in six complicated love-affairs, featuring many extravagantly farcical episodes, much repartee, a swordfight, a pursuit, two disguises, two dances, and four songs. The unities of time and place are both observed: the time is one day, the place, Madrid. Dryden specifies the day of the play, Mardi Gras. This choice of day lends verisimilitude to the holiday spirit of the play, with its numerous songs and dances, and also to the rapidity with which the love-affairs progress: the marriages must take place immediately or be postponed until after Lent. In thus choosing a special day for his play Dryden is using a modification of a device which Neander mentions approvingly in the *Essay*: "viz. the making choice of some signal and long-expected day, whereon the action of the play is to depend." *Liaison des scènes* is maintained except for a break between the first two scenes in Act I and a virtual break in Act IV, where Dryden has to open and shut the backdrop to maintain the continuity.

Dryden has also sought to achieve unity of action by making the characters in the two plots acquainted with or related to one another and by making some of them agents in both plots. The play focuses on the amours of two visiting English gallants. One of them, Wildblood, has a stormy but gay affair with a Spanish girl, Jacinta. There is a parallel affair between Maskall and Beatrix, their respective servants. In the other plot, Wildblood's friend Bellamy finds his love for Jacinta's sister Theodosia complicated by a rival, Don Melchor. Melchor is deceitfully dividing his affections between Theodosia and her cousin Aurelia, who is loved by the Englishmen's host, Don Lopez. Maskall engineers a scheme whereby Bellamy passes himself off as an astrologer and uses his position to reveal the duplicity of Melchor.

The sources of the play are numerous. The principal ones are, for the Wildblood-Jacinta plot, Molière's *Le Dépit amoureux;* for the mock-astrologer plot, Thomas Corneille's *Le Feint astrologue* and a portion of Mlle de Scudéry's romance, *Ibrahim ou l'Illustre Bassa,* both of them derived from a play by Calderón, *El Astrologo Fingido.*[27]

The regularity and variety of the play are in accord with Dryden's theory. So are Wildblood and Jacinta. They are not at all like the earnest young lovers of *Le Dépit amoureux,* but are a witty, professedly profligate couple like Celadon and Florimel. They manifest the same extravagant "wildness" that is the distinguishing characteristic of Celadon and Florimel, and that, I believe, Dryden worked out in accord with his conception of humours characterization. Since a principal advantage of a humours character is that it affords the variety of novelty, Dryden is not, strictly speaking, abiding by his theory in repeating the humour of Celadon and Florimel in Wildblood and Jacinta. However, Dryden considered correspondence to theory not an end in itself but a means to the end of pleasing the audience; it is for this reason that Neander objects to slavish adherence to the unities. As long as discriminating playgoers liked a humour, he was no doubt willing to give it to them. Furthermore, Dryden does provide some variety by a change of setting. The setting of *Secret Love,* though nominally Sicily, is actually England; but the setting of *An Evening's Love* is intended to be Spanish. In the play English and Spanish manners are often deliberately contrasted for comic effect. This Spanish flavoring adds a new ingredient to the wild couple. The Wildblood-Jacinta plot is the best part of the play, and Dryden's preface shows that he considered Wildblood and Jacinta his two most important characters. Bellamy, the other Englishman, is only moderately wild and witty; Theodosia is only rarely witty and hardly wild at all in comparison to Jacinta. The male Spanish lovers are nondescript and unimportant, serving mainly as butts for Wildblood and Bellamy.

Aurelia, the third Spanish lady, is of considerable interest. She is a character new in Dryden's comedy, a female fop, analogous to the affected ladies in Molière's *Les Précieuses ridicules*. Dryden borrows a detail or two from Molière's play, but other characteristics of Aurelia seem to be taken from the affectations of English ladies. She instructs her maid to say "Parn me mam" instead of "Pardon me, Madam," and uses French words which Molière would not have considered precious. She is foolish rather than witty and is therefore inconsistent with Dryden's preference for witty comedy. On the other hand, she is in accord with Dryden's theory in that hers is not a low but an elevated sort of folly which might be called pseudo-wit and which might be included to set off, by contrast, the true wit. Aurelia's affected discourse contrasts with the wit of Jacinta. Their attitudes towards love are also contrasting. Aurelia takes her amours very seriously, affecting the idealized, "platonic" kind of love conventional in the heroic plays and the French romances. Jacinta, like Florimel, wittily makes fun of this attitude. Compare, for example, their views concerning jealousy and constancy and "deserving." In Act II, Jacinta, having met Wildblood just once, tells Beatrix that she loves him "most vehemently." Their conversation continues as follows:

BEAT. But are you sure he will deserve this kindness?

JAC. I never trouble my self so long before hand: Jealousies and disquiets are the dregs of an amour; but I'll leave mine before I have drawn it off so low.

Beatrix, however, persuades her to test Wildblood for "the two great virtues of a Lover . . . constancy and liberality." Jacinta tests him twice by disguising herself, but when he fails both tests she marries him anyway. Aurelia, in similar circumstances, is seen to have the true platonic attitude. Don Lopez tells her that her lover Melchor is at this very minute at an assignation with your Cousin in the Garden. . . .

AUR. I swear this Evenings Air begins to incommode me extremely with a cold; but yet in hope of detecting this perjur'd man I am content to stay abroad.

LOP. But withal you must permit me to tell you, Madam, that it is but just I should have some share in a heart which I endeavour to redeem. . . .

AUR. This prize is so very inconsiderable that 'tis not worth the claiming.

LOP. If I thought the boon were small, I would not importune my Princess with the asking it. . . .

CAM. [Aurelia's maid] Mam, I must needs tell your Laship that *Don Lopez* has deserv'd you: for he has acted all along like a Cavalier. . . .

AUR. Don *Lopez* go along with me, I can promise nothing, but I swear I will do my best to disingage my heart from this furious tender which I have for him.

Aurelia in another way does deviate from Dryden's theory: since she is a Spaniard, it is not natural that she should exhibit the affectations of an English lady.

Don Alonzo, father to Theodosia and Jacinta, is in accord with Dryden's theory as a humours character, but deviates from it in that his is a mechanic humour. He is inordinately loquacious and has the habit of taking the words out of other people's mouths. The lowness of his humour is manifest in Dryden's exploitation of it in farcical episodes. In Act III, Lopez tries to tell Alonzo something, but Alonzo so loquaciously accuses him of loquacity that Lopez cannot make himself heard. The two begin to shout at each other simultaneously, and finally Lopez drives

Alonzo off by ringing a bell in his ear. This episode is taken from *Le Dépit amoureux* and is probably the source of Alonzo's humour. But the loquacity of Molière's character, unlike that of Alonzo, is confined to this single episode.

The play abounds in similar foolishness. The last act is the most absurd of all. At one point four men, one to a limb, carry Melchor off the stage while he yells Murder. Much of the farce in the play is taken from the French sources. The use of farce is of course inconsistent with Dryden's theory.

The witty servants, Maskall and Beatrix, probably are also inconsistent. Though Dryden was in favor of witty comedy, he seems to have considered wit appropriate only to gentlefolk. Furthermore, "servingmen" are one of the species of stock characters to which Neander objects.

Pepys, who admired *Secret Love* and *The Tempest,* found *An Evening's Love* "very smutty."[28] As in *Secret Love,* the indecency occurs mainly in the form of double meanings; but here the double meanings are often less witty than vulgar. From the point of view of Dryden's theory, the vulgarity is an aesthetic, not a moral, fault. Refined bawdry is neither more nor less justifiable morally than vulgar bawdry; aesthetically, the latter is inferior to the former, and Dryden, with his admiration for wit, certainly knew that it was.

John Evelyn considered the play "very profane."[29] The profaneness consists mainly of mockery of Roman Catholicism. It reaches a low point in a disagreeable scene in which the two gallants accost the Spanish ladies while the latter are supposedly at prayer in a chapel. However, in partial justification of Dryden it should be said that this scene is probably closer to Restoration reality than the modern reader might suppose. In Wycherley's *Love in*

a Wood two London churches are named along with the
playhouses, Hyde Park, and the Mulberry Garden as "Publick Marts where Widows and Mayds are expos'd."[30] Apparently Bellamy and Wildblood are simply carrying an
English custom to a foreign land. The life of Francis Sey-
mour, Fifth Duke of Somerset, affords an interesting historical parallel to their missionary efforts. In Italy in the
spring of 1678 His Grace was shot and killed by an irate
husband because, it was said, he had affronted the latter's
wife, a lady of quality, in a local church.[31] Another possible excuse for the profaneness is that Dryden may have
regarded the slurs on Catholicism as justifiable satire. He
was an Anglican at the time, and there was anti-Catholic
feeling in England.[32]

Whether or not Dryden considered the profaneness a
defect, he was well aware that the play is a spotty performance. Haste and weariness were probably the main
reasons for its poor quality. In 1667 four plays that he
had written or helped write were produced, and in the
same year he published *Annus Mirabilis*. In the prologue
to the play he says that he has lost the zestfulness of a beginning dramatist and now regards the writing of plays
as "ungrateful drudgery" at which he must "strain himself"
to please the audience. In the epilogue, answering the
charge that he "eas'd his half-tir'd Muse" "betwixt a
French and *English* Plot," he "most unlike an Author,
vow'd 'twas true." He hopes that "His haste his other
errors might excuse."

In the preface to the play Dryden acknowledges the
principal deviation from his theory—the use of farce,
much of it taken from French sources:

most of those comedies, which have been lately written, have
been allied too much to Farce: and this must of necessity fall
out, till we forbear the translation of French plays: for their

poets, wanting judgment to make or to maintain true characters, strive to cover their defects with ridiculous figures and grimaces. While I say this, I accuse myself as well as others: and this very play would rise up in judgment against me, if I would defend all things I have written to be natural: but I confess I have given too much to the people in it, and am ashamed for them as well as for myself, that I have pleased them at so cheap a rate.

Dryden deserves commendation for this candid acknowledgment of his faults; the play was not a failure, and he could easily have justified it if he had wished to be insincere. The passage is also significant for its implication of artistic standards in comedy. The comic dramatist should aim to please, but he should not aim to please too cheaply.

5.

When he deviated from his theory of comedy to write *The Rival Ladies*, Dryden was probably motivated by the fear of failure. His deviation from his theory during the period from 1667 to 1668 may be ascribed to the temptations created by success.[33] Having acquired a reputation as a dramatist, he was given the opportunity to collaborate with Newcastle and with Davenant. He deviated from his critical principles in order to suit the tastes of his collaborators. Perhaps it was a combination of self-confidence and desire to make hay while the sun shone which tempted him to undertake so many plays during this short period.

But he did not abandon his theory entirely. The humours and wit of *Sir Martin* are partly in line with his critical principles, although the play as a whole is far from his ideal of comedy. The lovers in *The Tempest* are, when allowance is made for their fantastic situation, rather like the constrasting heroic and comic lovers of *Secret Love*. In *An Evening's Love* Wildblood and Jacinta are manifestly a wild couple like Celadon and Florimel.

V. 1668-1672: RETURN TO THE THEORY; HIGHER COMEDY

1.

IN "A DEFENCE of an Essay of Dramatic Poesy," first printed in September, 1668, Dryden occupies himself chiefly with replying to Sir Robert Howard's attack, in the preface to *The Duke of Lerma,* on the *Essay.* He is especially concerned with Howard's remarks on the unities and on the use of rhyme in serious plays. At one point Dryden defends his use of rhyme in serious drama by citing his concept of "heightening":

One great reason why prose is not to be used in serious plays, is, because it is too near the nature of converse: there may be too great a likeness; as the most skilful painters affirm, that there may be too near a resemblance in a picture: to take every lineament and feature is not to make an excellent piece, but to take so much only as will make a beautiful resemblance of the whole: and, with an ingenious flattery of nature, to heighten the beauties of some parts, and hide the deformities of the rest. . . .

In *Bartholomew Fair,* or the lowest kind of comedy, that degree of heightening is used, which is proper to set off that subject: . . . the author . . . does so raise his matter . . . as to render it delightful; which he could never have performed, had he only said or done those very things, that are daily spoken or practised in the fair: for then the fair itself would be as full of pleasure to an ingenious person as the play, which we manifestly see it is not. But he hath made an excellent Lazar of it; the copy is of price, though the original be vile.

This concept of heightening, or "ingenious flattery of nature," is a very important feature of Dryden's theory.

Applied to the composition of serious plays, it would produce the tremendous deeds and elevated sentiments of love and honor, expressed in rhyme, of fictional heroes and heroines, as a heightened version of the deeds and words of actual heroes and heroines. Applied to the composition of comedy, it would produce the "wildness" and sustained repartee of Celadons and Florimels as a heightened version of the less airy and profligate discourse and behavior of actual Restoration gallants and their ladies. Clearly, the idea of comic heightening is related to Dryden's concept of a humour. One kind of humour included in Neander's definition is the humour of extravagance in degree: for example, Morose's extreme dislike of noise. This humour could be regarded as a heightened version of the average man's dislike of noise. The heightening, by exaggerating the ridiculous aspects of the average man's dislike of noise, helps the dramatist achieve his two ends of delight and instruction. We are more amused by Morose than we would be by an average man, and Morose also teaches us, better than could an average man, the folly of peevish insistence on quiet. Similarly, Celadon and Florimel, who also have a humour of extravagance in degree, could be regarded as heightened versions of the average Restoration gallant and his lady; and their heightened wildness makes them more delightful than the average.

In the *Essay* Dryden's definition of a play had given both the delight and the instruction of mankind as functions of a play, but in the discussion of drama which followed he was concerned far more with delight than with instruction. Not surprisingly, in the "Defence" we find him saying, "delight is the chief, if not the only, end of poesy." Elsewhere in the "Defence" he requires of poesy in general that it be moral: "moral truth is the mistress of the poet as much as of the philosopher; Poesy must re-

semble natural truth, but it must *be* ethical." Apparently
Dryden, though interested chiefly in delighting his audience, did not sanction unethical modes of delighting.

In the *Essay* Neander had approved of adherence to the
unities of time and place, but had disapproved of the servile regularity that results in barrenness. In the "Defence"
Dryden requires unity of place in both comedy and tragedy, but unity of time only in comedy, since the weighty
events of tragedy naturally require more time than the
small events of comedy. He does not say what should be
done about the unity of time in a two-plot tragicomedy,
where there are both weighty and small events. He conceives tolerantly of both unities: for place, "several places
in the same town or city, or places adjacent to each other
in the same country" will do, but the nearer and fewer
these places, the better; for time, "twenty-four or thirty
hours" at the most. A play should not contain more events
than can naturally take place in the time allotted, but better
too many events than too few: "I think that error the most
pardonable, which in too strait a compass crowds together
many accidents, since it produces more variety, and, consequently, more pleasure to the audience; and because the
nearness of proportion betwixt the imaginary and real time,
does speciously cover the compression of the accidents."
Obviously Dryden still retained his regard for variety as a
source of pleasure. He also retained his regard for Jonson;
he says in the "Defence" that he prefers "the *Silent Woman* before all other plays . . . as I do its author, in judgment, above all other poets."

2.

The preface to *An Evening's Love* (1671) must be
considered in the light of Dryden's quarrel with a rival
dramatist, Thomas Shadwell.[1]

In 1668 Shadwell began to turn out plays for the
Duke's Company. He had most of his success with what
Dryden must have considered low comedy, or even farce,
done in close imitation of Jonson's humours comedy. Shadwell evidently enjoyed the continued patronage of the Duke
of Newcastle. He dedicated his first play, *The Sullen
Lovers,* to Newcastle and praised him profusely in the
epistles of four of his subsequent plays.[2] Newcastle had
formerly shown favor to Jonson, and the plays attributed
to Newcastle have a strong Jonsonian flavor. It is likely
that Newcastle thought well of Jonson, and that he trans-
ferred his benevolence to Shadwell largely because Shadwell was the most fanatical adulator and imitator of Jonson in the Restoration period. Dryden qualified his praise
of Jonson; Shadwell praised him unreservedly.

In the preface to *The Sullen Lovers,* along with much
immoderate praise of Jonson ("the man, of all the World,
I most passionately admire for his Excellency in Dram-
matick-*Poetry*")[3] are passages attacking Dryden. Shadwell does not mention Dryden by name, but his allusions
are clear enough. Significantly, he compares Dryden's
plays unfavorably to Jonson's and attacks Dryden as anti-
Jonsonian. In the *Essay,* first published in the same year
as *The Sullen Lovers,* Neander says of Jonson, "One cannot say he wanted wit, but rather that he was frugal of
it. . . . Humour was his proper sphere," and, later, "as he
did not want imagination, so none ever said he had much
to spare." Shadwell replied:

I have known some of late so Insolent to say, that *Ben Johnson* wrote his best *Playes* without Wit; imagining, that all the
Wit in *Playes* consisted in bringing two persons upon the
Stage to break Jests, and to bob one another, which they call
Repartie, not considering that there is more wit and invention
requir'd in the finding out good Humor, and Matter proper for
it, then in all their smart reparties. For, in the Writing of a

Humor, a Man is confin'd not to swerve from the Character, . . . but in the *Playes* which have been wrote of late, there
is no such thing as perfect Character, but the two chief persons are most commonly a Swearing, Drinking, Whoring Ruffian for a Lover, and an impudent ill-bred *tomrig* for a Mistress . . . almost any thing is proper for them to say; but their
chief Subject is bawdy, and profaneness.[4]

The ruffian and the tomrig are, of course, Dryden's wild
couples: Celadon and Florimel, Wildblood and Jacinta—
especially the latter pair, who are more bawdy and profane than the former and who had appeared on the stage
less than three months before Shadwell wrote his attack.

Elsewhere in Shadwell's preface there is a contemptuous reference to dramatists "that never yet wrote Play
without stealing most of it."[5] This too is probably aimed
at Dryden; he borrowed freely, and at least some of his
extensive borrowings in *An Evening's Love* must have been
known, for he admitted them in the epilogue, and an
English translation of the most important source appeared
in the same year as the play itself.

There is in the "Defence of an Essay" a passage in
which Dryden seems to be taking cognizance of Shadwell's
attack: "I confess my chief endeavours are to delight the
age in which I live. If the humour of this be for low comedy, small accidents, and raillery, I will force my genius
to obey it, though with more reputation I could write in
verse. I know I am not so fitted by nature to write comedy: I want that gaiety of humour which is required to
it. . . . So that those, who decry my comedies, do me no
injury, except it be in point of profit: reputation in them
is the last thing to which I shall pretend." This statement,
which is sometimes cited as representative of Dryden's attitude towards the writing of comedy throughout his career,
was provoked by unusual circumstances. His comedies
had just been severely attacked by Shadwell at a time when

he was occupied with Howard's attack on the *Essay*. His two previous comedies, *Sir Martin* and *An Evening's Love*, are largely foreign to his theory, and the former probably had been written to suit Newcastle, who was now showing favor to the uncouth upstart who had attacked him. In such depressing circumstances Dryden might well take a jaundiced view of his activities as a comic dramatist.

Shadwell continued his attack on Dryden in the preface to his second play, *The Royal Shepherdess*, published in 1669. Here Shadwell assumes a lofty moral tone, speaking censoriously of those modern plays that encourage vice by representing "debauch'd People" as "fine Gentlemen," and their depraved and criminal behavior ("Swearing, Drinking, Whoring, breaking Windows, beating Constables, &c.") as "a Gentile gayety of Humour." "But it is said by some," continues Shadwell (and here he probably has reference to the passage of the "Defence of an Essay" which has just been quoted), "that this pleases the people, and a Poets business is only to endeavour that: But he that debases himself to think of nothing but pleasing the Rabble, loses the Dignity of a Poet, and becomes as little as a Jugler, or Rope-Dancer."[6]

In 1671 Dryden published *An Evening's Love* along with a preface, in which he replied to Shadwell's attacks, and a dedicatory epistle addressed to Newcastle, praising him and thanking him for certain "favours." Probably these "favours" were money given either for his work on *Sir Martin*, or for the dedication of *An Evening's Love*, or for both. In both plays Dryden had successfully produced the comedy of folly, full of farce and mechanic humours, which his rival Shadwell advocated and which Newcastle apparently liked. In the preface to *An Evening's Love*, with good assurance of popular approval and Newcastle's continued patronage, he could have abandoned his critical

principles, outdone Shadwell in extravagant adulation of
Jonson, and advocated the comedy of folly he had written
in *Sir Martin, The Wild Gallant,* and *An Evening's Love.*
Instead, he chose to defend his principles and the sort of
comedy he had written in *Secret Love,* even though in so
doing he had to condemn parts of *An Evening's Love* and
risk offending Newcastle, to whom his play was dedicated.
Dryden did not dedicate anything to Newcastle after 1671,
possibly because he saw little chance of "favours" from
him after the publication of the preface. Shadwell, on the
other hand, continued to eulogize Newcastle and his wife
in print and presumably did not go unrewarded.

As he had done in the "Defence of an Essay," Dryden
in the preface says that he is not much interested in comedy: "Neither . . . do I value a reputation gained from
Comedy, so far as to concern myself about it, any more
than I needs must in my own defence: for I think it, in its
own nature, inferior to all sorts of dramatic writing."
Dryden's belief that comedy is an inferior genre did not
always keep him from admiring his own comedies. His
statement here was probably provoked in part by his recent
unpleasant experiences with comedy, in part by a wish to
score against Shadwell by pointing out that comedy, which
was Shadwell's specialty, was for him a contemptible side-
line.

He distinguishes thus between comedy and farce:
"Comedy consists, though of low persons, yet of natural
actions and characters; I mean such humours, adventures,
and designs, as are to be . . . met with in the world.
Farce, on the other side, consists of forced humours, and
unnatural events. . . . The one causes laughter in those
who can judge of men and manners, by the lively representation of their folly or corruption: the other produces
the same effect in those who can judge of neither, and

that only by its extravagances." This distinction is implicit in the *Essay,* where Neander disparages the unnatural characters of the "Old Comedy" and the French plays imitating it.

In the preface Dryden also provides for a distinction between low comedy and high comedy. Giving reasons for his dislike of comedy, he says, "Low comedy especially requires, on the writer's part, much of conversation with the vulgar, and much of ill nature in the observation of their follies." The statement clearly implies the conception of a high comedy that requires less ill nature and less conversation with the vulgar, or conversation with the less vulgar. All comedy, of course, deals with low persons, but that term includes all social levels from the mechanic people of Jonson's comedies up to gentlemen, and even members of the nobility, who are of less than tragic or heroic stature. In the *Essay* Dryden expressed approval of gentlemen and the repartee he associated with them. In the epilogue to Part Two of *The Conquest of Granada,* performed in 1671, he objected to the "Mechanique humour" and "conversation low" in Jonson's comedies; and in the "Defence of the Epilogue," published in the following year, he again expressed a strong preference for comedy involving gentlefolk and repartee. Clearly he conceived of high comedy as dealing with the activities of gentlefolk (the chief activity being love, of course) whose follies or petty vices are tempered with wit: the sort of comedy, in short, afforded by the wild couples of *Secret Love* and *An Evening's Love.*

In the preface Dryden admits that "my disgust of low comedy proceeds not so much from my judgment as from my temper." Even thus qualified, his sentiments would not have recommended him to Newcastle, since Jonson's comedies are low comedy. Of his own low comedy Dry-

den says, "I . . . seldom write it; and . . . when I succeed
in it, (I mean so far as to please the Audience) yet I am
nothing satisfied with what I have done; but am often
vexed to hear the people laugh, and clap, as they perpetually do, where I intended 'em no jest; while they let
pass the better things without taking notice of them."

Dryden says categorically that he "detests" farce. He
goes on to blame the translating of French plays for the
prevalence of farce in England. He had made the same
point in the prologue to Part I of *The Conquest of Granada:*

> And may those drudges of the Stage, whose fate
> Is damn'd dull farce more dully to translate,
> Fall under that excize the State thinks fit
> To set on all French wares. . . .
> French farce worn out at home is sent abroad;
> And, patch'd up here, is made our English mode.

The English versions of French plays were adaptations, not
literal translations. Furthermore, "patch'd up" implies
modification other than literal translation. When Dryden
wrote "to translate," he probably meant "to adapt."[7] Consequently, in attacking the translation of French comedies
Dryden is attacking his own work. He had not publicly
acknowledged the authorship of *Sir Martin,* but it was
generally known that *An Evening's Love* had a French
source. Dryden confesses his guilt and says that he is
ashamed of the audience and of himself because he has
pleased them "at so cheap a rate." His attack on the
translation of French comedy also strikes a blow against
Shadwell, whose *Sullen Lovers* is an acknowledged adaptation of Molière; but if his only purpose had been to asperse
Shadwell, he could easily have found some means that did
not involve disparagement of his own work; Shadwell's

comedies are not flawless. Far from manipulating his theory to justify his practice, Dryden is here upholding his theory at the expense of his practice.

In the *Essay of Dramatic Poesy* Dryden had devoted a great deal of space to analysis of the comedy of Ben Jonson, showing particular interest in Jonson's humours characterization. I have attempted to show that although he did not approve of the lowness of Jonson's humours, he did approve of the theory of humours characterization, as he conceived it, and used it to create, in his wild couples, a blend of the characteristic excellences of Jonsonian and Fletcherian comedy.

In the preface to *An Evening's Love* his discussion of Jonson and of humours is conditioned by his desire to answer Shadwell effectively. In the *Essay* Neander says, not at all accusingly, that Jonson's humours characters were modeled on actual persons. In the preface Dryden says of Jonson, "Neither was it more allowable in him, than it is in our present poets, to represent the follies of particular persons; of which many have accused him." This remark is aimed at Shadwell, who in *The Sullen Lovers* had caricatured Sir Robert Howard as Sir Positive At-All.

Replying to Shadwell's charge that he is a decrier of Jonson, Dryden says, "I know I have been accused as an enemy of his writings; but without any other reason, than that I do not admire him blindly . . . I admire . . . him where I ought: those who do more . . . by telling you they extol Ben Johnson's way, would insinuate to you that they can practise it. For my part, I declare that I want judgment to imitate him; and should think it a great impudence in myself to attempt it." Here Dryden is obviously (and perhaps justly) implying that Shadwell in setting himself up as a disciple of Jonson is presumptuously and unscrupulously trying to enhance his own inferior plays with Jon-

son's reflected glory. The better to bring out Shadwell's
"great impudence," he plays down his own imitation of
Jonson—somewhat unfairly, perhaps; though it is true that
his comedies are not so sedulously Jonsonian as Shadwell's.

As to the matter of Jonson's wit, Dryden stands to his
guns. Though Jonson's plays are pleasant, he says, "that
pleasantness was not properly wit, or the sharpness of conceit; but the natural imitation of folly." He defends wit,
particularly repartee, against Shadwell's attack on it. To
Shadwell's charge that it is easier to write wit than humour,
he replies that "there are as different characters in wit as
in folly," and that wit, like the discourse of a humours
character, must be appropriate to the speaker.

In order sharply to contrast Shadwell's comedy and
his own and to demonstrate the superiority of the latter,
Dryden presents "characters of wit" and "characters of
humour" as though they were two different species. When
he says, "to entertain an audience perpetually with humour, is to carry them from the conversation of gentlemen,
and treat them with the follies and extravagancies of Bed-
lam," he is clearly putting across the superiority of his
witty gentlefolk to Shadwell's fools. In this statement he
tacitly equates "humour" and "mechanic humour," and
excludes both wit and gentlefolk from the province of
humour. Here again, I think, he is oversimplifying. His
discussion of humour in the *Essay* excludes neither wit nor
gentlefolk, and another passage in the preface indicates that
his conception of a humour had not changed. He says that
he prefers

the mixed way of Comedy; that which is neither all wit, nor
all humour, but the result of both. Neither so little of humour
as Fletcher shows, nor so little of love and wit as Johnson. . . .
I would have the characters well chosen, and kept distant
from interfering with each other; which is more than Fletcher

or Shakespeare did: but I would have more of the . . . orna-
ments of wit; and these are extremely wanting in Ben Johnson. As for repartie, in particular; as it is the very soul of
conversation, so it is the greatest grace of Comedy, where it
is proper to the characters.

Here we have an explicit statement of the idea of combining Fletcherian and Jonsonian comedy, an idea which
Dryden hinted at in the prologue to his first play and implies in the *Essay*, and which he was to develop further in
the "Defence of the Epilogue"; an idea which had strongly
affected his practice and would continue to do so.

In the preface Dryden defends himself against Shadwell's accusation of immorality. "It is charged upon me,"
he says, "that I make debauched persons . . . my protagonists . . . and that I make them happy in the conclusion
of my play; against the law of Comedy, which is to reward
virtue, and punish vice." He first points out that Terence,
Plautus, Jonson, and Fletcher all fail to provide poetic
justice in some of their comedies. Then he argues that
delight is the chief end of comedy:

the business of the poet is to make you laugh: when he writes
humour, he makes folly ridiculous; when wit, he moves you,
if not always to laughter, yet to a pleasure that is more noble.
And if he works a cure on folly, and the small imperfections
in mankind, by exposing them to public view, that cure is not
performed by an immediate operation. For it works first on
the ill nature of the audience; they are moved to laugh by the
representation of deformity; and the shame of that laughter
teaches us to amend what is ridiculous in our manners.

He then observes that in comedy "the faults and vices are
but the sallies of youth, and the frailties of human nature . . . such, in short, as may be forgiven." He concludes
his discussion of morality as follows:

lest any man should think that I write this to make libertinism
amiable, or that I cared not to debase the end and institution

of Comedy, . . . I must further declare . . . that we [Dryden and certain "better poets"] make not vicious persons happy, but only as Heaven makes sinners so; that is, by reclaiming them first from vice. For so it is to be supposed they are, when they resolve to marry; for then, enjoying what they desire in one, they cease to pursue the love of many.

Since the above is Dryden's first detailed discussion of morality in comedy, this is a convenient place to consider the morality of the comedies he had written.

Dryden's profligates, male and female, engage in much immoral talk but little or no immoral action. There are no scenes like that in Etherege's *Man of Mode* where Dorimant and Bellinda, the former "in his gown," emerge from a bedroom, or like the celebrated china-collection episode in Wycherley's *Country Wife*. The profligates of Dryden's early comedies boast of past exploits and make great promises for the future, but when they meet during the play they do little but talk bawdy. If they ever show signs of suiting their actions to their words, they are interrupted.

Furthermore, Dryden might argue with some justice that he performs the duty of a comic poet by making "folly ridiculous." His gallants are repeatedly thwarted and embarrassed in their amours. Loveby is teased by Constance, arrested by bailiffs, and perplexed by what he supposes to be the supernatural; Celadon is out-gallanted by Florimel in disguise; and Wildblood is twice befooled by Jacinta in disguise. It is true that the gallants are embarrassed only temporarily. They quickly revert to their habitual attitude of cynical complacency, and, on the whole, Dryden seems to be on their side. But, as Dryden says, their vices are "the sallies of youth . . . such . . . as may be forgiven."

The off-color wit that is the principal indecency of these early comedies nearly always takes the form of double meanings. It is quite obvious that Dryden intended such wit not as ridiculous and disgusting but as clever and pleasing. He does not specifically defend it in the preface; probably he felt that it was taken care of by his defense of wit and of the morality of his persons. The wit apart from its indecency is admirable, and the bawdiness is justifiable because it is appropriate to the speaker and is a minor and forgivable vice.

A suspicious reader of the preface might imagine that his leg is being pulled when he peruses Dryden's remarks on morality, particularly Dryden's claim that he makes his profligates happy only when he has by marriage reclaimed them from vice. However, it is possible that Dryden meant what he said. Delight, as he said, was his primary end in comedy; but let us suppose that he had the secondary end of improving the morals of his audience. What means could he use? Among Restoration courtiers, the "noblesse" whom he especially aimed to please in his early comedies, conventional morality was sadly out of fashion; it was associated with the Commonwealth and condemned as hypocrisy.

Two far more popular lines of thought were skepticism and Hobbesian materialism.[8] Both philosophies—Hobbesian materialism directly, and skepticism through its offshoot libertinism—regarded self-interest as the root of all human action. With this doctrine prevalent, what better argument for sexual morality could Dryden use than witty professions of self-interest by gallants who have unsuccessfully tried the alternative? It is this argument that he does seem to use. In the preface he approves of marriage on grounds not of religion, or of virtue as desirable in itself, but of self-interest: "enjoying what they desire in one, they cease to pursue the love of many." In the comedies marriage is displayed in the same light. The gallants repeatedly attempt to "possess" their mistresses, but are thwarted, and sometimes made ridiculous, until they marry. In *Sir Martin* Lord Dartmouth does indeed succeed in possessing Mrs. Christian, but he finds that a mistress is more trouble than a wife. In *The Tempest* Hippolito, who may be taken as representing natural man, gives up his promiscuity not for the sake of virtue but for the selfish reason that he is disturbed by the thought of sharing Dorinda with other men. And in the comic plot of Dryden's next tragicomedy, *Marriage à la Mode,* this practical kind of morality was to be brought out very clearly. The bawdy wit of the gallants, which Dryden meant to be admired, not ridiculed, is not inconsistent with this moral purpose. By having his persons talk not like ministerial students but like genuine young rips, he could better lead the rips in the audience to see that strict monogamy is the best solution to man's sexual problems.[9]

In the last part of the preface Dryden defends himself against Shadwell's charge of plagiarism. He admits that "wherever I have liked any story in a romance, novel, or foreign play, I have made no difficulty . . . to take the foundation of it . . . and to make it proper for the English stage." But, he says, he so improves on this foundation that very little of the source remains in the final product: "I seldom use the wit and language of any romance or play, which I undertake to alter: because my own invention (as bad as it is) can furnish me with nothing so dull as what is there. . . . and, since no story can afford characters enough for the variety of the English stage, it follows, that it is to be altered and enlarged with new persons, accidents, and designs, which will almost make it new." Dryden's claim to originality in modifying and adding to his borrowings is well substantiated by Allen's study of the comedies in relation to their sources.[10]

Making allowance for some distortion resulting from Dryden's desire to thump Shadwell and defend himself, we find in the preface a valuable statement of Dryden's views on comedy, a statement consistent with his previous criticism and with his practice. The salient points are Dryden's preference for a high comedy of love, wit, and gentlefolk which is also a mixture of Jonsonian and Fletcherian elements; the advocacy of what might be called practical morality; and the original use of borrowed source-material.

3.

Dryden begins the epilogue to Part Two of *The Conquest of Granada* (1671) as follows:

> They, who have best succeeded on the Stage,
> Have still conform'd their Genius to their Age.
> Thus *Johnson* did Mechanique humour show,
> When men were dull, and conversation low.
> Then, Comedy was faultless, but 'twas course:
> *Cobbs* Tankard was a jest, and *Otter's* horse.

Later he says,

> Wit's new arriv'd to a more high degree;
> Our native Language more refin'd and free.
> Our Ladies and our men now speak more wit
> In conversation, than those Poets writ.
> Then, one of these is, consequently, true;
> That what this Poet writes comes short of you,
> And imitates you ill, (which most he fears)
> Or else his writing is not worse than theirs.

His "Defence of the Epilogue" (1672) elaborates on this argument. He blames the faults of preceding dramatists on the deficiencies of their age. In his own age, he says, the general improvement in language, wit, and "conversation" (by "conversation" he means not merely social talk but social intercourse in general) must mean an improvement in the drama that mirrors it.

He discusses separately the three elements, language, wit, and conversation. His discussion of language is, for the modern reader, the weakest of the three. His standards of correctness are too rigid and narrow. The "solecisms" he finds in the works of his predecessors would be excused by a modern linguist as justifiable license or as the standard practice of the time. But his remarks on language include one significant passage. Discussing the language of his own day, he objects to those who "corrupt our English idiom by mixing it too much with French: that is a sophistication of language, not an improvement of it. . . . We meet daily with those fops, who value themselves on their travelling, and pretend they cannot express their meaning in English, because they would put off to us some French phrase of the last edition." This passage indicates that in including Frenchified discourse in his own comedies Dryden was not merely following a dramatic convention but exposing to ridicule an actual fashion.

Dryden attributes the improved wit and conversation of his own age to the influence of the Court and especially the King, who brought back to England the refinements he had acquired, during his exile, in "the most polished courts of Europe." The idea of the Court as the center of refinement is consistent with the preference for the noblesse in his audience which Dryden expresses in the *Essay*. In conforming his genius to his age, the Restoration dramatist should not only aim to please the noblesse, but should imitate them in his plays.

It is easy for him to do so, because the free manners of the age permit the dramatist to mix with the nobility: "Greatness was not then [in the preceding age] so easy of access, nor conversation so free, as now it is. I cannot, therefore, conceive it any insolence to affirm, that, by the knowledge and pattern of their wit who writ before us, and by the advantage of our own conversation, the discourse and raillery of our comedies excel what has been written by them." Since his predecessors lacked these advantages, "their wit was not that of gentlemen; there was ever somewhat that was ill-bred and clownish in it."

This doctrine, with its ideals of elegant wit and freedom of manners, fits very well the sort of comedy which Dryden wrote in *Secret Love* and the witty portions of *An Evening's Love;* and I see no reason for doubting that in these comedies Dryden endeavored to present a suitably heightened version of the life of the noblesse.

In the "Defence of the Epilogue" Dryden discusses only three of his predecessors: Shakespeare, Jonson, and Fletcher (under whose name he presumably includes Beaumont)—the same three to whom he had devoted special attention in the *Essay,* and who at the time were generally regarded as the foremost dramatists of "the last age." His opinion of them is essentially the same in the "Defence of the Epilogue" as it was in the *Essay.*

As in the *Essay,* he finds Shakespeare brilliant but uneven: "Shakespeare, who many times has written better than any poet, in any language . . . writes, in many places, below the dullest writer of ours, or any precedent age." Again as in the *Essay,* Dryden views Fletcher and Jonson as complementary. He considers Fletcher excellent in wit but deficient in judgment, Jonson excellent in judgment but deficient in wit.[11] Fletcher "neither understood correct plotting, nor . . . *the decorum of the stage*"; his plots are unnatural and violate the unities; his hero Philaster stabs "his mistress, and afterwards his boy, to save himself; not to mention the Clown, who enters immediately, and not

only has the advantage of the combat against the hero,
but diverts you from your serious concernment, with his
ridiculous and absurd raillery."[12] His characterization was
faulty; his wit "was seldom so fixed, and made proper to
his character, as that the same things might not be spoken
by any person in the play."

Jonson, on the other hand, "always writ properly, and
as the character required," and displayed "the height and
accuracy of judgment in the ordering of his plots." But
Jonson's characters, though perfectly drawn, are low. He
is a "perfect pattern of imitation" only in humour, "and
for humour itself, the poets of this age will be more wary
than to imitate the meanness of his persons. Gentlemen
will now be entertained with the follies of each other."
(Here Dryden, no longer contrasting his own comedy and
Shadwell's, clearly implies that gentlemen can be humours
characters.) When, in Truewit, Jonson did try to portray
a gentleman, he produced "a scholar-like kind of man, a
gentleman with an allay of pedantry." But Fletcher, despite his imperfect characterization, could create gentlemen: his Don John is the only stage gentleman of the preceding age whom Dryden considers a serious rival to
those of his own age. And Fletcher excels in the portrayal
of love, whereas in Jonson's comedies "love . . . is scarcely
mentioned." In short, Dryden presents the two dramatists
as complementing each other almost perfectly. Even more
than the *Essay,* the "Defence of the Epilogue" shows that
Dryden's preference for comedy which is a mixture of
Fletcherian and Jonsonian elements is founded on a careful evaluation of the two dramatists.

4.

Marriage à la Mode was probably first performed late
in 1671.[13] In it Dryden followed, with certain modifica-

tions, the pattern of *Secret Love*. Both plays are set in Sicily; both contain two plots, one heroic, one comic; in both the principal comic ingredient is the wild couple.

Secret Love abides by the unities, in accord with Dryden's theory that regularity, if accompanied by sufficient variety, is desirable. *Marriage à la Mode* violates the unity of time; its action lasts three days. However, this violation is also in accord with Dryden's theory. In the "Defence of an Essay" he says that comedy should abide by the unity of time, but that the weighty design and great persons of tragedy require more than one day. The three-day duration of *Marriage à la Mode* seems to be a sensible compromise, allowing enough time for the great persons (a king, a prince, a princess, and two favorites) and weighty events (a usurpation, an heir to the throne lost and found, and a rebellion) of the serious plot, and coming reasonably close to satisfying the unity of time required in the comic plot. In both plots the unity of place is observed, but the scenes are not always linked. Dryden attempts to provide unity of action as he did in *Secret Love:* all of the characters are connected with the Sicilian court, and most of them are mutually acquainted; minor characters by figuring in both plots serve as links, and in the last act the two gallants of the comic plot fight on the side of beleaguered virtue in the serious plot.

The principle of decorum is more carefully observed in *Marriage à la Mode* than it is in *Secret Love*. Fault was found with *Secret Love,* according to Dryden, because Celadon and Florimel wittily debate the conditions of their marriage in the presence of the serious characters, interrupting the denouement of the serious plot. In *Marriage à la Mode* the four principal comic characters, unobserved by the serious characters, settle their marital difficulties before the final episode of the serious plot begins. There is, however, a possible violation of decorum in *Marriage à la Mode*. Melantha, one of the comic characters, forces her polite attentions on Palmyra, daughter of the usurping king of Sicily, just as Leonidas, Palmyra's lover, is led by in chains, on his way to be executed. But Melantha is characterized as a foolish social climber, and Dryden, by having her annoy Palmyra at such an inopportune moment, effectively ridicules this variety of pest. Furthermore, he both heightens the ridicule and minimizes the breach of decorum by having Palmyra squelch Melantha: "Away, impertinent," she says. Unlike Beaumont and Fletcher, who display Philaster wounding women and defeated by a clown, Dryden preserves the dignity of the serious character.

Marriage à la Mode is richer than *Secret Love* in what Dryden calls "pleasing variety." Its serious plot is more complex and fuller of vicissitudes than that of *Secret Love,* and in the comic plot we have not one pair of lovers, but two. Rhodophil and Doralice are a married Celadon and Florimel; they have reached the state of boredom prophesied by their predecessors in *Secret Love* when they set the conditions of their marriage. Palamede and Melantha are engaged to be married in three days; they wish to make the most of their brief remaining period of freedom. Rhodophil engages in an intrigue with Melantha, while Palamede occupies himself with Doralice. The two men are friends. Each soon learns what the other is up to, and each undertakes the difficult task of violating his friend's woman while preserving the chastity of his own. Both women are all too willing to be violated.

As in *Secret Love,* repartee is the principal source of comedy. Dryden employs some comic situations, but they are not extravagant and seem to be introduced less for their own sake than to serve as occasions for wit. In Act III the two couples meet unexpectedly, having inadvertently made assignations for the same place at the same time; in Act IV both ladies use a masquerade as an excuse for disguising themselves as boys and meeting their gallants, and the two couples meet at an inn. These episodes perhaps lean a little too heavily on coincidence, but they are certainly not unnatural in the same sense as are the pregnancy scene in *The Wild Gallant* and the "Frolick of the Altitudes" in *Sir Martin.* Dryden could reasonably contend that *Marriage à la Mode* is a comedy, not a farce.

As in *Secret Love,* the elevated love of the serious plot is deliberately contrasted with the earthy love of the comic plot. Marriage is regarded by the serious lovers as a state of transcendent and sacred bliss; the comic lovers treat it as a state of ineffable boredom. The serious lovers are true to one another under the most trying circumstances; the comic lovers are cheerfully promiscuous. William Empson points out that this contrast is epitomized in the word "die," which in the play has besides its ordinary meaning the bawdy meaning, made clear in a song in Act IV, "to expire (temporarily) as a result of the ecstacy of lovemaking."[14] The serious lovers are forever indicating their heroic willingness to die for love, while the comic lovers are unheroically busy trying to die of it. Dryden's use of contrast in this play, as in *Secret Love,* is consistent with Neander's theory that "contraries, when placed near, set off each other."

As in *Secret Love* and *An Evening's Love,* the repartee of the comic characters consists largely of double meanings—less gross, on the whole, than those of *An Evening's Love*—but their behavior is innocuous. Despite the efforts of all four, their chastity is preserved throughout the play, and, in the end, they conclude that monogamy is the best solution to their problems. Rhodophil discovers that jealousy of Palamede has reawakened his interest in Doralice;

she is well satisfied with her husband as long as he is attentive, and she refuses to share Palamede with Melantha. Palamede is willing to give up Doralice in order to avoid sharing Melantha with Rhodophil. The men therefore make a mutual non-aggression pact, with the proviso that if either violates it "by war abroad, or by neglect at home, both the Women shall revenge themselves, by the help of the other party."

This denouement is the best example in Dryden's comedies of the practical attitude towards morality which he presents in the preface to *An Evening's Love*. The selfish reasons that the four give for remaining faithful are in accord with the current notions of self-interest as the mainspring of human action. And in this play, far more than in his previous ones, Dryden stresses the fashionableness of the persons and their behavior. One of the fashions he includes is adultery. Early in the play Rhodophil points out that in being unfaithful to his wife he is at least partly motivated by the desire to be in fashion: "I lov'd her a whole half year, double the natural term of any Mistress, and think in my conscience I could have held out another quarter; but then the World began to laugh at me, and a certain shame of being out of fashion, seiz'd me." He therefore tries the fashionable alternative, adultery. His unfashionable marriage becomes, in the words of the title, a "marriage à la mode." But the results of the experiment are unsatisfactory; he decides that marital fidelity is the better alternative after all. It seems quite likely that Dryden in a pleasant and cautiously indirect fashion was trying to persuade his audience that marital fidelity ought to be the fashion instead of adultery.[15]

An interesting indication that some, at least, of Dryden's contemporaries were aware of the moral implications of the play is to be found in the following passage of a book called *Marriage Asserted: In Answer to a Book Entitled Conjugium Conjurgium,* written by "a Country Gentleman" and published in 1674:

What is either wicked or silly in modish colours he [Dryden] has . . . well painted, . . . more particularly this of shunning Marriage, and being entred perfidiously to break a vow so easy to be kept, in his Play of *Marriage a-la-Mode*: a more gentile Satyre against this sort of folly, no Pen can write, where he brings the very assignations that are commonly used about Town upon the stage; and to see both Boxes and Pitt so damnably crouded, in order to see themselves abused, and yet neither to be angry or ashamed, argues such excess of stupidity, that this great Pen it self . . . would be put to a nonplus to express it.[16]

Dryden probably did not share the Country Gentleman's disappointment at the audience's reaction. As he had said in the preface to *An Evening's Love,* the "cure is not performed by an immediate operation." It was his business as comic dramatist to amuse the audience with a representation of their follies; shame and reform would presumably come later.

In the dedicatory epistle, addressed to the Earl of Rochester, Dryden says:

I am sure, if there be any thing in this Play, wherein I have rais'd my self beyond the ordinary lowness of my Comedies, I ought wholly to acknowledge it to the favour, of being admitted into your Lordship's Conversation. . . . the best Comick Writers of our Age, will joyn with me to acknowledge, that they have copy'd the Gallantries of Courts, the Delicacy of Expression, and the Decencies of Behaviour, from your Lordship, with more Success, then if they had taken their Models from the Court of *France.*

This statement is consistent with the "Defence of the Epilogue," in which Dryden stresses the advantages of "imitating" the fashionable "conversation" of his day (in the dedication he is flattering Rochester by naming only him as model). It is also consistent with the caricature of Dryden in *The Rehearsal:* Bayes says in Act I that it is his practice to frequent witty men and record their *bons mots* for use in his plays. And in the play Dryden, as the "Country Gentleman" was well aware, was imitating contemporary manners. The setting, like that of *Secret Love,* is Sicily, but as in the earlier play it is evident that Sicily as an island stands for England.

In the affected Melantha, Dryden ridicules the Frenchified discourse that in the "Defence of the Epilogue" he attacks as a contemporary English fashion. He also ridicules Melantha as a sycophantic social climber. She repeatedly makes a fool of herself by thrusting herself into the company of the great. Palamede sees no hope of reforming her; he decides that he must "get her a place at Court; and when she is once there, she can be no longer ridiculous; for she is young enough, and pretty enough, and fool enough, and *French* enough, to bring up a fashion there to be affected." This satirical remark would have had little point unless it referred to contemporary conditions in England; nor would the fashionable mockery of the banality and pretense of life outside the inner circle which is expressed in the following passage:

Your little Courtiers wife, who speaks to the King but once a moneth, need but go to a Town-Lady; and there she may vapour, and cry, *The King and I,* at every word. Your Town-Lady, who is laugh'd at in the Circle, takes her Coach into the City, and there she's call'd your Honour. . . . as for my finical Cit, she removes but to her Countrey-house, and there insults over the Countrey Gentlewoman that never comes up; who treats her with Frumity and Custard, and opens her dear bottle of *Mirabilis* beside, for a Jill-glass of it at parting.

The high social station of the characters, their preoccupation with love, their wit, and their profligacy are all qualities that Dryden associates with the plays of Fletcher. The wild couple, Rhodophil and Doralice, are clearly lineal descendants of Celadon and Florimel, and, like them, were probably conceived in accord with Dryden's theory of Jonsonian humours characterization. Early in the play, when characters need to be established, Rhodophil says of Doralice, "[as] for her humour, she laughs, sings, and dances eternally; and, which is more, we never quarrel about it, for I do the same." Here Rhodophil credits himself and Doralice with the same extravagant insouciance that characterizes Celadon and Florimel, and he calls it a humour. As he had done with Wildblood and Jacinta, Dryden provides variety not by creating a new humour but by displaying the same humour in different circumstances: in this case, marriage.

Unlike the other three lovers Melantha is foolish, not witty. Apparently Dryden intended her, too, as a humours character. Her affectation is the same as that of Aurelia in *An Evening's Love,* but her character is much more fully developed than Aurelia's. Like Aurelia she is one of a kind—Dryden, as I have noted, stresses the fashionableness of her folly—but Dryden's definition of a humour includes deviations in degree as well as in kind. Melantha might qualify as a humours character by carrying fashionable behavior to extremes. Her behavior is indeed extravagant, more so than that of Aurelia. Dryden in presenting her uses the Jonsonian device of recommending her to the observation of the audience by a pleasant description of her before she first appears. In this description the use of superlatives, indicating humorous extravagance, is particularly striking: "she's the greatest Gossip in Nature: for, besides the Court, she's the most eternal Visiter of the Town; and yet manages her time so well, that she seems ubiquitary. . . . No Lady can be so curious of a new Fash-

ion, as she is of a new French-word; she's the very Mint
of the Nation; and as fast as any Bullion comes out of
France, coins it immediately into our Language." Just
after he has finished this description of Melantha, Rhodophil calls her extravagance a humour: "this insufferable
humour, of haunting the Court."

Unlike Jonson, Dryden never concerned himself with
distinguishing between true and false humours. I have
suggested that he considered such a distinction superfluous,
since what Jonson calls false humour—for example, the
affectation of a fop—is really the manifestation of a true
humour—the fop's extravagant desire to shine in public.
This theory fits Dryden's presentation of Melantha. Her
true humour, as defined by Rhodophil, is her extravagant
social ambition, which leads her to affect the latest modes
of speech and behavior, however hard they come for her
(she has to memorize French words from a list provided
by her maid).

Melantha's humour is certainly not one of the mechanic humours which Dryden disparaged. She is a lady, and
her behavior, though foolish, is refined. Like Aurelia, she
is really a sort of pseudo-wit. In her affected way she holds
her own in a wit-contest with Doralice. It is illuminating
to compare her with the unpolished Frances of *The Wild
Gallant,* who also has extravagant social ambitions.

Aside from the humours characterization, Dryden
seems to have followed Jonson in his plotting and characterization. He follows Jonson, not Fletcher, in conforming to the unities and to the principle of decorum. He also
follows Jonson in the "justness" of his characterization.
Unlike Fletcher, he does not subordinate the comic characters to the vicissitudes of an involved and improbable intrigue, or sacrifice their consistency in order to provide a
spectacular or farcical scene.

The comic plot of *Marriage à la Mode* appears to be just such a mixture of Fletcher and Jonson as Dryden prefers in the preface to *An Evening's Love*. He has eschewed the low comedy and farce that he condemns in the preface, and he has adhered to the concept of morality implicit in his discussion of morality in the preface. In accord with his remarks in the "Defence of the Epilogue," he has tried to combine Fletcherian excellence in wit with Jonsonian excellence in judgment and has founded the comedy on the fashionable life of his time.

Secret Love, An Evening's Love, and *Marriage à la Mode* contain common elements that fit Dryden's comic theory. *Marriage à la Mode* is better than either of its predecessors, and its improvements are always in line with the theory. In *Secret Love* Dryden provides a situation that involves one wild couple, contrasts with the serious plot, and includes a single scene ridiculing affectation (that in which Florimel disguised ridicules foppery). In *An Evening's Love* he once more provides a wild couple, varying it with a Spanish setting, and amplifies the element of fashionable affectation from a single scene to a new character, Aurelia. In *Marriage à la Mode* he provides the wild couple once more, this time varying it with marriage; exploits more skillfully the contrast between comic and serious plots; and evolves the rudimentary Aurelia into the polished Melantha.

Much of *An Evening's Love* was conceded to the vulgar tastes that Dryden deprecated, but *Secret Love* and *Marriage à la Mode* were both written entirely (except for the breach of decorum in *Secret Love*) in accord with Dryden's theory. It is significant that he speaks well of both of them. He said in the preface to *Secret Love* that he valued the play "above the rest of my Follies of this kind," and in his dedicatory epistle he called *Marriage à*

la Mode "perhaps . . . the best of my Comedies." After
successfully applying his comic theory in *Secret Love*, Dryden compromised with it during the period from 1667 to
1668; but he returned to it in *Marriage à la Mode*.

5.

The Assignation, or, Love in a Nunnery (October or
November, 1672) did not succeed on the stage. For nearly
three centuries it has also failed miserably in the opinions
of the majority of critics of Dryden's plays, who either
roundly condemn it or pointedly ignore it. But Dryden
himself defended the play. In his dedicatory epistle, addressed to Sir Charles Sedley, he suggests that its failure
on the stage was due, in part at least, to poor acting and
to the efforts of enemies "who came resolv'd to damn" the
play. Furthermore, some of Dryden's contemporaries
whose opinions he valued seem to have thought well of
the play. He says in the dedicatory epistle that the play
was approved by "many [of] the best Judges of our Age,"
to whom he read it before it was staged. And in 1673
Dryden's friend Charles Blount, replying to an attack on
Dryden, defended the play. "You are too severe to Railly
upon this last new Play . . . before you can have the
opportunity of Reading it," he said,[17] thus implying that
the play has excellences that were not brought out in the
performance.

While admitting that the play has defects (Dryden himself admits it, in the dedicatory epistle), I shall try to
justify the good opinion Dryden and some of his contemporaries had of *The Assignation* by showing that in it
Dryden made a bold attempt at a further development of
the idea of comedy which underlies *Secret Love* and *Marriage à la Mode*.

For variety Dryden has provided in the play two plots, with nine lovers and five love-affairs, each of them different from the others. In one plot Aurelian and Camillo, two young Roman gentlemen, engage in an amour with, respectively, Laura and Violetta, sisters, the wards of their Uncle Mario. Their courtship is obstructed by the countermeasures of Mario and the blunders of Aurelian's servant, Benito. In the other plot Prince Frederick enters into a platonic affair with Lucretia, a prospective nun. Frederick's adolescent page Ascanio simultaneously engages in an intrigue with the nun Hippolita. The activities of both couples are hampered by the women's residence in a nunnery. The affair of Frederick and Lucretia is further complicated when Frederick's father, the Duke of Mantua, becomes inflamed with lust by the beauty of Lucretia and seeks, in a decidedly un-platonic fashion, to possess her. The audience is also provided with the entertainment of songs, instrumental music, and a dance.

Like *Marriage à la Mode,* the play loosely observes the unities. The time of the action is two days; the place, Rome. Dryden has linked the two plots in his customary fashion. Aurelian and Camillo are friends and are acquainted with Frederick. Mario attempts to thwart Aurelian and Camillo by confining his two nieces in the nunnery occupied by Lucretia and Hippolita. The nunnery thus becomes an obstacle that confronts all nine lovers, and eight of them can plausibly co-operate in overcoming it (none of the other lovers care to assist the lustful Duke).

The characters are all Italians, not Englishmen, and the setting is Rome, not London. Obviously Dryden could not set a play about a nunnery in contemporary London, or show an English Duke attempting the seduction of a nun. Once established in Rome, he makes use of a few

Roman features besides the nunnery: the custom of keeping young women in seclusion, the practice of serenading
them with "Guittars," etc. In this play Rome does not
stand for London as Sicily does for England in *Secret Love*
and *Marriage à la Mode;* nor are there English travelers in
it as there are in *An Evening's Love.* But the characters,
despite their foreign names and residences, resemble Englishmen. They speak colloquial English. Like English
gallants, Aurelian and Camillo occupy themselves with
wenching. Frederick's unfleshly (at first) affair with
Lucretia is referred to as "Platonick"; platonic love-con-
ventions seem to have been a literary fashion in England at
that time.[18] Benito is a fop who sings French songs; the
affectation of things French is a characteristic of English
fops of the period. In *An Evening's Love* Dryden had en-
dowed the Spanish lady, Aurelia, with platonic and Frenchified affectation. Such mingling of English and foreign
manners is of course not true to life. However, Dryden
probably thought that it would be accepted by the audience as long as the English manners were not inconsistent
with the ages, ranks, and dispositions of the characters.

The plot dealing with the loves of Aurelian and Camillo and the blunders of Benito is, as James Rundle has
shown, adapted from a comedy by Calderón, *Con quien
vengo vengo.*[19] Dryden's Camillo surreptitiously courts
Violetta. His friend Aurelian decides to accompany him
to an assignation disguised as the servant Benito. Meanwhile Violetta's sister Laura decides to accompany her
to the assignation disguised as their maid. Each "servant" is much taken with the other's wit, but each is disillusioned upon encountering the genuine servant. This
situation is nearly identical with that in Calderón's play,
but otherwise the two are quite different. Calderón's four
lovers are serious, much preoccupied with jealousy and

honor; Dryden's plot is comic, and his lovers are like the witty gallants and ladies in his previous comedies.

In Dryden's play the servant Benito is, like Calderón's Celio, foolish and vain, and believes quite readily that the lady has really fallen in love with him. But Dryden makes much more of the servant's folly than does Calderón. He alters Calderón's plot in order to have Benito's blunders spoil the schemes of his masters. Like Sir Martin, Benito is a fop who is "fruitful of foolish plots" and who spoils the schemes concocted by others. It is clear that Dryden has included him to gratify the vulgar taste for farce, modeling him on the extraordinarily successful Sir Martin. Dryden virtually says as much in the prologue, which was spoken by Haynes, the actor who played Benito:

> He who made this [play], observ'd what Farces hit,
> And durst not disoblige you now with wit.
>
> . . . .
>
> You must have Fooles out of the common Rode.
> Th' unnatural strain'd Buffoon is onely taking
>
> . . . .
>
> . . . he hopes I'm Fool enough to please ye.

Mario, the girls' uncle and guardian, is not well individualized. He is a stock figure, the oldster who unsuccessfully opposes the progress of young love. As a stock figure, he is not in accord with Dryden's theory; but Dryden may be forgiven for this deviation, since he had his hands full with the five love-affairs in the play. He does show some care in characterizing Mario. In Calderón's play the love-affairs are opposed by the girls' brother, who is motivated by jealousy and by concern for honor. Near the end of the play he engages in a duel with the suitors. This conflict is too serious for Dryden's comic version of the plot, and he has accordingly changed the romantic young brother into the comic old uncle, whose motives in opposing young love are not at all heroic: he wants to get the girls' inheritance.

Aurelian and Laura are a wild couple, like Celadon and Florimel. Their relationship is slightly varied with the supposed-servant complication. Camillo is a gallant less extraordinary than Aurelian. Violetta is a young and supposedly innocent girl of fifteen. At the beginning of the play Laura tells her that she is too inexperienced to conduct an amour. Violetta vehemently disagrees: "Though I am not all Ayr and Fire, as you are, yet that little wit I have, will serve to conduct my Affairs. . . . I would have you to know, that I have kill'd my Man before I was Fourteen, and now am ready for another execution."

During their first assignation, the dialogue of Camillo and Violetta is excessively romantic. It begins thus:

CAM. *Violetta,* my Love!

VIO. My dear *Camillo*!

Later Camillo urges her to take advantage of their opportunity, whereupon the dialogue continues as follows:

VIO. You do not love me; if you did, you would not
Thus urge your satisfaction in my shame. . . .

CAM. I haste to take possession of my own.

VIO. E're Heaven and holy vows have made it so?

CAM. Then witness Heaven, and all these twinkling
Stars. . . .

VIO. I never will receive these Mid-night Vows;
But when I come hereafter to your Arms,
I'll bring you a sincere, full, perfect bliss;
Then you will thank me that I kept it so.

When next they meet, their dialogue is not romantic but witty and cynical, like that of Aurelian and Laura:

CAM. . . . let us take this opportunity for your escape . . .

VIO. This is the second time we e're have met; let us discourse, and know each other better first: that's the way to make sure of some love before-hand; for as the world goes, we know not how little we may have when we are Marry'd.

CAM. Losses of opportunity are fatal, in war, you know; and Love's a kind of warfare.

VIO. I shall keep you yet a while from close fighting.

This shift from lush romanticism to cynical wit is not an inconsistency in Dryden's characterization of the two lovers. As I have shown, he carefully presents Violetta as a very young girl and raises in the minds of the audience doubt as to her ability to conduct an amour. In subsequent scenes she proves herself. Camillo, quite sensibly, first woos her with romantic platitudes likely to appeal to a young girl; but she shows that she is a match for him by repulsing him in the same romantic language. Finding that she is maturer than she seems to be, Camillo when they next meet tries another approach, profligate wit; again she beats him at his own game. The actress who played Violetta could have made the first assignation pleasantly comic by overacting so as to show that Violetta too was playing a part.

The other plot of *The Assignation* is especially interesting. It is a curious mixture of heroic and comic elements. As Allen points out, the basic situation—father and son rivals for the love of the same woman—is precisely that which Dryden later used in his heroic play

Aureng-Zebe.[20] The chief psychological conflict is the standard heroic one of love versus duty, or honor: in this case, Frederick's love for Lucretia versus his filial obligation to his father. In the genuinely heroic *Aureng-Zebe* this basic situation produces the earthshaking political repercussions typical of the heroic plays; in *The Assignation* it chiefly produces comic nocturnal prowlings about a nunnery. The mighty passions of *Aureng-Zebe* may occasionally amuse a disrespectful reader, but Dryden meant them to be uniformly awesome; the passions in *The Assignation*, particularly the Duke's, are intended to be predominantly laughable. The dialogue of *Aureng-Zebe*, like that of Dryden's other heroic plays, is uniformly and excruciatingly elevated, impassioned, hyperbolic; the dialogue of *The Assignation* includes extended passages of comic repartee. The mixture of comic and heroic in *The Assignation* may be well observed in the final scene of the play, the "big" scene, from which the play gets its title. To get possession of a letter with which the Duke is blackmailing her, Lucretia meets him in the nunnery garden and by pretending that she loves him induces him to give her the letter. She then attempts to leave. When the Duke seizes her, she screams, thus alerting several women whom she has stationed in the shrubbery. They also scream, and Lucretia escapes from the thoroughly discomfited Duke. The action thus far is manifestly comic, as the Duke himself is well aware, for when Frederick enters at this point the Duke thinks he has come

> To laugh at . . .
> The weakness, and the follies of your Father.

Abruptly the action becomes heroic. Frederick has mustered up some followers and has come to the garden with the idea of using force against the Duke. Now, kneeling, he tells his father that passion had impelled him to rebel,

> But reason now has reassum'd its place,
> And makes me see how black a crime it is
> To use a force upon my Prince and Father.

Moved by his son's nobility, the Duke rises above his ignominious passion for Lucretia and turns her over to Frederick: love and duty are reconciled.

Dryden did not get this strange mixture of comic and heroic from his source, a story in an anonymous collection called *The Annals of Love*. The events of his plot follow those of its source quite closely, but Dryden has made important changes in the characters and in the tone. Dryden has repeatedly been accused of catering to obscene tastes in his comedies. Certainly he had a splendid opportunity to do so in this plot. The possibilities for indecent exploitation of "love in a nunnery" are practically unlimited, and the source provided any assistance he could possibly have needed. In *The Annals of Love* the disagreeable tone of the story is established by the author's preliminary comment on the behavior of nuns: "their Religious Civility is so great, they will not discourage any man's affection."[21] Prince Henry, the original of Frederick, "had every liberty he could wish" of Constance, the original of Lucretia. Furthermore, three gallants selected by Henry woo three of the other nuns, enjoying as much success as he does. "The Prince and his three Confidents past away whole nights with the four Nuns in the Garden."[22] When Henry suggests that the three gallants follow his example and marry the nuns they have seduced, they demur, saying that "they could not but fear the Laws of Wedlock might be as easily violated, as the Rules of a Convent."[23] Constance and Henry do marry, but the match is arranged in a sordid fashion. The Pope, who is Constance's uncle, falls out with the Emperor Frederick Barbarossa, Henry's father and rival, because of Barbarossa's attempt upon Constance. Henry, annoyed for the same reason, rebels against his father and sides with the Pope. Learning of Constance's "intrigues" with Henry and finding it "troublesom to conceal them," the Pope offers to make Henry emperor if he will marry Constance. Henry is extremely reluctant to do so; he loves Constance "most passionately," but the thought of marriage dampens his ardor. It is only the Pope's bribe that wins him over.[24]

Instead of making the most of this indecency and cynicism, Dryden has made his version considerably more chaste than the original. Constance has taken her vows, but Lucretia is still a novice; consequently, the same degree of misbehavior would be less reprehensible in Lucretia than in Constance. But Lucretia behaves much better than Constance does. Her affair with Frederick is platonic during most of the play. Presently they fall in love, of course, but then their thoughts are not of illicit love but of marriage. Furthermore, their repartee is never indecent. When in exclusively male company Frederick occasionally permits himself the use of a mildly indecent expression, but when he is in the presence of ladies his discourse is unexceptionable. For the three gallants who love as furiously as Prince Henry, Dryden substitutes the page Ascanio and his amour with the nun Hippolita. The two indulge in a good deal of bawdy talk, but their affair is more comic than indecent. The adolescent Ascanio brags repeatedly of his lovemaking ability, but when at last he has the opportunity to make good his boasts, he fails to take advantage of it. Nor do the four lovers in the other plot, after the girls are sent to the nunnery, supply the indecency provided by the subsidiary gallants and nuns in the original.

In the first place, Laura and Violetta are not nuns; in the second place, the lovers engage in no sexual misconduct; in the third place, they are ultimately married.

This novel comic-heroic mixture, in the achieving of which Dryden carefully modified his source material, can readily be accounted for as a further development of his conception of comedy. Dryden disapproved of low comedy, with its vulgar persons, mechanic humours, and dull conversation. He preferred high comedy involving witty and amorous gentlemen and ladies. He embodied his concept of high comedy in the wild couple, feebly begun in *The Wild Gallant,* perfected in *Secret Love,* and then varied: displayed against a Spanish background in *An Evening's Love* and shown married in *Marriage à la Mode.*

Having explored the possibilities of this sort of comedy pretty thoroughly, and feeling much encouraged by the success of *Marriage à la Mode,* his best comic effort up to this time, Dryden was ready to attempt, in *The Assignation,* a still higher comedy, founded on a more elevated wild couple. The earlier couples are gentlemen and ladies, but Frederick is a prince and Lucretia is a great lady, the niece of the Pope. The wildness of the earlier couples takes the form of insouciant profligacy. The wildness of Frederick and Lucretia is purer: they agree to "banish Love . . . [but] not Mirth, nor Gallantry"; they are "for all extravagancies, but . . . loving."[25] The repartee of the earlier couples is indecent; that of Frederick and Lucretia is not. The marriage of the earlier couples is opposed by the promiscuous inclinations of the lovers or by some absurd old man; the marriage of Frederick and Lucretia is opposed at first by their extravagant aversion to love, later by the rivalry of Frederick's father the Duke; and although the Duke too is an absurd old man, the conflict is elevated, quasi-heroic.

But although this portion of *The Assignation* is higher

than the high comedy Dryden had previously written, it is lower than the heroic plays. Its medial position is neatly epitomized in the reaction of Lucretia to the prospect of marriage. On the high-comedy level, Jacinta can't wait to be married to Wildblood; she insists that the ceremony be performed that very night, before the beginning of Lent. On the heroic level, in *The Conquest of Granada*, Almahide, free to marry her lover Almanzor at last, after ten acts of the most frightful vicissitudes, postpones their marriage for a year out of respect for her recently deceased husband. Lucretia, when all obstacles to her union with Frederick are removed, is seen to be just midway between the indecent haste of the comic heroine and the all-too-decent restraint of the heroic one:

> I am so fearful,
> That, though I gladly run to your embraces,
> Yet, ventring in the World a second time,
> Methinks I put to Sea in a rough storm,
> With Shipwracks round about me.

Dryden's dramatic criticism includes no discussion of this sort of comedy. But although he did not write such a discussion, he had read one. He must have been familiar with Corneille's three discourses on drama, for he refers to them repeatedly, and sometimes quotes from them, in the *Essay of Dramatic Poesy*. In the first discourse Corneille expresses dissatisfaction with Aristotle's definition of comedy as "une imitation des personnes basses et fourbes." He says,

La poésie dramatique, selon lui, est une imitation des actions, et il s'arrête ici à la condition des personnes, sans dire quelles doivent être ces actions. . . . cette définition avoit du rapport à l'usage de son temps . . . mais elle n'a pas une entière justesse pour le nôtre, où les rois même y peuvent entrer, quand leurs

actions ne sont au-dessus d'elle. Lorsqu'on met sur la scène
un simple intrique [une simple intrigue] d'amour entre des rois,
et qu'ils ne courent aucun péril, ni de leur vie, ni de leur État,
je ne crois pas que, bien que les personnes soient illustres,
l'action le soit assez pour s'élever jusqu'à la tragédie. . . .
    Je dirai plus. Bien qu'il y aye de grands intérêts d'État
dans un poëme, et que le soin qu'une personne royale doit
avoir de sa gloire fasse taire sa passion . . . s'il ne s'y rencontre
point de péril de vie, de pertes d'États, ou de bannissement, je
ne pense pas qu'il aye droit de prendre un nom plus relevé que
celui de comédie; mais pour répondre aucunement à la dignité
des personnes . . . je me suis hasardé d'y ajouter l'épithète
d'héroique, pour le distinguer d'avec les comédies ordinaires.[26]

The Frederick-Lucretia-Duke portion of *The Assignation,* with its mixture of comic and heroic elements, fits
admirably Corneille's conception of "comédie héroique."
The characters are illustrious enough. In the *Annals* the
amorous father is an emperor; Dryden, presumably for
the sake of decorum, reduces his rank to Duke, but he
is a king in everything but title. He has his own army,
and his son Frederick has the title of Prince. Lucretia,
as niece of the Pope, certainly qualifies as a "personne
illustre." The three of them are occupied not with weighty
affairs of state but with a fairly simple "intrigue d'amour."
    Dryden also seems to be aware of Corneille's stipula-
tion that in heroic comedy the "personnes illustres" must
not suffer "péril de vie," "pertes d'États," or "bannissement." In Dryden's heroic plays the characters are very
often imperilled, banished, dethroned, and slaughtered.
But he seems to have taken pains to avoid such calamities
in *The Assignation,* even modifying his source in order to
do so. To get rid of Frederick, the Duke orders him "to
travel into *Germany,*" but the order is never carried out.
Nor does the Duke undergo "péril de vie" or "perte
d'État." In the *Annals* Prince Henry actually rebels against

his father. In Dryden's version Frederick plans a rebellion, but his filial piety keeps him from putting the plan into effect.

Dryden's preference for high comedy and heroic drama might have brought him to attempt heroic comedy even if he had not read Corneille's discourses. But he had read them, and it is likely that Corneille's discussion of "comédie héroique" served as the theoretical basis for the Frederick-Lucretia-Duke portion of *The Assignation*.

Certain weaknesses in the play need to be considered. The farcical Benito was included to gratify the audience's taste for crude folly; but taken for what he is, he is on the whole effectively presented. Other parts of the play do not seem effective on any level. Of these the worst is the portion of Act IV which is justly satirized in *The Rehearsal* as the episode of "a petticoat and the bellyache." The Duke, having fallen in love with Lucretia at a masquerade without knowing who she is or that Frederick is acquainted with her, unexpectedly visits Frederick's rooms when the costume worn by Lucretia at the masquerade is lying on a chair. To keep his father from seeing it, Frederick feigns a sudden attack of illness and collapses on the chair. When the Duke goes to summon a doctor, Ascanio removes the costume. This incident is flat, and ill suited to the elevation of the characters involved, but its worst defect is its pointlessness; immediately afterwards the Duke finds a letter from Lucretia to Frederick which tells him everything. When the episode is described in *The Rehearsal* Smith asks, "Well, and what followed upon that?" Bayes replies, "Nothing, no earthly thing, I vow to gad."[27]

There is in Act V another episode almost as absurd and pointless. Laura and Violetta are escaping from the nunnery in disguise when, through Benito's blundering, they are intercepted by Mario and the Duke. Laura is wearing Lucretia's ubiquitous masquerade costume, and the Duke consequently thinks she is Lucretia, although she tells him that she is not. So absurdly positive is the Duke that when Laura offers to convince him by unmasking he says that if she unmasks he will not look at her. Benito then reappears and identifies the girls.

Probably Dryden filled out the play with these flabby episodes because he was in a hurry. In his dedicatory epistle he cites poor acting as a possible cause of the failure of the play. Now with only three exceptions the actors in *The Assignation* were the same ones who only a few months earlier had scored a success in *Marriage à la Mode*.[28] Furthermore, since they all hoped to profit from the play, they must have done the best they could. The likeliest remaining explanation for their inadequate performance is that they did not have time to rehearse sufficiently; and it is reasonable to suppose that if the actors were rushed, the author was also rushed. On the twenty-fifth of January the King's Company had suffered a great loss when a fire destroyed their theater and their entire stock of scenery and costumes. They moved temporarily to Lisle's Tennis Court (formerly occupied by the Duke's Company, who about a year earlier had moved to their splendid new Dorset Garden theater). There, on February 26, 1672, they "began to play after a fashion, with stock pieces and borrowed costumes, while they set about raising funds for a new theatre on the site of the old."[29] Clearly they were in no condition to wait patiently while their star dramatist polished *The Assignation* to the smoothness of *Marriage à la Mode*.

In *Secret Love* and *Marriage à la Mode* Dryden had successfully combined a high-comedy plot and a heroic plot. I believe that in *The Assignation* he tried a new combination: high comedy in the one plot and higher, heroic,

comedy in the other. As insurance against the failure of
his experiment, he included Benito to satisfy the vulgar
taste for farce. Under pressure of circumstances he wrote
the play too hastily, and as a result it is inferior to his best
comedies, though not quite so bad as the critics have made
it out.

For six years after the staging of *The Assignation,* no
new comedy by Dryden appeared. Probably he was dis-
couraged by the failure of *The Assignation.* After successfully embodying his idea of high comedy in *Marriage à la
Mode,* he had tried to rise to still greater heights in *The
Assignation,* only to have his attempt spoiled because of
the poor acting and the prejudiced audience to which he
alludes in the dedicatory epistle, and also, I think, because
the straitened circumstances of the King's Company forced
him to hurry his writing of the play.

VI. 1675-1681: THE THEORY MODIFIED

1.

THE COMEDIES and tragicomedies that Dryden produced during the last twenty years of his career as a practicing dramatist are markedly different from those which he produced during the first ten. This change in his practice is paralleled by a considerable modification of his dramatic theory.

Dryden acknowledges the change in his critical views. In the dedication of his adaptation of Shakespeare's *Troilus and Cressida* (1679), he says of his major critical essay, "The Grounds of Criticism in Tragedy," which was published along with the play, "I doubt not but I have contradicted some of my former opinions, [expressed] in my loose Essays of the like nature: but of this [essay], I dare affirm, that it is the fruit of my riper age and experience, and that self-love, or envy have no part in it." The *Essay of Dramatic Poesy*, written in 1665, was first published in 1668. In the dedication Dryden says of the *Essay*, "I confess I find many things in this discourse which I do not now approve; my judgment being a little altered since the writing of it." But when in 1684 the *Essay* was published again, "a little altered" had become "not a little alter'd."

A significant change is Dryden's increased admiration of Shakespeare. He had always praised Shakespeare as a great genius, but had deprecated his faults and had compared his plays unfavorably with the more polished drama of the Restoration. But in 1675, in the prologue to his last heroic play, *Aureng-Zebe,* he announced his dissatisfaction with heroic drama and pronounced it inferior to the less correct but more forceful, natural, and inspired drama of Shakespeare.

This change is reflected in Dryden's practice. I have suggested that formerly he eschewed Shakespeare as a model because he considered him inimitable at his best, unworthy of imitation at his worst. But one of the fruits of his "riper age and experience" was apparently the conviction that imitation of Shakespeare was both feasible and desirable. He wrote his tragedy *All for Love* (1677) in imitation of Shakespeare's style and adapted Shakespeare's *Troilus and Cressida.* Several of his subsequent plays also show traces of Shakespeare's influence.

The prologue to *Aureng-Zebe* indicates that Dryden's turning from the heroic play to Shakespeare is essentially a shift from artificiality towards naturalness in the representation of character, particularly character as manifest in passions. Dryden

> Grows weary of his long-lov'd Mistris, Rhyme

because

> Passion's too fierce to be in Fetters bound,
> And Nature flies him like Enchanted Ground.

Although he takes pride in *Aureng-Zebe* as the "most correct" of his plays,

>   a secret shame
> Invades his Breast at *Shakespear's* sacred name:
> Aw'd when he hears his Godlike *Romans* rage,
> He, in a just despair, would quit the Stage.

The "Fetters" that impede the natural representation of character in heroic drama are not only rhyme but other artificial conventions of the genre. Dryden had in the *Essay of Dramatic Poesy* regarded serious drama as an imitation not merely of nature but of nature "wrought up to an higher pitch." He cited this concept as justification for the use in serious drama of "heroic rhyme . . . the noblest kind of modern verse." The same concept applied to characterization justifies the superhuman qualities of the heroes and heroines who speak this heroic rhyme. In his "Defence of an Essay" Dryden again cited this concept (referring to it as "ingenious flattery of nature" or "heightening") as justification for the use of rhyme in serious drama, and extended the concept to include comedy by pointing out that "heightening" may be seen even in Jonson's low comedy *Bartholomew Fair.* His shift to naturalness under the influence of Shakespeare led him to reject rhyme in favor of blank verse and to endeavor to make his heroes behave as well as talk less like demigods and more like human beings. The former change became manifest in 1677, in *All for Love;* the latter two years earlier, in the last act of *Aureng-Zebe,* where the heroine Indamora is shown afraid of death. The ladies in the audience objected to Indamora's unheroic behavior, but Dryden defended it as natural: "I have onely represented a practicable Virtue, mix'd with the frailties and imperfections of humane life," he says in the dedication of the play.

Similarly, in his preface to *All for Love* he attacks the petty insistence on decorum, the "nicety of manners," which interferes with natural characterization and which as practiced by the French has transformed Hippolytus, "a rough young man . . . a jolly huntsman," into "Monsieur Hippolyte." Replying to the charge that in representing the quarrel of Octavia and Cleopatra he had offended "against the greatness of their characters, and the modesty of their sex," he says, "This objection I foresaw,

and at the same time contemned; for I judged it both natural and probable . . . that two exasperated rivals should
use such satire as I have put into their mouths; for, after
all, though the one were a Roman, and the other a queen,
they were both women."

Dryden's continued interest in character during this
period is seen in the fact that about three quarters of the
"Grounds of Criticism in Tragedy" is devoted to a discussion of it. The components of character, says Dryden, are
"manners," which he defines as "those inclinations, whether
natural or acquired, which move and carry us to actions,
good, bad, or indifferent, in a play; or which incline the
persons to such or such actions." "Character" Dryden defines as "that which distinguishes one man from another."
A person's character is simply the total of his manners.
And here Dryden makes a statement with an important
bearing on his theory of comedy:

A character . . . cannot be supposed to consist of one particular
virtue, or vice, or passion only; but 'tis a composition of qualities which are not contrary to one another in the same person;
thus, the same man may be liberal and valiant, but not liberal
and covetous; so in a comical character, or humour (which is
an inclination to this, or that particular folly), *Falstaff* is a liar,
and a coward, a glutton, and a buffoon, because all these
qualities may agree in the same man; yet . . . one virtue, vice,
and passion, ought to be shown in every man, as predominant
over all the rest.

This concept of a humour is quite different from Dryden's
previous one. He no longer requires the extravagant singularity that he had formerly regarded as the essence of a
humour. In the *Essay* he had defined a humour as "some
extravagant habit, passion, or affection, particular . . . to
some one person, by the oddness of which, he is immediately distinguished from the rest of men," and had dis-

qualified Falstaff as a humours character because "there are many men resembling him; old, fat, merry, cowardly, drunken, amorous, vain, and lying." Now he defines a humour as simply an "inclination"—not a uniquely extravagant inclination—"to this, or that particular folly"; says not that it is a person's extravagance but that it is the total pattern of his "manners" which distinguishes him from other persons; and regards Falstaff as a humours character.

This revision of his concept of a humour is probably a consequence of Dryden's shift from artificiality to naturalness. Humours characterization, as presented by Dryden in the *Essay,* is a sort of comic heightening related to the characterization in his heroic plays. As the heroic character is centered on extravagant notions of love or honor, the humours character is centered on one "extravagant habit, passion, or affection." The same desire for naturalness which led Dryden to add to Indamora's great love the ignoble fear of death, and to Octavia's great honor an ignoble jealousy of Cleopatra, probably also led him to adopt his new view of a humours character as less extravagant and more complex.

Dryden's rejection of artificial heightening is also apparent in his discussion of passions. In the *Essay* he had described the serious play as presenting nature "wrought up to an higher pitch." Here he uses the same musical metaphor with a quite different connotation: "the passions . . . suffer violence when they are perpetually maintained at the same height; for what melody can be made on that instrument, all whose strings are screwed up at first to their utmost stretch, and to the same sound [that is, to some one passion]? . . . the characters likewise bear a part in the general calamity . . . for . . . no man can be distinguished from another by his discourse, when every man is ranting, swaggering, and exclaiming with the same excess." He makes it clear that he has his own heroic plays in mind by citing a reprehensible passage from *The Indian Emperour*. Later, in his dedication of *The Spanish Friar,* he renounced "some verses of my own *Maximin* and *Almanzor,* which cry vengeance upon me for their extravagance."

Although in "The Grounds of Criticism in Tragedy" Dryden was primarily interested in serious characters, he considered his discussion applicable to comic characters as well, as is shown by his citing a comic character, Falstaff, to illustrate a principle of characterization which he had been discussing in relation to serious characters. His citing one of Shakespeare's comic characters to illustrate his point indicates that Shakespeare's influence affected his notions of comic as well as of serious characterization. He does not discuss the application of his modified theory to his own comic characters, but the application can be inferred. The same concept of heightening which produced the extravagantly and single-mindedly heroic Almanzor and Almahide also produced, on the comic level, the extravagantly and single-mindedly profligate Celadon and Florimel. The artificially sustained repartee of the profligates is the comic equivalent of the "pointed wit, and sentences affected out of season" of the heroes. In turning to more natural heroes and heroines, Dryden must also have turned to more natural mistresses and gallants.

It is not to be supposed that in his earlier theory Dryden entirely abandoned naturalness for the sake of heightening or that in his later theory he abandoned heightening for the sake of naturalness. His concern for naturalness in the earlier theory is manifest in his insistence on justness in the *Essay of Dramatic Poesy,* and in his condemnation of the absurdity of farce in the preface to *An Evening's Love.*

In 1672, in his essay "Of Heroic Plays," he defends Almanzor against the charge of being a "contemner of kings"
on the ground of naturalness, citing the precedent of
Homer and Tasso, who "made their heroes men of honour;
but so as not to divest them quite of human passions and
frailty." And in his "Apology for Heroic Poetry and Poetic
Licence" (1677) he defends hyperbole if it is used with
"coolness and discretion." In the dedication of *The Spanish Friar* (1681) he says, "Neither do I discommend the
lofty style in Tragedy, which is naturally pompous and
magnificent; but nothing is truly sublime that is not just
and proper." And a little further along in the dedication
he says, "as in a room contrived for state, the height of
the roof should bear a proportion to the area; so, in the
heightenings of Poetry, the strength and vehemence of
figures should be suited to the occasion, the subject, and
the persons. All beyond this is monstrous." The principles
of naturalness and heightening are to be found in both
major phases of development of Dryden's theory. With
respect to these two principles, the modification of his theory consists in a stricter regard for naturalness and a correspondingly more temperate use of heightening.

As in the *Essay of Dramatic Poesy,* Dryden in "The
Grounds for Criticism in Tragedy" regards character as
the most important element in a play. It must not be subordinated to plot: "Most comedies made up of accidents
or adventures are liable to fall into this error . . . for the
manners can never be evident, where the surprises of fortune take up all the business of the stage; and where the
poet is more in pain to tell you what happened to such a
man, than what he was." As in his previous criticism, he
praises the characters of Shakespeare and Jonson, and objects to those of Fletcher, calling attention once more to
the inconsistency of Fletcher's heroes in wounding women.

Another significant change in Dryden's dramatic theory during this period is his higher regard for regularity. Because of his increased admiration for Shakespeare's characterization he dwells less on Shakespeare's "incorrectness" than he had previously. But his disapproval of Shakespeare's irregularity is seen in his practice: he regularized *All for Love,* and did the best he could with *Troilus and Cressida* by reducing the number of shifts between the Greek camp and Troy. Probably his view of the unities of time and place was still tolerant. He says nothing of them that indicates a change in his opinion, and in *Troilus and Cressida* he violates the strict conception of both. But there are clear indications that he attached increasing importance to, and took a stricter view of, the unity of action. In the *Essay* he had justified subplots, if properly subordinated to and integrated with the main plot, on the ground that they afford variety. In his "Heads of an Answer to Rymer," written in 1678, he says the same. But the fact that he did not publish the "Answer to Rymer" perhaps indicates that he did not entirely approve of everything he had said in it.[1] Certainly his subsequent writings show a new awareness of the dangers of striving for variety and a corresponding increase in his regard for the unity of action. He says in his preface to *Oedipus* (1679), "Custom likewise has obtain'd [in English drama], that we must form an under-plot . . . which must be depending on the first. . . . Perhaps after all the ancient method [strict unity of action] as 'tis the easiest, is also the most Natural, and the best. For variety . . . is too often subject to breed distraction: and while we wou'd please too many ways, for want of art in the conduct, we please in none."

In "The Grounds of Criticism in Tragedy" he disapproves of multiple plots in stronger terms. Having cited Aristotle's doctrine that the action of a tragedy must be one and single, he continues, "this condemns . . . all double action of Plays . . . [including] my own *Marriage à la Mode,* where there are manifestly two actions, not depending on one another. . . . two different independent actions distract . . . the audience, and consequently destroy the intention of the poet; if his business be to move terror and pity, and one of his actions be comical, the other tragical, the former will divert the people, and utterly make void his greater purpose." This passage contradicts Dryden's assertion in the *Essay* that serious and comic plots enhance each other by contrast. But that Dryden now considers *Marriage à la Mode* disunified does not, of course, mean that he thought so at the time he wrote the play.

Dryden's efforts to unify the actions of his earlier two-plot tragicomedies were modified by his attention to the principle of decorum. He wished to link the two plots, but he wished also to preserve the heroic characters from the indignity of associating with the comic characters. The tightening of his standards of unity of action seems to be accompanied by a relaxation of his standards of decorum. This relaxation is implicit in his rejection of artificial heightening in favor of naturalness. If it is natural to adulterate the great love of a heroine with fear of death, it is also natural to show her involved now and then with low and even disrespectful persons.

In relaxing his standards of decorum Dryden may have been influenced by Shakespeare not only through his natural characterization but, more specifically, through his use of indecorous comic episodes in tragedy. In adapting *Troilus and Cressida,* Dryden not only retained but gave additional emphasis to the comic elements provided by Shakespeare in the characters Thersites and Pandarus. His tragedy *Oedipus* also contains a comic element in the Theban rabble. There are no such comic episodes in the heroic plays of his earlier period. In *The Rival Ladies* and in *Amboyna* (1673) he had injected comedy into a serious action; but in the former play he deviated from his theory to imitate Tuke, and in the latter, a political potboiler, he probably paid little attention to his theory, although it is possible that he had revised his standards of decorum by the time he wrote it. His inclusion of such comic episodes in the later plays is of course inconsistent with his belief that comedy weakens the effect of tragedy by distracting the audience. Probably he included the comic episodes as sops to the vulgar. Since they are less important than a full-fledged comic plot, they presumably would be less deleterious in their effect on the tragedy.

Another modification in Dryden's theory is his view of comedy as satirical. During the period of the first phase of his theory, he theoretically conceived of comedy as satirical in that it ridicules petty vices and follies; but actually, although there is some ridicule in the comedies that he wrote during this first period, his attitude towards his principal comic characters was prevailingly sympathetic. The audience, pleased by the wit and in agreement with the selfish motives of the wild couples, is supposed to accept their conclusion that monogamy is the best practical solution to human sexual problems. But after 1672 he came to regard comedy as more genuinely satirical. In "The Apology for Heroic Poetry" he says, "Comedy is both excellently instructive, and extremely pleasant; satire lashes vice into reformation, and humour represents folly so as to render it ridiculous. Many of our present writers are eminent in both these kinds; and, particularly, the author of the Plain Dealer, whom I am proud to call my friend, has obliged all honest and virtuous men, by one of the most bold, most general, and most useful satires, which has ever been presented on the English theatre." This passage indicates that Wycherley's *Plain Dealer* may have been a factor in Dryden's shift to a view of comedy as more genuinely satirical. Another possible factor is his contemporary interest in non-dramatic satire. *Absalom and Achitophel* and *MacFlecknoe* were published at the end of the period covered in this chapter, in 1681 and 1682, and the latter was probably written around 1678.

In this passage Dryden puts instruction before delight as an end of comedy. Similarly, in his "Heads of an Answer to Rymer" he says that "the chief end of the poet is to please; for his immediate reputation depends on it," but that "the great end of the poem is to instruct, which is performed by making pleasure the vehicle of that instruction." In "The Grounds of Criticism in Tragedy" he says that "To instruct delightfully is the general end of all poetry" and agrees with Bossu that the first obligation of the dramatic poet is to decide what shall be the moral of his play (though here he may be thinking only of serious drama). In both phases of his theory Dryden regarded delight and instruction as the two ends of drama and believed that the dramatist must please in order to instruct. During the first phase he tended to put more stress on delight; during the second, on instruction.

This shift in emphasis, as the passage quoted above indicates, is probably related to Dryden's view of comedy as more genuinely satirical. Both of these modifications of his theory are in accord with the changes in his religious and philosophical outlook. In the first phase of his theory, Dryden was probably influenced by the skeptical and materialistic attitude then current among the "noblesse." His sympathetic portrayal of the wild couples, with their ruling principle of self-interest, is in accord with this attitude. But subsequently Dryden began to take a more serious interest in religion, producing two religious works (*Religio*

Laici in 1682, *The Hind and the Panther* in 1687) and in 1685 joining the Roman Catholic Church. In view of this development, it seems natural that Dryden should adopt a less tolerant attitude towards vice and, accordingly, pay more serious attention to satire and instruction in comedy.

Another possible factor in Dryden's shift to a concept of comedy as more genuinely satirical is his disillusionment with courtiers and court life. Previously he had set up the conversation of the Court as a model for his comedies, and his imitation of that model had been on the whole flattering. In dedicating *Marriage à la Mode* to Rochester he had extravagantly praised that gentleman's wit and manners. In dedicating *The Assignation* to Sir Charles Sedley, he had defended the court wits against the attacks of "Pedants" who had accused them of "leudness, Atheism, Folly, ill-Reasoning, and all manner of Extravagances." What is more, he had classified himself as one of the wits, rhapsodizing over "our Genial Nights; where our discourse is neither too serious, nor too light; but alwayes pleasant, and, for the most part, instructive: the raillery neither too sharp upon the present, nor too censorious on the absent; and the Cups onely such as will raise the Conversation of the Night, without disturbing the business of the Morrow."

But in 1672 Buckingham and others lampooned him in *The Rehearsal*. In the dedication of *Marriage à la Mode* (1673), along with the immoderate praise of Rochester, is the complaint that at Court there is "much of Interest, and more of Detraction." Dryden goes on to define "a midling sort of Courtiers," witless and malicious, "who make it their business to chase Wit from the Knowledge of Princes, lest it should disgrace their ignorance." During the period from 1675 to 1677 his relations with Rochester, and possibly with other courtiers as well, took a definite turn for the worse. Through the agency of Rochester, John Crowne was commissioned to write a court masque, although Dryden had a much stronger claim to the commission, both as Poet Laureate and as a dramatic poet much more gifted than Crowne.

During this same period Dryden hoped to undertake the writing of an epic poem in honor of England. Although the King was generous with verbal encouragement, he did not grant the funds that Dryden needed to support himself while writing the epic. Possibly some unfriendly voices at Court helped frustrate the project, for in the dedication of *Aureng-Zebe* (1676), where Dryden asks Mulgrave to speak to the King on behalf of the epic project, he also remarks that "in all Courts, there are too many who make it their Business to ruine Wit," and proceeds to give a scathing characterization of these fawning and intriguing "Courtiers without Wit." Around 1677 Rochester attacked him in his "Allusion to the Tenth Satire of the First Book of Horace." Dryden replied bitingly to Rochester's attack in the preface to *All for Love.* Though aimed at Rochester, the reply may also express Dryden's disenchantment with some of the other court wits. It is illuminating to compare his description of "our Genial Nights" with the following:

Men of pleasant conversation (at least esteemed so), and endued with a trifling kind of fancy, perhaps helped out with some smattering of Latin, are ambitious to distinguish themselves from the herd of gentlemen, by their Poetry. . . . And is not this a wretched affectation, not to be contented with what fortune has done for them, and sit down quietly with their estates, but they must call their wits in question, and needlessly expose their nakedness to public view? Not considering that they are not to expect the same approbation from sober men, which they have found from their flatterers after the third bottle. If a little glittering in discourse has passed them on us for witty men, where was the necessity of undeceiving the world?

Dryden did not break with all the wits. He dedicated *Aureng-Zebe* to Mulgrave (who was at odds with Rochester) and *Limberham* to Vaughan. But his relations with courtiers were not the unmixed delight they seem to have been previously. Then, in 1679, came the mysterious Rose Alley incident, Dryden being attacked and badly beaten by three men, probably hired thugs. We do not know who was responsible for the attack,[2] but one or more courtiers may have been involved, and even if they were not, Dryden may have suspected them of being involved.

I do not mean to suggest that Dryden deliberately altered his dramatic theory to make it correspond to the state of his personal affairs. But it is human nature to see the best side of those who favor us and the worst of those who attack us. By all accounts Rochester and his fellows, when it was their whim to be agreeable, could be charming enough to deceive Dryden with what he later called their "little glittering," so that he was inspired honestly enough to heighten their wit and insouciance and gild their vices in his wild couples. But when his eyes were opened to their most disagreeable qualities, he might well have turned to a more naturalistic and satirical representation of their conversation.

Dryden's altered view of some of the court wits raises the question of his conception of the audience in the second phase of his theory. In the *Essay of Dramatic Poesy* he had divided the audience into the noblesse, whose opinion counts, and the populace, whose opinion does not count. Dryden must have included the wits among the noblesse, and indeed it is likely that he conceived of the noblesse as being composed wholly of the fashionable court coterie, which in the early days of the Restoration seems to have been the preponderant element of the theatrical audience.[3]

As the years went by, the composition of the audience changed. During the first half of the eighteenth century, people of the middle class were coming to the theaters in sufficient numbers to influence the plays then being written,[4] and it is possible that the influx of middle-class citizens began well before 1700, in spite of the many derisive references to the "cits" in Restoration comedy. Respectable ladies were surely not in good supply in the audiences of the early Restoration; but John Harrington Smith argues that from 1675 on they were a factor to be reckoned with.[5]

Dryden's disenchantment with some of the wits, then, must have meant some degree of disenchantment with the noblesse of the audience; and if during the latter part of his career the cits and the ladies did begin to make their presence felt in the theater, we have no reason to believe that he found this development encouraging. Apart from conventional allusions in his prologues and epilogues, we have, during this period of the second phase of his theory, two references in his writings to the theatrical audience. In the "Vindication of *The Duke of Guise*" (1683), answering the charge that *The Duke of Guise* was written to inflame the rabble, he asks a rhetorical question: "Are the *Audience* of a *Play-house* (which are generally Persons of Honour, Noblemen and Ladies, or at worst . . . Gallants . . .) . . . the *Rabble?*" of course this question is designed to score a point, not to describe the audience accurately; but if there had not been in the audiences at least a few of the "Persons of Honour," etc., the question would not have had a point.

In "A Parallel of Poetry and Painting" (1695) there is a passage which we may with more confidence accept as a description of the audience as Dryden saw it: "farce-scribblers . . . entertain citizens, country-gentlemen, and Covent Garden fops. . . . The better sort go thither [to the theater] too, but in despair of sense and the just images of Nature." Though the terms are different, we have here essentially the same distinction between coarse, undiscriminating populace and refined, discriminating noblesse that we find in the *Essay*. During the period of the second phase of his theory, Dryden may have to come to regard his audience less optimistically than he had regarded it when he wrote the *Essay* and the "Defence of the Epilogue"; but, I believe, he retained to the last his faith that the audience contained some of the noblesse, the "better sort," who were capable of fully appreciating his best work.[6]

But Dryden's new emphasis on naturalness and satire, along with the revised conception of the conversation of gentlemen to which he was brought by his own sad experience, placed him in something of a dilemma. The high comedy that he had advocated and written in the first phase of his theory is essentially a comedy of wit and extravagant wildness, sympathetically presented. The new emphasis on naturalness required him to play down both the extravagance and the wit; and the new emphasis on satire required him to play down the wit, since wit elicits admiration, or at least good-natured laughter, rather than scorn. How, then, could he keep his comedy high while conforming to his modified theory? This dilemma is, I believe, largely responsible for his dwindling interest in comedy in the second phase of his development. He had far less to say about comedy in his criticism, and he wrote fewer comedies and tragicomedies: in the first phase, nearly two-thirds of his plays were comedies or tragicomedies; in the second phase, only about a third were comedies or tragicomedies. When in the second phase he did write comedy, he turned, without apparent disapproval, to low comedy, or reverted to some extent to the wit and insouciance of his wild couples. Probably his new regard for naturalness and satire made him more tolerant of low comedy, but I think that he still preferred high comedy. His failure to write more of it I ascribe largely to the difficulty of making it conform to his modified theory.

2.

Dryden's next comedy, *The Kind Keeper, or Mr. Limberham,* appeared for three days in March, 1678, and then was banned from the stage. In his dedicatory epistle Dryden says that the play was intended as "an honest *Satyre* against our crying sin of *Keeping,*" and that it was proscribed because "it express'd too much of the Vice which it decry'd." Dryden probably eliminated some of the indecency from the printed version, but even in its present form the play is far more obnoxious than Dryden's other comedies.

Allen in 1935 hypothesized that in *Limberham* Dryden was imitating D'Urfey's indecent farce *A Fond Husband.*[7] His theory was corroborated in 1942 with the publication by C. E. Ward of Dryden's letter to Latimer, written in July, 1677, which contains the following passage: "the Kings Comedy lyes in the Sudds . . . it will be almost such another piece of businesse as the fond Husband, for such the King will have it, who is parcell poet with me in the plott; one of the designes being a story he was pleased formerly to tell me; . . . I hope he will keep the jeast in countenance by laughing at it."[8] The date of the letter and the obvious resemblance of *Limberham* to *A Fond Husband* make it virtually certain that *Limberham* is the play described in this passage. Responsibility for the nature of the play is explicitly placed on the King, and the tone of the passage quite clearly indicates Dryden's disapproval, which is consistent with his critical contempt for farce such as D'Urfey's.

I believe that as *Sir Martin* is the result of a compromise between Dryden's theory and the tastes of Newcastle, so *Limberham* is the result of a compromise between Dryden's modified theory and the tastes of Charles. In pleasing Charles, Dryden made the play like D'Urfey's farce; in conforming to his theory, he injected a considerable element of satire.

Like *A Fond Husband,* Dryden's play is founded on indecent farcical intrigue rather than on character. It abides strictly by the unities of action and place, but not of time: the numerous episodes require two days and a night. The action is of the same sort as that in D'Urfey's play. Woodall, a rake who is staying at a London boardinghouse, undertakes the seduction of two fellow-boarders, Mrs. Tricksy, mistress of the kind keeper Limberham, and the wife of the eccentric Mr. Brainsick. Mrs. Saintly, the elderly proprietress of the boardinghouse, tries to induce Woodall to seduce her, too. Mrs. Pleasance, her supposed daughter, falls in love with Woodall, and he subsequently finds time to fall in love with her. Father Aldo, an old man who is lecherous but impotent (as is Limberham), gratifies his prurience by acting as pander for Woodall, not knowing that Woodall is his son. Woodall's lovemaking is opposed by Limberham and Brainsick and also by the women—not by the one whom he is undertaking at the moment, but by the others, who jealously attempt to interfere. Most of the episodes are clandestine meetings of Woodall and one or another of the ladies, which are interrupted either in the nick of time or just too late by

the unexpected arrival of one or more of the other characters. An episode in Act III is typically absurd. Mrs.
Brainsick, for obvious reasons, comes into Woodall's bedroom. Hearing the approaching footsteps of not one but
two persons, she fears that her husband is with Woodall
and hides under the bed. However, it is Mrs. Tricksy who
enters with Woodall. They sit down on the edge of the
bed and commence their lovemaking. Mrs. Brainsick expresses her jealousy by pinching them. Each thinks that
the other, over-exuberantly amorous, is doing the pinching.
At this point Mrs. Saintly is heard approaching. Mrs.
Tricksy gets into the bed to hide, pulling the covers over
her. Mrs. Saintly enters and presently, for obvious reasons,
pretends to faint, collapsing heavily on the bed and thus,
to her astonishment, flushing the other two ladies.

In the course of a series of such vicissitudes Woodall
succeeds in accomplishing his purpose with both Mrs.
Tricksy and Mrs. Brainsick, and also takes advantage of
an unexpected turn of events which leaves him alone in a
bedroom with the young maid, Judith. He deputizes his
servant Gervase to perform the less pleasant task of sleep-
ing with Mrs. Saintly. At the end of the play Aldo discovers that Woodall is his son, and Woodall discovers that
Mrs. Pleasance is the heiress whom Aldo has arranged for
him to marry. Neither Woodall nor Mrs. Pleasance has
any objection to the arrangement. Gervase marries Mrs.
Saintly, and Limberham abjectly marries Mrs. Tricksy.
Though farcical and grossly indecent, the action of the
play is cleverly handled and lively.

The characters resemble D'Urfey's in being subordinated to the action and crudely drawn. Two of D'Urfey's
characters, Bubble (the counterpart of Limberham) and
old Fumble (the counterpart of Father Aldo), manifest
the mechanic humours to which Dryden objected. Fumble

is described in the dramatis personae as "a superannuated Alderman, that dotes on Black Women: He's very deaf, and almost blind; and seeking to cover his imperfection of not hearing what is said to him, answers quite contrarily."[9] Father Aldo has a similar humour. He wishes it supposed that he knows everything and everybody, and when, in the course of lying, other characters invent imaginary persons, Aldo unintentionally assists the lie by claiming that he knows those persons well. Dryden outdoes D'Urfey in imitating him: he provides not two but several humours characters.[10]

Dryden called the play "an honest *Satyre* against our crying Sin of *Keeping*," and I see no reason to doubt that in accord with his new interest in satirical comedy he attempted to ameliorate the indecent intrigue that Charles required by adding an element of satire. Langbaine, a contemporary, wrote that the play was damned because it "so much expos'd the keeping part of the Town."[11] The satire seems to be general. In his dedicatory epistle Dryden denies the charge of "particular *Satyre*" made by "some Criticks." He continues, "I have known so many of the same humour, in every folly which is here expos'd, as may serve to warrant it from a particular Reflection."

D'Urfey's *Fond Husband* contains some satirical incidents. The main plot is concerned with the repeatedly successful efforts of Emilia and Rashley to cuckold Emilia's preposterously gullible husband, Bubble. Ranger, who loves Emilia, and Maria, who loves Rashley, jealously endeavor to expose the amour. Now and then Ranger and Maria rail at the brazen wickedness of the lovers, but this railing is primarily an expression of their jealous rage rather than satire. It is clear that the audience is supposed to sympathize with the adulterers until the last scene of the play, when, more for the sake of a dramatic ending than for the sake of morality, they are surprised in a guilty embrace. Ranger concludes the play with a soliloquy on wenching which may be meant as a satirical comment on the omnipresent wickedness of the age. Wenching, he says, is a "damn'd thing," but " 'tis such a damnable Age we live in, that, Gad, he that does not follow it is either accounted sordidly unnatural, or ridiculously impotent." Ranger therefore resolves that he will follow the fashion himself and never again try to keep others from following it. In one subsidiary plot Old Fumble is ridiculed for pursuing women despite his age and decrepitude. In another, Sir Roger Petulant discovers that his nephew Sneak has contracted a venereal disease by consorting with prostitutes, and Sneak avoids punishment by pointing out that Sir Roger has patronized several of the same prostitutes. Dryden used these incidents in his play, but modified them to make them more manifestly satirical, and added other satirical elements, so that Limberham is much more a satire than *A Fond Husband* is. The primary influence on *Limberham* as a satire is, I believe, not the essentially farcical *Fond Husband* but Wycherley's *Plain Dealer,* which Dryden praised in his "Apology for Heroic Poetry" in 1677, the year he was writing *Limberham.*

The disgusting atmosphere of *Limberham* resembles (though it is worse than) that of *The Plain Dealer.* In both plays the atmosphere is well suited to inspire in the audience contempt for the vices depicted. It seems rather unjust that Dryden, who had been charged with making "vice amiable," should now be condemned for making vice disgusting.

As in *The Plain Dealer,* some of the satire is imparted through railing. There is in *Limberham* no single outstanding pillar of virtue comparable to Manly, who does most of the railing against vice and folly in Wycherley's play. But Dryden does provide two comparatively virtuous characters who rail a little. One is Woodall's servant Gervase. By way of exposition, he rails against Woodall's past wickedness at the beginning of Act I. He gives good advice to Woodall during most of the play. One of his remarks has a manifest satirical purpose. Having urged Woodall to marry, he says, "Debauchery is upon its last Legs in *England:* witty men began the Fashion; and, now the Fops are got into't, 'tis time to leave it." But instead of Gervase reforming Woodall, Woodall corrupts Gervase by appointing him his substitute as Mrs. Saintly's paramour. This corruption of Gervase is part of Dryden's satire, for Gervase's moral downfall is the occasion of his material prosperity as the husband of the well-to-do Mrs. Saintly. Dryden calls attention to this circumstance by contrasting Gervase with Woodall's former servant, Giles, whom for his uncompromising honesty Woodall has discharged. At the end of the play, when Gervase enters in triumph as "Mr. Saintly," he says, "When will *Giles,* with his honesty, come to this?"

Mrs. Pleasance, the other railer, is also comparatively virtuous; she is the only woman in the play who remains chaste. She is described in the dramatis personae as "spightful and Satyrical" and rails much more bitingly than Gervase does. However, her attacks on vice are more the results of her spiteful nature and her jealousy of the other two women than of her concern for morality. Dryden leaves no one in the play (except poor Giles, who appears only once) wholly untainted.

Again as in *The Plain Dealer,* most of the satire is afforded through the revealing behavior and discourse of the characters. In the first scene of Act IV the satire is particularly explicit. The satirical purpose is indicated by the fact that this scene is only tenuously connected with the plot, which is otherwise well-knit. In this scene Father Aldo, who like Justice Trice of *The Wild Gallant* takes a benevolent interest in prostitutes, hears the complaints of a number of his protégées. There is a similar scene in *The Wild Gallant,* but in the earlier play the treatment is not satirical. In its satirical method the scene in *Limberham* resembles the Westminster Hall episode in *The Plain Dealer,* which satirizes the legal profession in the persons of representative members of the profession. Dryden's recollection of the *Wild Gallant* episode gave him the means of applying Wycherley's method to another profession. First enters a procuress and former prostitute, Mrs. Overdon, and her daughter Pru, sixteen years old, who since the age of fourteen has been sold as a virgin at least three times, at successively lower prices, until now she earns very little. Aldo suggests that it is time to find her a husband in the City, but Mrs. Overdon, unwilling to have the girl's talents (she has been taught French and singing) "thrown away upon a Husband," decides to "let her try her fortune a little longer." The next prostitute to enter, Mrs. Pad, is in need of a new "keeper," her previous one having been hanged. Aldo suggests that she take up with the judge who hanged him. Next enters Mrs. Termagant, who had as keeper a professional gambler. He used her as bait to attract "young Cullies" to fleece, but discarded her when she became pregnant. A Mrs. Hackney now enters, and a dispute ensues. Mrs. Hackney accuses Mrs. Termagant of having "violated the Law of Nations; for yesterday she inveigled my own natural *Cully* from me, a marri'd Lord, and made him false to my Bed." Mrs. Termagant replies, "He's my Lord now; and, though you call him a Fool, 'tis well known he's a Critick. . . . You never read a Play in all your life; and I gain'd him by my Wit."

In *Limberham* satire is also provided through the behavior of the major characters. The rake Woodall is vulgar and disagreeable, far beneath the polished Celadon. Mrs. Pleasance, though not quite so vulgar as Woodall, is much more sordid than Florimel, as may be seen in the comparison of her coarse and spiteful railing with Florimel's airy repartee. Father Aldo, the lecherous and debilitated ancient who panders for Woodall, is exceedingly unappetizing. In the dramatis personae he is ironically described as "an honest, good-natur'd, free-hearted old Gentleman of the Town." Similarly, the treacherous Vernish is described in the dramatis personae of *The Plain Dealer* as "Manly's only and bosom friend." Vernish shows his friendship by betraying Manly. Aldo shows his honesty and good nature by offering to pander for Woodall and his free-heartedness by contributing to the support of prostitutes. Both Aldo and Limberham are characterized by a combination of lechery and physical debility; and in both this characteristic is mordantly ridiculed.

The father-son relationship of Aldo and Woodall seems to be intended as the vehicle of additional satire. Aldo, admiring Woodall's prodigious lechery, says that he is "As right as if I had begot thee," and asks permission, which Woodall grants, to call him son, not knowing that Woodall actually is his son. This chip-off-the-old-block presentation implies that Aldo in his youth was like Woodall; conversely, it has the biting implication that when Woodall grows old he will be like Aldo. When Pleasance learns that Woodall is Aldo's son she refers to him as "young Father *Aldo.*"

It is obvious that in Mrs. Saintly Dryden is satirizing puritanical hypocrisy. Mrs. Saintly is a nonconformist who attends a conventicle, and throughout the play her pretended piety is contrasted with her genuine wickedness. "Keepers" and their mistresses are ridiculed in Limberham and Mrs. Tricksy. Satirical elements in the character of Mrs. Tricksy include lofty pretensions despite low birth (she is the illegitimate daughter of a prostitute) and gross infidelity to the "keeper." In Limberham are satirized the keeper's total and abject subjection to his mistress—what Dryden ironically refers to as his "kindness." Though he knows that Tricksy has been and will be unfaithful to him, Limberham cannot break with her, and ultimately he sinks to his lowest depth by marrying her. Mrs. Brainsick is even more sketchily characterized than are the other principal persons. In Dryden's portrayal of her a possible satirical element is the alacrity and hypocrisy with which she undertakes to deceive her husband; in Act III she soothes him with endearments at a time when she has Woodall concealed in an adjacent room. Brainsick's grandiloquent discourse, which as Allen has pointed out resembles that of Puntarvolo in *Every Man Out of his Humour,* is probably not a satirical element. But at one point he also manifests Frenchified foppery and literary pretensions, and here Dryden is probably ridiculing fashionable literary affectation.

A weakness in the play's satire is its violation of poetic justice. The two biggest fools, Brainsick and Limberham, are punished for their folly, but the other characters escape virtually unscathed, and some are even rewarded. Woodall is married to Pleasance, who turns out to be an heiress and the daughter of a gentleman. Mrs. Tricksy achieves wealth and social standing as the wife of Limberham. Gervase and Mrs. Saintly both seem satisfied with their marriage. Mrs. Brainsick's adultery is unpunished and undiscovered. But there is reason to believe that Dryden meant the poetic injustice in the denouement as part of the satire.

As I have said, all his characters except the luckless Giles are tainted; he seems to be interested in showing the prevalence of vice and folly by demonstrating that the downfall of one fool or rascal simply means the exaltation of another. Jonson does the same sort of thing in *The Alchemist,* where the villain Face successfully outwits his not more villainous but less astute colleagues; and Dryden in the preface to *An Evening's Love* had cited *The Alchemist* as a precedent for the violation of poetic justice in comedy. In *Limberham* the elevation of Tricksy adds to the degradation of her keeper, who reaches his low point as her acquiescent husband. Gervase achieves worldly success only by the abandonment of his virtue. The same satirical idea is expressed in the resolution of the marital difficulties of the Brainsicks. Mr. Brainsick has been a cold and highly inconsiderate husband, but because he believes that his wife has remained faithful to him while both Tricksy and Mrs. Saintly have allowed themselves to be seduced, he vows to reform and to be a good husband. Woodall comments, "A most excellent Reformation, and at a most seasonable time! The Moral on't is pleasant, if well considered." The moral is the same as Gervase's: only wickedness succeeds in the world. As long as Mrs. Brainsick was virtuous she was unhappy.

Father Aldo and Woodall are both temporarily embarrassed when the former discovers that the latter is his son, but their embarrassment is hardly painful enough to be described as punishment for either of them. However, Dryden makes the discovery another illustration of the prevalence of vice. When Aldo attempts to assert his parental authority by upbraiding Woodall for his profligacy, Woodall silences him by reminding him of his own activities as procurer.

The weakest part of the denouement is the triumph of Woodall. It is difficult to understand how a woman of any self-respect could bring herself to marry him. But in Dryden's time the double standard of premarital sexual

conduct seems to have been pretty generally accepted.[12]
The aggressively virtuous Manly of *The Plain Dealer* is an
avowed wencher, but the chaste Fidelia shows no hesitation in agreeing to marry him. Dryden seems to be exhibiting the relationship of Woodall and Pleasance in the best
light he can. He has Woodall say of Pleasance, "I have
another kind of Love to this Girl, than to either of the
other two." In Act V may be seen the practical morality
implicit in the preface to *An Evening's Love*. When
Pleasance says she is afraid that Woodall will be unfaithful to her, he replies, "You'll find me so much imployment
in my own Family, that I shall have little need to look out
for Journey-work." And in the closing lines of the play
Woodall says,

> Mistress, and Wife, by turns, I have Possess'd:
> He who enjoys 'em both, in one, is bless'd.

These lines are not quite so flippant as a modern reader
might suppose, for Dryden in his epitaph on Lady Whit-
more describes her quite seriously as "A wife, a mistress,
and a friend in one." But although this practical morality
serves pretty well to justify Celadon, who after all seems
not such a bad fellow, it is unconvincing when applied to
the more manifestly depraved Woodall. Probably Dryden
weakened his satire for the sake of a conventional happy
ending.

In his dedicatory epistle Dryden speaks highly of
Limberham: "I will be bold enough to say, that this *Comedy* is of the first Rank of those which I have written, and
that Posterity will be of my Opinion." This statement is
probably conditioned by the fact that Charles had a hand
in the play; it would not have been tactful for Dryden to
disparage it publicly. But there is also some justification
for Dryden's good opinion. The play is an excellent speci-

men of its disagreeable kind, and Dryden partly atoned
for the farce and indecency by adding satire.

A truer appraisal of the play by Dryden is, I think, to
be found in the prologue. What he did not dare to say
explicitly he concealed in conventional railing at English
drama and English tastes. The speaker of the prologue
addresses the audience:

> True Wit has seen its best days long ago,
>
> . . . .
>
> And Comedy is sunk to Trick and Pun.
>
> . . . .
>
> What Stuff will please you next, the Lord can tell.
> Let them, who the Rebellion first began,
> To wit, restore the Monarch if they can;
> Our Author dares not be the first bold Man,

but follows the fashionable taste for Tricks, and

> If now and then he takes a small pretence
> To forrage for a little Wit and Sense,
> Pray pardon him, he means you no offence.

"Trick and Pun," of course, refers to farce like D'Urfey's.
The lines

> Let them, who the Rebellion first began,
> To wit, restore the Monarch if they can

are ingeniously ambiguous. "Them" refers to farce-scribblers like D'Urfey. The key word is "Monarch." If it is
taken metaphorically, the lines may be paraphrased, "Let
D'Urfey and the others who first rebelled against the monarch wit by writing farce restore wit to the stage if they
can." But if "Monarch" is taken literally, in the light of
Charles's deplorable influence on *Limberham,* the meaning of the lines becomes, "Let D'Urfey and the others who

first rebelled against the Monarch Charles II by corrupting his taste with farce restore him to wit (that is, bring him back to his senses) if they can." The allusion to rebellion and restoration insults the farce-scribblers by identifying them with the detested Puritans and also serves as a clue to the identification of the "Monarch" as Charles. In the following lines Dryden tells the audience that he dares not undertake the cure of Charles, but in *Limberham* gratifies the Monarch's taste for D'Urfeyan farce. He does, however, "forrage for a little Wit and Sense" by providing satire, and ironically begs the audience's pardon for doing so.

3.

Of his tragicomedy *The Spanish Friar, or the Double Discovery* (1680), Dryden remarks in the dedicatory epistle,

When I first designed this play, I found . . . somewhat so moving in the serious part of it, and so pleasant in the comic, as might deserve a more than ordinary care in both; accordingly, I used the best of my endeavour, in the management of two plots, so very different from each other, that it was not perhaps the talent of every writer to have made them of a piece. Neither have I attempted other plays of the same nature, in my opinion, with the same judgment, though with like success. . . . the care and pains I have bestowed on this, beyond my other tragicomedies, may reasonably make the world conclude, that either I can do nothing tolerably, or that this poem is not much amiss.

Fifteen years later, in "A Parallel of Poetry and Painting," he made a less complimentary reference to the play: "The faults of that drama are in the kind of it, which is tragicomedy. But it was given to the people: and I never writ anything for myself but Antony and Cleopatra." In this statement Dryden is not condemning all his plays, serious as well as comic, except *All for Love*. "Given to the people" means "written to please the audience," and Dryden regarded pleasing the audience as a legitimate end of drama, if the pleasing was accomplished by artistically justifiable means. Furthermore, "for myself" means "entirely for myself." That Dryden personally liked, in part, some of his plays other than *All for Love* is evident when he says earlier in "A Parallel" that he is "fond" of *The Spanish Friar*, apart from its "unnatural mingle" of comic and serious, and that its "comical parts are diverting." His remarks in "A Parallel" indicate that Dryden, in writing *The Spanish Friar*, deviated from his own aesthetic standards only in making the play a tragicomedy.

The serious plot has to do with love of Leonora, Queen of Aragon, and the heroic Torrismond, supposedly a commoner but actually the son of Sancho, formerly King of Aragon, whose throne was usurped by Leonora's father and who now languishes in a dungeon. Leonora is engaged to marry Prince Bertran, but her love for Torrismond overcomes the obstacles interposed by their unequal stations and her previous commitment. She attempts to gain the support of the people by inducing poor Bertran to murder Sancho. When Torrismond learns the secret of his birth, he finds himself married to the woman who is supposedly guilty of the murder of his father. Nevertheless his love for Leonora compels him to fight for her against a rebel force led by Raymond, his foster-father and a loyal adherent of Sancho. All ends well when it is discovered that Bertran, suspicious of Leonora's motives, has not murdered Sancho after all. In the comic plot Lorenzo, a colonel in the Aragonian army, undertakes an amorous intrigue with Elvira, the young wife of a decrepit old usurer, Gomez. The lovers are assisted by Dominic, a hypocritical friar. Their schemes are all thwarted—fortunately, for in the last act it is revealed that the would-be adulterers are brother and sister.

The play adheres approximately to the unities of time and place. The action lasts for two or three days and takes place in two or three different parts of the same city. Although Dryden has deviated from his modified theory in making the play a tragicomedy, in accord with his theory he has taken special pains to integrate the two plots, as he says in his dedicatory epistle. In linking the two plots he mingles serious and comic elements, showing a disregard for decorum not manifest in his earlier tragicomedies. Alphonso, who is Lorenzo's father and Gomez's father-in-law, is also a city official of some sort. At the beginning of the play he and an officer, Pedro, give the exposition of the serious plot. Pedro also gives a satirical description of the principal comic character, Dominic. The arrival of Lorenzo with Torrismond's army is announced by a serious character, Bertran. Lorenzo gives a humorous account of Torrismond's victory over the Moors. A little later Lorenzo and Pedro get the comic plot under way with Lorenzo asking Pedro to direct him to some wenches. At the end of this episode Pedro, Lorenzo, and Alphonso comment on the serious situation. Later in Act I, at the beginning of a comic episode, Pedro enters to inform Lorenzo of a development in the serious plot, on which Lorenzo humorously comments. In Act IV, Dominic makes use of another development in the serious plot. He suggests that Lorenzo get Gomez out of the way by having him arrested as one of the assassins of Sancho. Lorenzo does so, but Alphonso spoils the project by ordering the release of his son-in-law. Later in Act IV Alphonso and Pedro are both leaders in the rebellion against the Queen instigated by Raymond. Pedro wishes for Lorenzo on their side to raise "a mighty Faction" through his influence

with the "City Wives." But Lorenzo, in Act V, warns
Torrismond of the rebellion, and subsequently fights on his
side. Later in Act V Alphonso and Pedro participate in
the denouement of the comic plot as the officials to whom
Gomez appeals for justice against Lorenzo, Elvira, and
Dominic.

In the serious plot Dryden has conformed to his modified theory by striving for naturalness. The serious characters express their passions in language remarkably free
from bombast. The serious plot is written in blank verse
which, like that of *All for Love,* is probably modeled on
Shakespeare's.

The comic plot also fits Dryden's modified theory. The
principal comic figure is the friar, Dominic. In accord
with Dryden's specifications in "The Grounds of Criticism
in Tragedy," he is "a composition of qualities," with one
vice predominant: primarily he is a hypocrite, but he is
also covetous, gluttonous, lecherous, cowardly, vindictive,
and witty. Secondly, it is pretty clear that he is in part a
product of Shakespearean influence: he bears a marked
resemblance to Falstaff. Allen has shown that Dominic is
partly derived from a friar in *Le Pelerin,* a novel by Gabriel
de Bremond.[13] But Dryden used Bremond's novel mainly
for details of Dominic's activities as go-between. Bremond's friar is a good runner and is not represented as
inordinately obese; Dominic, like Falstaff, is a huge, fat
man who walks with difficulty. There is in Bremond's
friar little or no basis for Dominic's lechery, cowardice, and
fluent lying. In the *Essay of Dramatic Poesy* Neander calls
Falstaff "the best of comical characters," describes him
as cowardly, notes the comic appeal of his profligacy and
bulk ("the very sight of such an unwieldy old debauched
fellow is a comedy alone"), and cites his "quick evasions"
as a diverting manifestation of his wit. Dryden praises

Shakespeare's characters and discusses Falstaff in "The Grounds of Criticism in Tragedy," which was probably written in 1679; *The Spanish Friar* was probably written in that same year (it was first performed in March, 1680). I see no reason to doubt that Falstaff was an important influence on Dominic.[14]

Dominic also fits Dryden's modified theory in serving as the vehicle of satire. In him Dryden attacks the Roman Catholic clergy. Near the end of the play Alphonso, passing judgment on Dominic, says "your Bishop's my Friend, and is too honest to let such as you infect a Cloister." This is the only line in the play which presents the clergy as other than corrupt, and Dryden probably made the bishop honest merely as a means of punishing Dominic. Elsewhere Dominic's behavior is presented as typical. Pedro calls him "A true Son of the Church"; Lorenzo calls him "a true Church-man." Gomez, having itemized Dominic's vices, observes that if "Sins come to be divided once, the Clergy puts in for nine parts, and scarce leaves the Laity a tythe."

This satire, as well as other satire in the play, needs to be seen in the light of the sensational political developments of the time. This was the era of the notorious Popish Plot, unveiled by the perjurer Titus Oates late in 1678. The King was to be murdered (said Oates), England was to be invaded by the French, and all obstinate Protestants were to be massacred. Oates's lies, assisted by the mysterious murder of Godfrey, the magistrate to whom he reported the plot, produced a terrifying wave of anti-Catholic hysteria which was exploited by the Whigs in their struggle for power with Charles II and the Tories. A hero of the anti-Catholic citizenry was the "Protestant Duke," the Duke of Monmouth, Charles's illegitimate son. Shaftesbury and the other Whigs energetically promoted Monmouth in the hope of putting him on the throne instead of the legitimate successor, Charles's Catholic brother James, Duke of York. This, of course, is the situation that Dryden brilliantly satirized in Part I of *Absalom and Achitophel*, where Charles is represented as King David, Monmouth as Absalom, Shaftesbury as Achitophel, and Oates as Corah. The poem was published in 1681, only a year after the first appearance of *The Spanish Friar*. And most of the satirical allusions of *The Spanish Friar* were probably provoked by the same situation.

By the time *Absalom and Achitophel* was published, the King's party clearly had the upper hand; but in 1680, when *The Spanish Friar* appeared, the issue was very much in doubt. In view of the anti-Catholic hysteria, the Tories (whose side Dryden took) certainly would have wished to make it clear that Protestantism was not a Whig monopoly. It would therefore be a mistake to assume, on the basis of the satire of the Catholic Church through the character of Dominic, that Dryden had gone over to the Whigs.[15] Implicit in the serious plot, as G. W. Whiting has pointed out, is "an argument for established authority."[16] The frustrated plot against the life of King Sancho and, in particular, the closing lines of the play,

> But let the bold Conspirator beware,
> For Heaven makes Princes its peculiar Care,

may be taken as references not only to the alleged Popish Plot against Charles, but also to the Shaftesbury-Monmouth collusion.

The Whigs seem to have encouraged anti-Catholic mob demonstrations,[17] and probably these lie behind several satirical references to the rabble in *The Spanish Friar*. Leonora's reference to the people as

That hot mouth'd Beast, that bears against the Curb,
Hard to be broken even by lawfull Kings[18]

is reminiscent of Dryden's description of the rebellious
Jews in *Absalom and Achitophel:*

> . . . a Headstrong, Moody, Murm'ring race
> As ever tri'd th'extent and stretch of grace;
> God's pamper'd People, whom, debauch'd with ease,
> No King could govern nor no God could please.

In the serious plot Sancho, like David in *Absalom and
Achitophel,* is represented as encouraging rebellion by his
mild and benevolent rule; Bertran, like Absalom and
Achitophel, is accused of making a pretended concern for
the welfare of his sovereign and his state the pretext for
seditious activities. In the comic plot Gomez, like the
many victims of Corah's lies, is falsely accused of participating in a plot against the state. He protests as follows: "Who, I in a Plot! . . . I never durst be in a Plot:
Why, how can you in conscience suspect a rich Citizen of
so much wit as to make a Plotter? There are none but
poor Rogues, and those that can't live without it, that are
in Plots." This seems to be double-barreled satire. The
last sentence clearly refers to the crowd of informers (Oates
was followed by a swarm of others) who were paid for
their anti-Catholic revelations.[19] The rest of Gomez's pro-
test seems to satirize the rich citizens of London. From
them the Whigs drew much of their support, and (in the
Tory view) they along with the rest of the Whigs were
busily plotting not for the Pope but against the King.[20]

Lorenzo, like Absalom, decides to oppose his own father and consequently is a little troubled by his conscience.
He soliloquizes,

> Let me consider;
> Bear Arms against my Father? he begat me;
> That's true; but for whose sake did he beget me?
> For his own sure enough: for me he knew not.
> Oh! but says Conscience: Fly in Nature's Face?
> But how if Nature fly in my Face first?
> Then Nature's the Aggressor: Let her look to't—
> —He gave me Life, and he may take it back:—
> No, that's Boys play, say I.—
> 'Tis policy for Son and Father to take different sides:
> For then, Lands and Tenements commit no Treason.

This is like Absalom's wavering reply to Achitophel's blandishments—

> And what Pretence have I
> To take up Arms for Publick Liberty?
> My Father Governs with unquestion'd Right . . .

—and even more like one of Achitophel's casuistical counter-arguments:

> Nor let his Love enchant your generous Mind;
> 'Tis Natures trick to propagate her Kind.
> Our fond Begetters, who would never die,
> Love but themselves in their Posterity.

Incidentally, Lorenzo's soliloquy may be another result of Shakespeare's influence: it resembles Falstaff's soliloquy on honor in *Henry IV,* Part One. In modeling Dominic on Falstaff, Dryden probably re-examined the plays in which Falstaff figures. Lorenzo uses the phrase "Boys play." Falstaff, not long after delivering his soliloquy, uses the same phrase in cheering on Prince Hal against Hotspur.

Torrismond, like Lorenzo, intends to fight against his supposed father, Raymond, of whom he says, "I no more must call him Father now." Of this remark Lorenzo observes,

> How! not call him Father?
> I see Preferment alters a man strangely,
> This may serve me for a Use of Instruction,
> To cast off my Father when I am great.

Probably Dryden intended this as a reference both to Monmouth's great popularity and to his unfilial exploitation of it.

Other bits of satire in the play (most of them seemingly unrelated to the political situation) are afforded by Pedro, who, like Thersites in *Troilus and Cressida* and Manly in *The Plain Dealer,* is a railer. He rails briefly but incisively against religious hypocrisy, the clergy, courtiers, travel as a nourisher of vices in young men, the foolish subservience of a man to the woman he loves, the flightiness of women, and the rabble.

Gomez, the elderly husband of Elvira, fits Dryden's modified theory. The characters of the oldsters in Dryden's earlier comedies are founded on extravagant humours—Nonsuch's gullibility, Moody's downrightness, Alonzo's loquacity, Aldo's superannuated lechery and affectation of omniscience. But Gomez, like Dominic, is more naturally represented as a "composition of qualities." He is miserly, cowardly, and jealous. He is also a good deal more clever than the earlier oldsters. He rails rather wittily at his wife, her lover, and the friar and sees through their stratagems.

Lorenzo and Elvira resemble the wild couples of the earlier comedies, but are less artificial, just as Torrismond and Leonora are less artificial than the earlier heroic couples. Lorenzo is as professedly polygynous as the earlier gallants, but his pursuit of women is made more natural

by the circumstance that as an officer campaigning with
Torrismond's army he has, as he puts it, "kept a tedious
Fast." Unlike Palamede, he does not begin an intrigue
with a married woman only three days before his marriage;
unlike Celadon and Wildblood, he does not pursue other
women whenever his mistress is out of sight. Elvira is
forward, like the earlier ladies (it is she, not Lorenzo, who
opens negotiations); but her amorous inclinations, like Lorenzo's, are made more natural by her circumstances: she
is the young wife of a debilitated old man who guards her
jealously. At her first meeting with Lorenzo, she says,
"Perhaps . . . you may accuse my forwardness; but . . .
there is nothing so extravagant as a Prisoner, when he gets
loose a little, and is immediately to return into his Fetters."
Unlike Doralice, she does not begin an amour only a year
after her marriage to a handsome young man. There are
only two passages of repartee between Lorenzo and Elvira.
They spend much of their time plotting, with the assistance
of Dominic, the escape of Elvira, or inventing lies to mis-
lead Gomez when he inopportunely appears. This varying
of repartee with other manifestations of wit makes Lorenzo
and Elvira appear more natural than the earlier couples,
who sometimes give the impression that they consider an
amour primarily an occasion for witty talk. Furthermore,
their repartee is less extravagant than that of the wild couples in *Secret Love* and *Marriage à la Mode*. Compare, for
example, these two discussions of constancy:

The Spanish Friar:

LOR. To confess freely to you, Madam, I was never in
love with less than your whole Sex before: but now I have
seen you, I am in the direct road of languishing and sigh-
ing. . . . perhaps I may go shufflingly at first; for I was
never before walk'd in Trammels; yet I shall drudge and

moil at Constancy, till I have worn off the hitching in my pace.

ELV. Oh, sir, there are Arts to reclaim the wildest Men, as there are to make Spaniels fetch and carry: chide 'em often, and feed 'em seldom: now I know your temper, you may thank your self if you are kept to hard meat:— you are in for years if you make love to me.

Secret Love:

FLA. . . . could you not be constant to one?

CEL. Constant to one! . . . give me some Twenty, some Forty, some a Hundred Mistresses: I have more Love than any one woman can turn her to.

FLOR. . . . he's as constant as the Sun, he would see all the world round in 24 hours.

CEL. 'Tis very true, Madam, but, like him, I would visit and away.

FLOR. For what an unreasonable thing it were to stay long, be troublesome, and hinder a Lady of a fresh Lover.

Dryden seems also to have endeavoured to diversify the interests of Lorenzo and Elvira. The earlier couples' monomaniac pursuit of love is one of the principal manifestations of their artificial extravagance. Lorenzo and Elvira are more natural in exhibiting some interest in other matters. Elvira is as anxious to escape from the tyranny of Gomez as she is to be Lorenzo's mistress; she acquiesces only on the condition that he run off with her. Lorenzo displays interest in his social and financial position; when told that his cousin Torrismond has been ruined, he says, "not that I wish my Kinsman's ruin; that were Unchristian: but, if the General's ruin'd, I am Heir; there's comfort for a Christian." Later he is concerned with a problem of filial duty: he must decide whether to fight for or against his father.

The comic plot contains some low and improbable episodes. In Act I Lorenzo, not knowing that Gomez is Elvira's husband, asks him to assist their amour. In Act II Dominic, on the pretext of hearing confession, orders Gomez to stand out of earshot while he gives Elvira a mes-; sage from Lorenzo. In Act III Lorenzo by disguising himself as a friar gains admission to Elvira's room. Gomez returns unexpectedly and, grappling with Lorenzo, pulls off his disguise. In Act IV Gomez, having been arrested for treason, is carried off the stage on the backs of two soldiers. He returns a minute or two later to find Lorenzo and Elvira about to steal his gold and jewels. When he threatens legal action, Lorenzo beats him. After the others leave, Gomez beats his own head as punishment for marrying a young wife. In Act V Gomez before Alphonso as judge alternately makes and denies charges as Lorenzo from a place of concealment frowns and shakes his fist. Some of these episodes, especially the last two, go pretty far, but it is conceivable that Dryden regarded them as low comedy rather than farce. None of them go as far as *Limberham*.

Jeremy Collier, in the course of his attack on Dryden's treatment of the clergy, complains that "Lewd *Lorenzo* comes off with *Flying Colours*. 'Tis not the Fault which is corrected but the Priest. The Authors Discipline is seldom without a Biass. He commonly gives the *Laity* the pleasure of an ill Action, and the *Clergy* the Punishment."[21] This complaint is more witty than just. It is true that Dominic and poor Gomez are severely treated and that Lorenzo and Elvira are not. But Elvira's misconduct and Gomez's misfortunes are justified in part by Gomez's de-

ficiencies as a husband. Furthermore, Dryden has taken
pains to justify the punishment of Dominic by making him
more wicked than the others. His hypocrisy and his violation of his obligations as a cleric make him a worse sinner
than Lorenzo or Elvira, and at one point in the play Dryden emphasizes his greater depravity. Just before Lorenzo
sends in his soldiers to carry off Gomez, Dominic suggests
that they not only abduct but murder the old man. Lorenzo says, "What, take away a man's Wife, and kill him
too! the Wickedness of this old Villain startles me, and
gives me a twinge for my own Sin, though it come far short
of his."

The denouement of the comic plot, in which Lorenzo
and Elvira learn they are brother and sister, is highly improbable, and one wonders why Dryden used it. He seems
to have been actuated partly by moral considerations. The
discovery deepens Dominic's sin, for his pandering nearly
results in incest as well as adultery. Moreover, although
Lorenzo and Elvira seem not at all chastened by the
revelation of their relationship (Elvira says, "You see,
Brother, I had a natural affection to you," and Lorenzo
replies, "What a delicious Harlot have I lost!"), the fact
remains that wenching is here presented in a more disagreeable light than it is in the comedy which Dryden
wrote before 1675. Another possible indication of Dryden's concern for morality is the relative decency of the
play. Lorenzo and Elvira are always interrupted before
their lovemaking progresses beyond preliminaries. The
dialogue includes a few double meanings, but it is for
the most part free from bawdiness.

VII. 1685-1700: THE LAST PERIOD; HIGHER COMEDY AGAIN

1.

DRYDEN'S BRIEF and infrequent discussions of the drama during this final period of his career indicate that his modified theory remained basically unchanged, although in some respects it seems to have developed a little further. Many of his remarks express an increasing concern for morality and decency. His conversion in 1685 to Catholicism was probably an important factor in this development. In the same year, in his preface to *Sylvae,* he says that "barefaced bawdry is the poorest pretence to wit imaginable." In the following year, in a passage of his ode to Anne Killigrew, he deplores the lubricity of the stage and his own contributions to it. In the preface to *Don Sebastian* (1690) he agrees with Rymer that poets should observe "Poetical justice," and calls attention to the morality of the play. In "The Original and Progress of Satire" (1693) he speaks of the "scurrility and profaneness" of the stage and the "licentious insolence" of dramatists and actors. In the dedication of *Examen Poeticum* (1693) he argues that pleasing the audience is a worthy function, but that "religion and good manners" must not be sacrificed to it. In "A Parallel of Poetry and Painting" (1695) he says that "the chief design of Poetry is to instruct," and that comedy is "a sharp manner of instruction for the vulgar." His preface to *Fables Ancient and Modern* (1700) contains an admission of guilt occasioned by Collier's charge of immorality and profaneness: "in many things he has taxed me justly; and I have pleaded guilty to all thoughts and expressions of mine, which can be truly argued of obscenity, profaneness, or immorality, and retract them." The same moral tendency may be seen in his private correspondence during this period. In 1699 he urged Elizabeth Thomas to eschew in her writings "the Licenses which Mrs. Behn allowed herself," and continued, "I confess, I am the last Man who ought, in Justice to arraign her, who have been myself too much a Libertine in most of my Poems, which I should be well contented I had Time either to purge or to see them fairly burned."

But the moral protestations that Dryden made during the last fifteen years of his life should not be taken as evidence of his venality as a comic dramatist throughout his career. It is unwarranted to assume that in 1671 or 1672, when he wrote *Marriage à la Mode,* Dryden had the same moral standards that he had in 1700, when, in the epilogue to *The Pilgrim,* he implied that he had been a literary prostitute to the lewd Restoration Court. The skeptical practical morality and the admiration for the conversation of the Restoration Court which Dryden professed in the preface to *An Evening's Love* and the "Defence of the Epilogue," and embodied in his earlier comedies, were probably as sincere as his subsequent disillusioned condemnation of them. The tightening of moral standards with increasing age is not uncommon.

Furthermore, we must not assume that Dryden's standards of decency and morality were the same as ours. Dryden in condemning the indecency of his works was neither wholesale nor specific. Consequently we do not know how many of his comedies, or what features of his comedies, he considered reprehensible. The indications are that his standards, even towards the end of his life, were less strict than those of subsequent generations. In his "Preface to

Ovid's Epistles" (1680) he says that the epistles he has translated "may be read, as he [Ovid] intended them, by matrons without a blush." One of these epistles ("Canace to Macareus") is a chronicle of incestuous love, attempted abortion, and childbirth which, though highly poetized, would have made a Victorian matron blush, or at least feel as though she ought to. Dryden's song, "Sylvia the Fair, in the Bloom of Fifteen," published in 1685, is founded on a double meaning potent enough to raise the eyebrows of some modern readers. But such songs do not seem to have been considered vulgar by sophisticated Restoration readers.[1] In the dedication of *Examen Poeticum* Dryden announces that he has read his translations of Ovid to Lord and Lady Radcliffe, who "seemed not to be displeased with them." These translations include several rather inflammatory accounts of the amours of the gods. In the preface to the *Fables* Dryden says that in translating the fables "I have written nothing which savours of immorality or profaneness; at least, I am not conscious to myself of any such intention." Some of his translations of Boccaccio in the *Fables* contain lush descriptions of love and women.

Dryden seems to have had a decidedly unromantic conception of love and women. In the preface to *Sylvae* (1685) he admits the obscenity of Lucretius' very clinical account of love in the fourth book of *De Rerum Natura,* but defends it as "honest and instructive," and says that in this book Lucretius "has given the truest and most philosophical account, both of the disease [love] and remedy, which I ever found in any author." Similarly, in his "Preface to the Translation of Ovid's Epistles" (1680) Dryden admits that Ovid's highly practical *Ars Amoris* is lascivious, but he also says that "no man has ever treated the passion of love with so much delicacy of thought, and of

expression, or searched into the nature of it more phil-
osophically, than he [Ovid]." The episode of Dido and
Aeneas, which many sensitive and high-minded persons
no doubt have contemplated with tearful rapture, was regarded by Dryden from a more matter-of-fact point of
view. In the dedication of his translation of the *Aeneid*
(1697) he summarizes the conclusion of the affair as follows: "possession having cooled his love, as it increased
hers, she soon perceived the change, or at least grew suspicious of a change; this suspicion soon turned to jealousy,
and jealousy to rage; then she disdains and threatens, and
again is humble, and entreats, and, nothing availing, de-
spairs, curses, and at last becomes her own executioner."

Dryden also translated the sixth satire of Juvenal, a
savage attack on women, in which lust is represented as
the dominant drive in the female psyche. In the "Argument" of this satire Dryden says that Juvenal's charges are
unjust and that no English lady could possibly be guilty
of the vices that Juvenal catalogues. That Dryden hoped
to fool his lady readers with such obvious flattery is still
another indication of his not idealistic conception of
women. When we consider that Dryden studied Lucretius,
Ovid, and Juvenal, that to him (as to his educated contemporaries) these were respectable authors, and that he lived
in a society that included such notorious women as the
Countess of Castlemaine, the Countess of Shrewsbury,
and Nell Gwyn, his unchivalrous ideas about love and
marriage seem quite natural. We may find his attitude deplorable, but we must admit that it was probably sincere.[2]

Against the passages in which Dryden submits to the
strictures of Jeremy Collier and other guardians of morality must be weighed other passages in which he defends
himself with some vigor against their attacks. In the preface to the *Fables* he justifies the ridicule of the clergy, for

which he had been accused of profaneness: "A satirical poet is the check of the laymen on bad priests. We are only to take care, that we involve not the innocent with the guilty. . . . [I reserve] to myself the right . . . to describe another sort of priests . . . more easily to be found than the Good Parson; such as have given the last blow to Christianity in this age, by a practice so contrary to their doctrine." At the beginning of one of the fables, "Cymon and Iphigenia," he unregenerately defends himself against Collier:

Old as I am, for ladies' love unfit,
The power of beauty I remember yet,
Which once inflamed my soul, and still inspires my wit.
If love be folly, the severe divine
Has felt that folly, though he censures mine.

. . . .

The world will think that what we loosly write,
Though now arraigned, he read with some delight;
Because he seems to chew the cud again,
When his broad comment makes the text too plain;
And teaches more in one explaining page,
Than all the double meanings of the stage.
　　What needs he paraphrase on what we mean?
We were at worst but wanton; he's obscene.
I, nor my fellows, nor myself excuse;
But love's the subject of the comick muse;
Nor can we write without it, nor would you
A tale of only dry instruction view.

Dryden did not intend all his remarks on decency and morality to apply to comedy. In the "Parallel of Poetry and Painting" he says that the subjects of an epic poem or a tragedy "ought to have nothing of immoral, low, or filthy in them," but he obviously does not mean to impose the same restrictions on comedy, since elsewhere in the same essay he observes that the subjects of comedy are low, and presents comedy as instructive in exposing the vices and follies of the vulgar, which are certain to be immoral and low, and are apt to be filthy as well. When in the preface to *Don Sebastian* he says that poets should observe poetic justice, he is probably thinking only of serious poets. His concept of comedy as satirical admits of violations of poetic justice, and both privately (in a letter to Walsh) and publicly (in his commendatory verses addressed to Congreve) he spoke well of Congreve's satirical comedy *The Double Dealer,* in which two adulteries go unpunished.

I believe that Dryden was sincere in professing a stricter concern for morality and decency during the period from 1685 to 1700. But I believe that his earlier "practical" moral attitude was also sincere. And, when considering the morality and decency of the comedy of his last period, we must remember that even at that time his standards were tolerant; that his conception of love and women was honestly unromantic; and that his conception of comedy as satirical involves the representation of vice and folly.

During this period Dryden had a good deal to say about satire. His most important discussion of this subject, the essay "On the Original and Progress of Satire" (1693), is concerned primarily with non-dramatic satire, but portions of it are applicable to the drama. He prefers general satire to satire of individuals, which he calls "lampoon" and which, he says, is permissible only when one has no other means of replying to the attack of another lampooner, or when the target of the lampoon is a "public nuisance." Commenting on Heinsius' definition of satire, he observes that Heinsius' phrase "without a series of action" "distinguishes satire properly from stage-plays, which

are all of one action, and one continued series of action."
But Dryden is here speaking of satire as a genre, not a style;
he does not mean that comedy cannot be satirical. In his
commendatory verses to Congreve, published only about
a year after this essay, he praises the satire of Congreve
and Wycherley.

Distinguishing among the satires of Persius, Juvenal,
and Horace, Dryden says that those of the first two are
grave, severe, and elevated, while those of Horace are
comic, mild, and low, dealing with the follies of "fools and
fops" rather than the vices of "notoriously wicked men."
This distinction places Horace's satire the closest of the
three to Dryden's idea of comedy, and Dryden probably
thought of the satire in his comedies as primarily Horatian.
It is possible, however, that once in a while he attempted
Juvenalian satire—for example, in the vehement and elevated railing of Dorax in *Don Sebastian*. Dryden also
holds that satire must "be confined to one particular
theme," but concludes that other vices may be "transiently
lashed" if they are kept subordinate to the main satirical
theme, as, in a play, subplots are kept subordinate to the
main plot. I believe that here again Dryden is speaking of
satire as a nondramatic genre. If he is not, he has violated
this principle in his comedies, where the satire is sometimes multiple and incidental.

In several of the prologues that Dryden wrote during
this period—the ones to *Albion and Albanius* (1685), *Don
Sebastian* (1689), *Amphitryon* (1690), and *The Pilgrim*
(1700)—are remarks to the effect that dramatic satire is
forbidden, dangerous to the author, and futile, and that
he intends to write no more of it. Although these passages
perhaps reflect an increasingly strict censorship of the
stage,[3] they probably refer primarily to Dryden's own circumstances. He found himself in trouble, with *Limber-*

ham, even during the reign of Charles. *The Spanish Friar* was forbidden during the reign of James, probably because of its anti-Catholicism. Then the Revolution of 1688 unseated the Catholic James and established the Whiggish and Protestant régime of William and Mary. Dryden, a Catholic and a Tory, was not in an enviable situation. He lost his pension, of course, along with the laureateship, to which Shadwell succeeded.

In May, 1689, *The Spanish Friar* was performed for Queen Mary, but instead of pleasing her as a Protestant play it seems to have caused her embarrassment because of the usurper Leonora.[4] In 1692 his tragedy *Cleomenes* was forbidden by the Queen. With the help of some influential friends, he was able to get the ban lifted. At some time before the performance the play was censored by the management of the United Company. In his preface to the play Dryden wryly comments on this censorship: "I cannot reasonably blame them for their Caution; because they are answerable for any thing that is publickly represented: And their Zeal for the Government is such, that they had rather lose the best Poetry in the World, than give the least Suspicion of their Loyalty." He wrote for his son's comedy, *The Husband his own Cuckold* (1696), an epilogue in which the clergy are ridiculed; but he also wrote an alternative, less mordant version of the epilogue, to be used in case the first should give offense.[5] In his postscript to the *Aeneid* (1697) he describes his situation as follows: "curbed in my genius, liable to be misconstrued in all I write; and my judges . . . prejudiced against me, by the lying character which has been given them of my morals." A little later in the postscript, speaking of bad poets, he says, "Here is a field of satire opened to me: but, since the Revolution, I have wholly renounced that talent." What he wholly renounced, I think, is non-dramatic satire;

the three plays he wrote after the Revolution contain satire that is unmistakable. Of course he had discretion. Probably the exotic locales and characters of these last three plays are due partly to his wish to avoid offense. He also made much of the satire general or retrospective. But on the whole, when we consider his adverse circumstances, it seems remarkable that Dryden incorporated in his later plays as much and as strong satire as he did. John Robert Moore pays tribute to his courage and honesty in doing so.[6] Dryden also deserves credit, I believe, for his fidelity to his revised theory of comedy.

In discussing the three unities during this period, Dryden exhibits some tolerance in his conceptions of the unities of time and place. In the preface to *Don Sebastian* he says of the play, "I have taken the time of two days, because the variety of accidents . . . cou'd not naturally be suppos'd to arrive in one: But to gain a greater Beauty [presumably he means variety], 'tis lawful for a Poet to supersede a less." In the dedication of *Love Triumphant* he defends, citing Corneille as a precedent, his approximation of the unity of place, " a Street and Palace, not far distant from each other in the same City."

But his view of the unity of action seems even stricter than it was during the preceding period. He now condemns tragicomedy as "wholly Gothic"[7] and repeatedly says that he writes it, against his better judgment, only to please the tastes of his audience.[8] He calls *Cleomenes* "a bold Attempt of mine, to write upon a single Plott, unmix'd with *Comedy;* which though it be the natural and true way, yet is not to the *Genius* of the Nation." Although variety is a "beauty" and a legitimate excuse for moderate stretching of the unity of time and, presumably, the unity of place, it does not excuse violation of the unity of action: when carried to the extreme of in-

sistence on tragicomedy, the English taste for variety becomes a "debauchery of Pleasure"[9] and a "publick Vice."[10]
In the *Essay of Dramatic Poesy* Neander had defended
tragicomedy on the ground that "contraries, when placed
near, set off each other"; now, in "A Parallel of Poetry
and Painting," Dryden holds that in the "unnatural mingle"
of tragicomedy "mirth and gravity destroy each other, and
are no more to be allowed for decent than a gay widow
laughing in a mourning habit." However, it is only tragicomic conrast that Dryden condemns. Otherwise, he seems
to have retained his faith in the dramatic effectiveness of
contrast. On this same page of "A Parallel" he advocates
the juxtaposition of contrary characters, such as a miser
and a prodigal, and quotes the "old maxim," *"contraria
juxta se posita magis elucescunt."*

Dryden continues to prefer English dramatists to
French and "ancient" dramatists on the ground that the
English afford more variety. "Our poets," he says in the
dedication of *Examen Poeticum,* "could more easily com-
ply with [the French taste for barren regularity] . . . than
the French writers could come up to the sublimity of our
thoughts, or to the difficult variety of our designs." But
although he charges the French with following the ancients
"too servilely in the mechanic rules," he also charges the
English with assuming "too much licence" in following the
rules "at too great a distance." Consequently his preference of English dramatists is not inconsistent with his
stricter regard for the unity of action.

Despite his disparagement of French dramatists, Dryden in the dedication of *Amphitryon* praises Molière as the
greatest modern comic dramatist. This evaluation is probably conditioned by Dryden's desire to promote his play,
which is an adaptation of Molière. But it is possible that
the modification of his theory in the direction of satire,

naturalness, and regularity led him to acquire increased respect for Molière. Probably the modification of his theory also lies behind his references in the dedication of *Examen Poeticum* to his English predecessors: "Peace be to the venerable shades of Shakespeare and Ben Johnson! none of the living will presume to have any competition with them; as they were our predecessors, so they were our masters . . . we have not arriv'd to the pitch of Shakespeare and Ben Johnson." Dryden no longer claims, as he did in the "Defence of the Epilogue," that the superior conversation of his own age has raised contemporary drama above that of the preceding age. It is true that in his commendatory verses on *The Double Dealer* he had credited Congreve with being Shakespeare's equal in "Genius," Jonson's equal in judgment, and Jonson's and Fletcher's superior in wit; but this is probably the sort of hyperbole conventional in eulogistic verse, meant to be taken with reservations, like Dryden's similar contention that Nature combined in Milton the particular excellences of Homer and Virgil.

Jonson and Shakespeare are mentioned again in "The Original and Progress of Satire." Dryden deplores the shortage, before his time, of English studies of the art of poetry. He continues, "Shakespeare, who created the stage among us, had rather written happily, than knowingly and justly, and Johnson, who, by studying Horace, had been acquainted with the rules, yet seemed to envy to posterity that knowledge . . . [I learned the art of poetry without] other help than the polestar of the Ancients, and the rules of the French stage amongst the Moderns." This statement should not be taken as meaning that Dryden had no literary obligation at all to Shakespeare and Jonson. He is here speaking of precept, not example. Even so, the statement is unfair to Jonson, of whom Dryden had said, in the *Essay of Dramatic Poesy,* "in the precepts which he has laid down in his Discoveries, we have as many and profitable rules for perfecting the stage, as any wherewith the French can furnish us." Dryden's lapse of memory perhaps was caused by his shift from Jonson to Shakespeare as primary dramatic model.

A passage in the "Parallel of Poetry and Painting" shows that Dryden still retained his views on the position in poetry of comedy and farce: "comedy is a representation of human life in inferior persons, and low subjects, and by that means creeps into the nature of poetry. . . . There is yet a lower sort of poetry . . . farce. . . . The persons and action of a farce are all unnatural." Dryden does not here state a preference for high comedy, but such a preference may be inferred. Since lowness is objectionable, it is to the advantage of the dramatist to make his comedy as high as he can without transcending the limits of the genre.

Dryden proceeds in the "Parallel" bitterly to attack laughter:

Laughter is indeed the propriety of a man, but just enough to distinguish him from his elder brother with four legs. 'Tis a kind of bastard-pleasure too, taken in at the eyes of the vulgar gazers, and at the ears of the beastly audience. . . . farce-scribblers . . . entertain citizens, country-gentlemen, and Covent Garden fops. . . . The better sort go thither [to the theater] too, but in despair of sense and the just images of Nature, which are the adequate pleasures of the mind. . . . After all, 'tis a good thing to laugh at any rate; and if a straw can tickle a man, it is an instrument of happiness.

Dryden in attacking laughter is not attacking comedy. His objection to laughter is the one which Jonson had made in his *Discoveries* and which Dryden himself had made in the *Essay of Dramatic Poesy*: laughter is a vulgar pleasure because it is provoked as readily by a farce or by a straw as by comedy. But of the three only the comedy affords the higher pleasure which one experiences upon beholding a just image of Nature. Dryden expresses the same opinion in his preface to his son's play, *The Husband his own Cuckold:* "the taste of the age is wretchedly depraved in all sorts of poetry. . . . poets, worthy of such an audience, know not how to distinguish their characters; the manners are all alike inconsistent, and interfering with each other. There is scarce a man or woman of God's making in all their farces, yet they raise an unnatural sort of laughter, the common effect of buffoonery."

Since the deformities represented in farce are unnatural, the laughter that they provoke has no value other than that of a vulgar pleasure. But the vices and follies represented in comedy are natural deformities, and consequently the laughter that greets them may have a corrective function: the comedy may serve as a mirror in which persons guilty of those vices or follies may see themselves and in consequence be shamed into reform. This notion is behind another passage of the "Parallel": "Comedy . . . is often to produce laughter, which is occasioned by the sight of some deformity; but for this I refer the reader to Aristotle. 'Tis a sharp manner of instruction for the vulgar, who are never well amended till they are more than sufficiently exposed." This idea is expressed once more when Dryden in "The Original and Progress of Satire" describes "the best and finest manner of Satire" as "that sharp, well-mannered way of laughing a folly out of countenance."

Since laughter, though an indiscriminate reaction, does have this corrective function, one might justifiably ask why Dryden treats it so contemptuously, why he does not at least distinguish between the worthless laughter aroused by farce and the corrective laughter aroused by comedy.

The answer is, I think, that Dryden was by nature un-
sympathetic towards laughter. "My humour," he says in
the "Defence of an Essay," "[is] saturnine and reserved."

It is significant that he speaks, somewhat vaguely and
uncertainly, of a pleasure "nobler" than laughter which is,
or may be, produced by comedy and satire. In the preface
to *An Evening's Love,* in the very passage in which he
speaks of corrective laughter, he says, "the business of the
[comic] poet is to make you laugh: when he writes humour, he makes folly ridiculous; when wit, he moves you,
if not always to laughter, yet to a pleasure that is more
noble." And in his "Life of Lucian" (*c.* 1696) he says,
"if the pleasure arising from comedy and satire be either
laughter, or some nobler sort of delight, which is above
it, no man is so great a master of irony as our author
[Lucian]." Now in the preface to *An Evening's Love*
Dryden conceives of wit in comedy as repartee. Accordingly, he probably conceived of the "more noble pleasure" which such wit inspires as delight in the rhetorical
felicity of the repartee.[11] Apparently he had the same conception of the "nobler sort of delight" arising from satire.
In the "Life of Lucian" he goes on to say that Lucian's
irony "is not only a keen, but a shining weapon in his
hand; it glitters in the eyes of those it kills; . . . his greatest
enemies, are not butchered by him, but fairly slain." This
is reminiscent of a passage in "The Original and Progress
of Satire" in which Dryden, speaking of satire, says, "There
is . . . a vast difference betwixt the slovenly butchering of
a man, and the fineness of a stroke that separates the head
from the body, and leaves it standing in its place."

This "nobler pleasure" of delight in rhetorical felicity
is consistent with Dryden's earlier conception of a high
comedy of witty gentlefolk, and with his conception of
non-dramatic satire, but it is inconsistent with his later

conception of satirical comedy. In non-dramatic satire the author does the talking and is free to use all the wit he can command; but in satirical comedy the fool or rascal does the talking. It is true that witty persons may have follies or vices, but the satirical dramatist who tries to represent a character as both admirable (in his wit) and contemptible (in his vice or folly) undertakes a very ticklish task, and will probably lose the admiration in the contempt, or vice versa. Of course the dramatist may invent a witty and moral spokesman to ridicule the other characters, but he cannot make the comedy a monologue; the spokesman must often be silenced so that the fools and rascals may display their failings. Dryden's preference for the "nobler pleasure" of admiration for rhetorical felicity, his realization that the end of comedy is after all the lower pleasure of scornful laughter at vice or folly, and his recognition of the difficulty of reconciling the conflicting requirements of the two sorts of pleasure are largely responsible, I think, for his decreasing interest in his own comedy in the period of the second phase of his theory.

During the period from 1685 to 1700 Dryden made a few scattered observations on characterization. In the "Parallel" he says that "the characters of Comedy and Tragedy . . . are never to be made perfect, but always to be drawn with some specks of frailty and deficience. . . . [Their] perfection consists chiefly in their likeness to the deficient faulty nature, which is their original . . . there will always be found a better likeness and a worse . . . the better is constantly to be chosen . . . in tragedy, which represents the figures of the highest form among mankind. . . . In Comedy there is somewhat more of the worse likeness to be taken" in order (Dryden continues) to make some impression on the thick-skinned vulgar, who mend their manners only if they are "more than sufficiently exposed." In this passage may be seen Dryden's modified conception of naturalness and heightening. The perfection of a character consists chiefly in its naturalness, yet some heightening is desirable: the better side of a character should be emphasized in tragedy, the worse in comedy.

Dryden's idea of natural characterization is logically extended in the preface to *Albion and Albanius*. He says, "The suppos'd Persons of this musical Drama, are generally supernatural. . . . The Subject therefore . . . admits of that sort of marvellous and surprizing conduct, which is rejected in other Plays. . . . Yet propriety is to be observ'd even here. The Gods are all to manage their peculiar Provinces: and what was attributed by the Heathens to one Power, ought not to be perform'd by any other." This doctrine has a respectable ancestry; both Aristotle and Horace permit use of the supernatural, and both require fidelity to established tradition.

In "The Original and Progress of Satire" Dryden says of the translation of Juvenal,

If sometimes any of us [Dryden and his collaborators] . . . make him [Juvenal] express the customs and manners of our native country rather than of Rome, 'tis either when there was some kind of analogy betwixt their customs and ours, or when, to make him more easy to vulgar understandings, we give him those manners which are familiar to us. But I defend not this innovation, 'tis enough if I can excuse it. For to speak sincerely, the manners of nations and ages are not to be confounded; we should either make them English, or leave them Roman. If this can neither be defended nor excused, let it be pardoned . . . as being a fault which is never committed without some pleasure to the reader.

In the plays of this last period Dryden mingles national manners, and the excuses given in this passage are applicable to his practice. For example, in *Amphitryon*, which is set in ancient Greece, one of the characters makes a similitude involving a "Six-pence" and two "Three-pences." Since the Greeks had a monetary system, there is an "analogy between their customs and ours"; by using English coins instead of Greek ones, Dryden made his similitude "more easy to vulgar understandings"; and being more easily understandable, the similitude was more pleasing. For the comedies Dryden had an additional excuse, which he probably did not care to mention: the precariousness of his position made it advisable to disguise with a foreign setting his satire of English manners.

2.

The comic plot of *Don Sebastian* (1689) is much less important than the serious plot. Dryden says in his preface that he included a comic plot to suit the tastes of his audience. In thus adulterating tragedy with comedy he deviated from his dramatic theory, but in accord with his theory he took special pains, as he had done in writing *The Spanish Friar,* to unify the action. He says in the preface, "It had been easie for me to have given my Audience a better course of Comedy, I mean a more diverting, than that of *Antonio* and *Morayma.* But I dare appeal, even to my Enemies, if I or any man cou'd have invented one which had been more of a piece, and more depending, on the serious part of the design." As in *The Spanish Friar,* the integration of the two plots involves an intermingling of serious and comic elements indicative of a relaxation of Dryden's standards of decorum.

In the serious plot Muley-Moluch, Emperor of Barbary, has taken prisoner Don Sebastian, King of Portugal. The two are rivals for the affections of Almeyda. She and Don Sebastian marry, only to discover in Act V that they are guilty of incest, Almeyda being the illegitimate child of Sebastian's father. Meanwhile Muley-Moluch has had his head cut off as the result of a rebellion engineered by Benducar, his favorite. In the service of Muley-Moluch is Dorax, a Portuguese noble who has turned renegade because he thinks he has been unjustly treated by Don Sebastian. In a big scene in Act V, Dorax and Don Sebastian are reconciled.

In the comic plot Antonio, a young Portuguese noble who has been taken prisoner along with Don Sebastian, becomes the slave of the Mufti Abdalla. He and Morayma, daughter of the Mufti, fall in love at first sight. Their efforts to steal the Mufti's jewels and elope are opposed by the Mufti and by his "Chief Wife," Johayma, who has taken a fancy to Antonio and wants to keep him for herself. Antonio first appears as one of a band of prisoners which also includes three of the serious characters—Sebastian, Almeyda, and Alvarez (the Old Counsellor who reveals the secret of Almeyda's parentage). Antonio is characterized as an "Amorous airy spark" by the serious character Dorax. Along with Sebastian and Alvarez, Antonio draws lots to see whether he will be executed. The first two face the prospect of death with great nobility; Antonio, with comic trepidation. In charge of the prisoners is Mustapha, Captain of the Rabble. Both Mustapha and his rabble are comic, but they play an important part in the wars of the serious plot. The comic Mufti plays an even more important part in the serious plot as advisor to Muley-Moluch and confederate of the treacherous Benducar. Antonio and Morayma escape from the Mufti just when Mustapha and his rabble have risen against Muley-Moluch. Antonio joins the rebels, who presently capture the Mufti. When Almeyda swoons upon hearing that she is guilty of incest, Morayma is among the women who carry her off the stage. When she next appears she is led by Morayma.

In his preface Dryden admits that for the sake of the variety which suits the "Genius of the *English*" he has followed the unities of place and time "only at a distance": "My Scenes are therefore sometimes broken, because my Under-plot requir'd them so to be; though the General Scene remains of the same Castle; and I have taken the time of two days, because the variety of accidents, which are here represented, cou'd not naturally be suppos'd to arrive in one: But to gain a greater Beauty, 'tis lawful for a Poet to supersede a less."

The influence of Shakespeare is discernible in the play. The blank-verse passions of the serious plot were probably composed in imitation of Shakespeare. The reconciliation of Dorax and Don Sebastian, like Dryden's other big reconciliation episodes (Antony and Ventidius in *All for Love,* Hector and Troilus in *Troilus and Cressida*), is reminiscent of the quarrel and reconciliation of Brutus and Cassius in *Julius Caesar.* However, in the preface to *Troilus and Cressida* Dryden denies that the Hector-Troilus scene is an imitation of the Brutus-Cassius one, though he praises the latter highly. His actual model, he says, was the quarrel of Agamemnon and Menelaus in Euripides' *Iphigenia.* Possibly he would have denied Shakespearean influence on the other two reconciliations as well.

In other respects *Don Sebastian* seems to have been influenced by *Coriolanus.* In both plays there is a good deal of political intrigue in the course of which demagogues exploit the ignorance and fickleness of the populace. In Act IV, Mustapha and the Mufti contend with one another in attempting to sway the rabble with oratory. This episode was perhaps suggested to Dryden by the orations of Brutus and Antony in *Julius Caesar,* but the ludicrous rhetoric of Dryden's speech-makers is of the same sort as that employed by the ignorant citizenry in *Coriolanus.* Compare, for example, the following:

Coriolanus:

1. CIT. . . . Let us revenge this with our pikes ere we become rakes; for the gods know I speak this in hunger for bread, not in thirst for revenge.

3. CIT. We have power in our selves to do it, but it is a power that we have no power to do. . . . Ingratitude is monstrous; and for the multitude to be ingrateful were to make a monster of the multitude, of the which we being members, should bring ourselves to be monstrous members.

Don Sebastian:

MUF. . . . though your Tyrant is a lawful Emperor, yet your lawful Emperor is but a Tyrant. . . . you were born to be *Turks,* but he has played the *Turk* with you. . . . Yes, true Believers, you may believe me, that he is going to beget a Race of Misbelievers. . . . Therefore . . . Believers pluck up your Hearts, and pluck down the Tyrant.[12]

Both passages make lavish use of puns. Dryden regarded puns as the lowest form of wit, and in the *Essay of Dramatic Poesy* and the "Defence of the Epilogue" deplored Shakespeare's use of them. But his increased regard for naturalness justifies both his and Shakespeare's use of puns in these passages; as a low form of wit, they are appropriate to the low characters who use them.

In *Don Sebastian,* as in *Coriolanus,* the rabble are derided and discomfited by the nobility. Dorax resembles Coriolanus. Both are great warriors, both are haughty malcontents. Although Dorax, unlike Coriolanus, is not injured by the populace, he shares Coriolanus' aristocratic sentiments and like Coriolanus rails at the multitude. According to John Dennis, Dryden thought highly of *Coriolanus,* saying "more than once" that it contains "something . . . truly great and truly *Roman.*"[13]

Dryden's depiction of the rabble is obviously satirical. For example, in Act IV Mustapha tells his mob to demonstrate their loyalty by cheering. They oblige. Mustapha then asks them for whom they are cheering. One replies, "Even who you please, Captain," and another adds, "We are not bound to know who is to Live and Reign; our business is only to rise upon command, and plunder." The rabble are also satirized in some of Dorax's seemingly Juvenalian railing. Dismissing them unpunished after their rebellion fizzles, Dorax says,

> . . . Justice cannot stoop so low, to reach
> The grovelling sin of Crowds: but curst be they
> Who trust revenge with such mad Instruments,
> Whose blindfold bus'ness is but to destroy:
>
> . . . .
>
> . . . Away ye skum,
> That still rise upmost when the Nation boyls:
> Ye mungrill work of Heav'n . . .
>
> . . . .
>
> That have but just enough of sence, to know
> The masters voice when rated, to depart.

Dryden provided a rabble scene in his next tragedy, *Cleomenes* (1692), of which he said, "to gratifie the barbarous Party of my Audience, I gave them a short Rabble-Scene, because the Mobb (as they call them) are represented by *Plutarch* and *Polybius,* with the same Character of Baseness and Cowardice, which are here describ'd." This statement is, I believe, applicable to the rabble in *Don*

Sebastian. Their low-comedy activities were probably included to gratify the audience, but Dryden considered his inclusion of such behavior artistically justifiable because it was, though low, natural. His satire of the rabble, which is couched not only in such low-comedy features as the competitive speeches of Mustapha and the Mufti but in the high-toned railing of Dorax, is undoubtedly sincere; Dryden's skeptical and conservative sentiments involved distrust of and even contempt for the mob. In *The Hind and the Panther,* which appeared only about three years before *Don Sebastian,* he sees as one of the horrid consequences of Protestantism the reduction of the nation to "the dregs of a democracy."[14]

John Robert Moore has found the play to be rich in satirical allusions to the politics surrounding the Glorious Revolution. The Mufti carries much of the satire. Like Dominic in *The Spanish Friar,* he is a religious hypocrite. At one point he soliloquizes, "by this I have got to be chief of my Religion; that is, honestly speaking, to teach others what I neither know nor believe my self." He has accumulated a fortune by the "Rapines, Simony, and Extortions . . . of thirty Years Muftiship." The Mufti is a Mohammedan, but he of course stands for the corrupt clergy in general. It is likely that Dryden had the Protestant clergy, Anglicans as well as Dissenters, especially in mind. In *The Hind and the Panther* he twice associates Mohammedanism with Protestantism.[15] The Mufti as fomenter of a rebellion also fits Dryden's notion of the Protestant clergy.[16]

But in representing the Mufti as the corrupt and bungling adviser of his monarch, Dryden probably had a different satirical aim. Dorax scolds the Mufti in the following dialogue:

DOR. Why then these forein thoughts of State-Employ-
    ments,
Abhorrent to your Function and your Breeding?
Poor droaning Truants of unpractis'd Cells,
Bred in the Fellowship of bearded Boys,
What wonder is it if you know not Men?

.   .   .   .

... when let loose from thence to live at large,
Your little tincture of Devotion dies:

.   .   .   .

Of all your College Vertues, nothing now
But your Original Ignorance remains;
Bloated with Pride, Ambition, Avarice,
You swell, to counsel Kings and govern Kingdoms.

MUF. He prates as if Kings had not Consciences,
And none requir'd Directors but the Crowd.

DOR. As private men they want you, not as Kings.

"Cells" and "Directors of Conscience" suggest not Mohammedanism or Protestantism, but Catholicism. I believe that
here the primary target of Dryden's satire is Father Petre,
the Jesuit confessor of James II. Bredvold shows that
many moderate Catholics, Dryden among them, disapproved of the rash policies of James and of Petre's influence on James. Bredvold interprets the fable of the
martin and the swallows, in Part III of *The Hind and the
Panther*, as an allusion to Petre and his disastrous counsel.[17] The characteristics of the Martin are very like those
of the Mufti, as presented in the passage quoted above.
Like the Mufti, the Martin is the ignorant product of a
narrow ecclesiastical training: "church-begot," a "dunce"
who quotes the Fathers of the Church without understanding them. Like the Mufti, he is unqualified for a part in
the world of affairs: "unfit himself to fly," he presumes to

advise the swallows concerning their migration. And, like the Mufti, he presumptuously assumes a high position in the world of affairs: "from a Priest became a Prince."

In his prologue Dryden promises the audience

That he for once, wou'd sheath his cutting Satyr:
Sign but his peace, he vows he'll ne'er again
The sacred Names of Fops and Beaus profane.

This disingenuous renunciation is, I think, a result of Dryden's ambivalent attitude towards satire. His conception of comedy obliged him to include satire; the unpopularity of his politics and religion made it risky for him to do so. Consequently he included the satire, but disguised and denied it.

Since the comic plot is brief, the characterization is sketchy, and it is difficult to detect any signs of the application of Dryden's new principles governing character. But there are a few indications that he made some attempt to avoid extravagance and achieve naturalness. None of the characters is dominated by a humour. The Mufti is notably complex: he is hypocritical, ambitious, avaricious, jealous, and cowardly. Mustapha too is somewhat complex, manifesting the rapacity, ignorance, cowardice, and fickleness of the rabble he leads, as well as a prodigious vanity as their leader. The Mufti's wife, Johayma, is conventionally and very sketchily characterized as a lady past her youth, professedly virtuous but actually lascivious. Antonio and Morayma resemble the wild couples of Dryden's earlier comedies, but, like Lorenzo and Elvira in *The Spanish Friar,* they are more natural. Antonio's amorous proclivities are varied with his fear of death and his discomfiture as a slave. In depicting the affair of Antonio and Morayma, Dryden puts less emphasis on repartee than he had done in the earlier comedies; there is an extended

passage of repartee in Act III and a short one in Act V,
but most of the time the lovers apply their wits to stealing
the Mufti's jewels and extricating themselves from difficulties interposed by the unexpected appearances of the
Mufti or Johayma. What repartee there is is less ingenious
than that of the better earlier comedies. The reduction in
cleverness may be the result of Dryden's dwindling powers
or his diminishing interest in comedy, but it may also be
the result of his desire to make his comic lovers more natural.

The comedy in *Don Sebastian* is sometimes low. When
Antonio is being sold as a slave, he is treated as though
he were a horse, led about with a bridle and put through
his paces. The Mufti, having disguised himself as Antonio
to trap his errant wife, is captured by his own servants;
fearing disgrace, he does not tell them who he is. The
servants beat him, getting vicarious (they think) revenge
for the Mufti's ill-treatment of them. It can hardly be denied that in providing such incidents Dryden contravened
his theory to cater to the tastes of his audience. However,
most of the comic plot is on a higher level.

The play seems reasonably consistent with Dryden's
standards of morality and decency.[18] His use of incest as
a dramatic theme has the highly respectable precedent of
Oedipus the King, and his handling of the theme is morally
unexceptionable. Almeyda and Don Sebastian sin un-
wittingly. When informed of their guilt, they are more
than adequately horrified and penitent. Don Sebastian becomes a hermit, Almeyda retires to a convent. The comic
plot is far less indecent than *Limberham* and a good deal
less indecent than *An Evening's Love* and *Marriage à la
Mode.* It contains double meanings, but none that are
especially shocking. The behavior of the characters is reasonably innocuous. As the source of some of his comic

episodes Dryden used Bremond's *Pelerin,* the same source
he had used in *The Spanish Friar.* His handling of the
source indicates some concern for decency. In both Dryden and Bremond an older lady and a younger one are
rivals for the affections of a young man, and in both the
older lady once comes close to seducing him. But in Bremond the encounter occurs in bed, whereas in Dryden it
occurs in a garden. If Dryden had wished to exploit indecency, he would not have missed this fine opportunity
for a bedroom scene like those in *Limberham.*

In Bremond the ladies are not related, whereas in Dryden the older one is the younger one's stepmother. Probably Dryden related them for the sake of naturalness and
unity (he could thus naturally account for the presence of
both in the same house) and also to add to the comic discomfiture of the Mufti, the husband of one and the father
of the other. Certainly we should not suppose that his purpose was indecent exploitation of incest. If it had been, he
would surely have come up with something spicier than the
unconsummated encounter of Antonio and one of three
stepmothers of a girl whom at the time he has seen only
once, at a distance. Indeed, Dryden's making Johayma the
stepmother of Morayma, when he could just as easily have
made her the mother, indicates that he wished to avoid any
suggestion of incest in this triangle.

In Bremond, as in Dryden, the jealous husband disguises himself as his wife's lover and lurks under her win-
dow. In Bremond a chamber pot is dropped on his head.
But Dryden's Mufti suffers no such fate; Morayma only
tells him that he deserves "to be saluted . . . with a Piss-
pot." If Dryden had wished to vulgarize the play, he could
easily have followed the source.[19]

Both of Bremond's ladies are wives. Dryden's Morayma is unmarried, and, though somewhat free-spoken,

she virtuously insists on marriage to Antonio as the prerequisite to any familiarity beyond an occasional kiss. Johayma is a wife, but her wicked plans for Antonio are always thwarted, and furthermore her wickedness is somewhat palliated by the circumstance that hers is not a Christian but a Mohammedan marriage; besides her, the Mufti has three wives and six concubines. And Dryden, not even satisfied with getting Antonio and Morayma legally united, enjoins on them morality after marriage. The original cause of the unwitting incest of Sebastian and Almeyda is the sin of Sebastian's father, for Almeyda is his illegitimate and therefore unacknowledged child. In the concluding lines of the play, Dorax holds up to Antonio and Morayma the fate of Sebastian and Almeyda as an example of the consequences of adultery:

> . . . be happy both;
> And let *Sebastian* and *Almeyda's* Fate,
> This dreadfull Sentence to the World relate,
> That unrepented Crimes of Parents dead,
> Are justly punish'd on their Childrens head.

In the epilogue, it is true, Antonio and Morayma wittily and cynically comment on the affair of Sebastian and Almeyda, accusing them of being too queasy of conscience. But this, like the epilogue to *Marriage à la Mode,* was meant, I believe, as a means of ironically and pleasingly emphasizing a moral to a hard-bitten audience. Near the end of the epilogue Morayma once more wittily insists on marriage.

3.

Dryden's next play, *Amphitryon, or the two Sosias* (1690) is to the second phase of Dryden's development as

a comic dramatist what *The Assignation* is to the first
phase. In each play Dryden attempted a higher comedy
than he had written previously. In each he also provided
high comedy of the sort he had written previously, and in
each he included, probably as insurance against failure, a
liberal helping of farce. The differences between the earlier play and the later one are in accord with the intervening modification of Dryden's theory.

Amphitryon has two plots, both comic. One, which I
shall refer to as the high plot, has to do with Jupiter's assumption of the shape of Amphitryon as a means of enjoying the love of his wife, Alcmena. The other, which I
shall refer to as the low plot, has to do with Mercury's assumption of the shape of Amphitryon's servant, Sosia, in
order to assist the amorous Jupiter. In this plot the genuine Sosia is mercilessly browbeaten by Mercury, who also
ambitiously undertakes the task of pursuing Alcmena's
avaricious but attractive maid, Phaedra, while evading the
approaches of Sosia's libidinous but unattractive wife,
Bromia. Also paying court to Phaedra is Gripus, a wealthy
and corrupt old judge.

Dryden's objection to two-plot tragicomedy during this
period is founded on the idea that a mingling of serious
and comic is unnatural and distracting. A two-plot play
in which both actions were comic would not have these
faults. Furthermore, the two plots could be tightly inter-
twined without incongruity, so that disunity would be min-
imized. Although Dryden apologizes for the double action
of each of the three tragicomedies (*The Spanish Friar,
Don Sebastian,* and *Love Triumphant*) that he wrote during this period, he nowhere even mentions the double action of *Amphitryon.*

The two plots are well integrated. *Liaison des scènes*
is observed everywhere except between the first two scenes,

and the opening scene is actually a kind of prologue, introductory to rather than a part of the subsequent action. Mercury, Sosia, Bromia, and Phaedra, as the servants of Jupiter, Amphitryon, and Alcmena, have important parts in the high plot, serving not only to advance the action but to provide comedy in their own right, so that some episodes are neither wholly high nor wholly low, but a mixture of high and low involving both high and low characters. For example, in Act I the love-dialogue of Jupiter and Alcmena, in romantic blank verse, is interrupted by the impertinent questions of Phaedra and Bromia, who at one point seize Jupiter and pull him from side to side. The play also observes the other two unities. The action begins at night and ends at dinnertime on the following day. The place is Thebes, either inside or in front of the house of Amphitryon.

In writing *Amphitryon* Dryden borrowed from two plays on the same subject by Plautus and Molière.[20] In his dedicatory epistle Dryden acknowledges his indebtedness, saying that more than half the play is his own, and the rest "rather a lame Imitation of their [Plautus' and Molière's] Excellencies than a just Translation." The latter statement is Dryden's conventionally modest way of saying that he has handled the sources freely.

Comparison of the play and its sources corroborates Dryden's statements in the dedicatory epistle. Phaedra and Gripus, and the episodes involving them, are Dryden's. So is his representation of the first meeting of Jupiter and Alcmena. So is much of his introductory scene. Plautus introduces his play with a prologue spoken by Mercury. Molière has a more elaborate prologue in the form of a dialogue between Mercury and Night. Dryden in his opening scene expands Molière's prologue into a still more elaborate dialogue involving Mercury, Night, Jupiter, and a new character, Phoebus. These major additions agree with Dryden's theory in that they afford variety. Dryden is probably referring to them when in his dedicatory epistle he says that he has altered the play in accord with the differences between the English and the French and Roman stages.

In Dryden the Jupiter-Alcmena-Amphitryon triangle gets a more elevated treatment than it does in Molière or Plautus. The elevation is accomplished almost wholly with blank-verse expressions of passion, done in Dryden's Shakespearean manner. But Dryden did not aim to turn this portion of the play into a serious plot; he consistently stressed the comic aspects of the triangle, sometimes going further than Plautus or Molière in his comic treatment. Throughout the play the high characters are treated with extreme disrespect by the low characters, especially by Mercury and Phaedra. There is not nearly so much of this disrespectful treatment in either Molière or Plautus.

For example, the comedy of Dryden's opening scene is founded almost wholly on irreverent treatment of the gods. Mercury's description of a quarrel between Jupiter and Juno is typical: "She threaten'd to sue him in the Spiritual Court, for some Matrimonial Omissions; and he stood upon his Prerogative. Then she hit him on the Teeth of all his Bastards. . . . They were both in their Cups; and at the last the matter grew so high, that they were ready to throw Stars at one anothers Heads." Mercury is just as disrespectful when he is actually speaking to Jupiter: "I was considering into what form your Almighty-ship would be pleas'd to transform your self to night. . . . what Bird or Beast you wou'd please to honour, by transgressing your own Laws, in his Likeness; or in short, whether you wou'd recreate your self in Feathers, or in Leather?" One has only to compare this scene with Molière's and Plautus' prologues to see how much Dryden has amplified this comic irreverence.

The comic treatment of the high characters continues throughout the play. The ardent Jupiter, meeting Alcmena for the first time, is plagued with impertinent questions by Bromia and Phaedra. In the same scene he and Alcmena are victimized by Phaedra. Alcmena, not knowing that her husband (really Jupiter) has returned, promises that Phaedra shall sleep with her that night, as she has been doing in Amphitryon's absence. When Jupiter and Alcmena, after expressing the incandescence of their love in a highly romantic dialogue, are about to retire, Phaedra reminds Alcmena of her promise. She gets the better of the ensuing argument, being silenced only when Jupiter bribes her with a diamond ring. This episode, which is Dryden's own, obviously exhibits Jupiter in a comic light, and Jupiter knows it: "This Love," he observes, "can make a Fool of *Jupiter*."

Amphitryon is also thoroughly ridiculed. In an episode taken from Molière, Jupiter and Alcmena make love in Amphitryon's house while Amphitryon's servant (really Mercury in disguise) makes fun of Amphitryon from the balcony and refuses to let him in. In another episode taken from Molière, Amphitryon, having been absent for weeks on a campaign, comes home shortly after Jupiter has left Alcmena. She greets him by saying, "So soon return'd!" He scolds her for her coldness and a quarrel ensues, in the course of which he learns that he is probably a cuckold. This is all in Molière; but Dryden of his own accord heightens the comic irony of Amphitryon's position by having Alcmena accuse her husband, who is actually ravenous for love, of being "Pall'd in Desires, and surfeited of Bliss." Phaedra also attributes his behavior to satiety;

he is picking a quarrel, she says, as a means of evading subsequent nuptial obligations to Alcmena.

The high plot is markedly satirical. As Allen suggests, Dryden by his treatment of the amorous activities of Jupiter ridicules the similar activities of Charles II and his courtiers. Dryden's opening scene differs from the corresponding prologues of Plautus and Molière not only in that Jupiter is more irreverently ridiculed but also in that Jupiter and Olympus are clearly represented as a king and his court. Towards the end of the scene Mercury in the course of a conversation with Night gives the following satirical account of conditions on Olympus: "the Deities in Heav'n . . . are all given to the Flesh most damnably. . . . 'tis the way to be Popular to Whore and Love. For what do'st thou think old *Saturn* was depos'd, but that he was cold and impotent; and made no court to the fair Ladies. *Pallas* and *Juno* themselves, as chaste as they are, cry'd shame on him. I say unto thee, *Old Night,* Wo be to the Monarch that has not the Women on his side."

The reign of Saturn stands pretty well for the moral Puritan régime that preceded the Restoration. Earlier in the same scene Jupiter and Phoebus argue about the morality of Jupiter's amours, while Mercury makes satirical comments on both disputants. When Phoebus accuses him of sin, Jupiter defends himself by saying that "pow'r Omnipotent can do no wrong." Mercury says, "Here's Omnipotence with a Vengeance, to make a Man a Cuckold, and yet not to do him wrong. . . . you Kings never Enact a Law, but you have a kind of an Eye to your own Prerogative." The god's omnipotence is explicitly equated with the king's prerogative. A little later Mercury ridicules Phoebus in terms applicable to Restoration England: "you, Brother *Phoebus,* are but a meer Country Gentleman, that never comes to Court; that are abroad all day on Horse-

back, making Visits about the World; are drinking all
Night, and in your Cups are still rayling at the Government: O these Patriots, these bumpkin Patriots, are a very
silly sort of Animals." There must have been a good
many of these bumpkin patriots deploring the behavior of
Charles.

The epilogue, spoken by Phaedra, pretty clearly alludes
to the reign of Charles. Phaedra says,

I'm thinking (and it almost makes me mad,)
How sweet a time, those Heathen Ladies had.

. . . .

When the sweet Nymph, held up the Lilly hand,
Jove was her humble Servant, at Command.
The Treasury of Heav'n was ne're so bare,
But still there was a Pension for the Fair.
In all his Reign, Adultry was no Sin;
For *Jove,* the good Example did begin.

. . . .

You teize your Cuckolds; to their face torment 'em;
But *Jove* gave his, new Honours to content 'em.
And, in the kind Remembrance of the Fair,
On each exalted Son, bestow'd a Star.

. . . .

Severity of Life did next begin;
(And always does, when we no more can Sin.)
That Doctrine, too, so hard, in Practice, lyes,
That, the next Age may see another rise.
Then, Pagan Gods may, once again, succeed;
And *Jove,* or *Mars,* be ready, at our need
To get young Godlings; and, so, mend our breed.

This longing for the good old days is satirical. The epilogue is oriented to the point of view of the speaker,
Phaedra, whose aim in life is to turn her charms to profit.

In the play Mercury ridicules the sanctimonious Phoebus and the cuckolded Amphitryon, but he also ridicules the profligate Jupiter. I have called attention to some of this ridicule which occurs in the opening scene. At the end of the play Dryden follows Molière in having Jupiter maintain that he has brought honor, not disgrace, to Amphitryon and Alcmena; but Dryden also follows Molière in having Sosia observe that Jupiter is simply gilding a bitter pill, and that the less said about the affair the better. And Dryden concludes his play with the following lines by Sosia, which have no counterpart in Plautus or Molière and in which Jupiter cuts a very poor figure:

> The fair Wife makes her Husband live at ease:
> The Lover keeps him too; and but receives
> Like *Jove,* the remnants that *Amphitryon* leaves:
> . . . .
> In fine, the Man, who weighs the matter fully,
> Wou'd rather be the Cuckold, than the Cully.

In the first phase of his theory Dryden regarded tragicomic contrast as desirable, and accordingly he made use of it in his earlier tragicomedies. He not only provided one serious and one comic plot but also contrasted the extraordinary chasteness and fidelity of the serious characters with the extraordinary profligacy and infidelity of the comic characters. In the second phase of his theory he regarded tragicomic contrast as undesirable. Accordingly, he made both plots of *Amphitryon* comic.

Furthermore, he did not contrast but paralleled the two sets of characters. In the earlier tragicomedies two different patterns of behavior are shown in operation; in *Amphitryon* the same pattern of behavior is shown operating on two different levels. Jupiter's sinful appetite for Alcmena is paralleled with Mercury's for Phaedra. Both Amphitryon and Sosia have good reason to believe that their wives have betrayed them; both are motivated by jealousy and by concern for their reputations; both seek to learn the truth by pretending that it was they and not impostors who arrived the night before, and by asking their wives to tell them in detail what happened. In Dryden as in Molière the comic point of the two episodes lies not in their different outcomes but in their similarity; Sosia's jealousy is a caricature of Amphitryon's. Alcmena and Bromia are also more parallel than contrasting. Both manifest a strong sexual appetite and an equally strong concern for their reputations. Alcmena is young, beautiful, and newly married, while Bromia is plain and elderly, and has been married for fifteen years; consequently Alcmena is the pursued, and her appetite is satisfied, while Bromia is the pursuer, and hers is not. Their marriages are on different levels and at different stages, but are essentially the same.

By showing the same motives and patterns of behavior at work on different levels Dryden has made *Amphitryon* more natural than the earlier two-plot tragicomedies, in which the two contrasting sets of characters seem to be of two different species, neither of which is quite human.

Dryden probably intended portions of the low plot of *Amphitryon* primarily to appeal to the audience's taste for low comedy. However, given the supernatural situation of the play, he might justifiably argue that he had not descended from low comedy to farce in any of his episodes. Extravagant but conceivably natural are two episodes that he took from Molière. In one, Sosia, addressing his lantern, rehearses the speech that he intends to deliver to Alcmena. In the other, Sosia is bullied by Mercury into denying his own identity. More extravagant are three episodes original with Dryden. In one, Mercury puts the indignant Bromia to sleep by waving his wand; in the other

two, he uses his supernatural powers to see through Phaedra's clothing. But even these might be excused by Dryden as naturally supernatural, and in accord with his contention in the preface to *Albion and Albanius* that "The
Subject . . . being extended beyond the Limits of Humane
Nature, admits of that sort of marvellous and surprizing
conduct, which is rejected in other Plays." He adds the
restriction that "The Gods are all to manage their peculiar
Provinces; and what was attributed by the Heathens to one
Power, ought not to be perform'd by any other. *Phoebus*
must foretel, *Mercury* must charm with his *Caduceus*."

Dryden's presentation of the gods in *Amphitryon* shows
his awareness of this restriction. Mercury does indeed
charm with his caduceus. His wit is appropriate to his
status as god of wit, to which Dryden calls attention in
Act IV. As god of eloquence, he judges Sosia's oration;
as god of thieves, he steals Gripus' goblet; and in the opening scene he performs his function as messenger of the
gods. Even his generally low behavior is consistent with
pagan tradition, or at least with Dryden's view of it, for
in his translation of the tenth satire of Juvenal, Dryden
alludes to Mercury as a "mean" god and in a footnote ex-
plains that "Mercury . . . was a god of the lowest size."
Dryden does not have Phoebus foretell in *Amphitryon,*
but he uses Phoebus' prophetical function as a source of
comic incongruity. Wondering why Jupiter has sent for
him, Phoebus says,

> They call me God of Wisdom,
> But Mars and Vulcan, the two Fools of Heav'n,
>
> .   .   .   .
>
> Know full as much as I.

Phoebus and Night are appropriately designated by Jupiter
to see that the night of his amour with Alcmena is an extra-

ordinarily long one. Jupiter's philandering is of course in accord with his traditional character. The irreverent treatment of Jupiter, essential to Dryden's satire, is not consistent with his majesty as ruler of the gods, but Dryden provides explanation for it. After impertinent comments by Mercury and Phoebus, Jupiter says,

> Well, my familiar Sons, this sawcy Carriage
> I have deserv'd; for he who trusts a Secret
> Makes his own Man his Master.
> I read your Thoughts;
> Therefore you may as safely speak as think.

And when victimized and insulted by Phaedra, Jupiter informs the audience in an aside,

> Now I cou'd call my Thunder to revenge me,
> But that were to confess my self a God,
> And then I lost my Love!

Like the episodes, the characters of the low plot seem reasonably natural, and they also fit Dryden's theory in affording a little satire now and then. Dryden's Sosia, like Molière's, is discontented, henpecked, cowardly, and vain. But Dryden, acting on a hint or two in Molière, has transformed the vanity of Molière's Sosia into foppery. In both Dryden and Molière, Sosia comments with immoderate admiration on the eloquence of his speech to Alcmena, but only in Dryden does Mercury define this behavior as foppery, saying of Sosia that "he has all the natural Endowments of a Fop; and only wants the Education."

A little later Dryden's Sosia, like Molière's, sings to keep his courage up and is silenced by Mercury. The comment of Molière's Sosia on this interruption is simply, "Cet homme assurement n'aime pas la musique," but the comment of Dryden's Sosia has a distinctly foppish flavor:

"I wou'd I had Courage . . . that I might teach him to call my singing Catterwawling, an Illiterate Rogue; an Enemy to the Muses and to Musick." In Dryden the foppery of Sosia is again seen when he narrates his adventure to Amphitryon. He employs absurd similitudes, and calls himself "a Man of Honour in every thing, but just Fighting." In his cowardice, his foppery, and particularly in his conceited admiration for his ability as a musician, Sosia resembles the servant Benito in *The Assignation*. Comparison of the two shows the greater naturalness of Sosia. For example, Benito absurdly continues to play and sing while his master kicks him, but Sosia is silenced at once by Mercury.

Mercury and Phaedra constitute a kind of witty couple. Though hampered by his assumption of Sosia's identity, Mercury is actually a gallant, as is seen in his wit, in his uninhibited pursuit of Phaedra, and in his challenging his rival, Judge Gripus, to a duel. Though she too is a servant, Phaedra exhibits the wit and the cynical and emancipated attitude towards love which is characteristic of the witty ladies. Their relationship includes some repartee and culminates in a witty proviso passage in Act V, in which they set the conditions of their liaison.

But in accord with his modified theory Dryden has made Mercury and Phaedra more natural than the earlier wild couples. When the attention of the earlier couples is given entirely to love, Mercury's and Phaedra's status as servants diversifies their interests. Their wit, unlike that of the earlier couples, is not manifest wholly or almost wholly in amorous repartee, but often takes the form of satirical comments on the other characters. And their relationship has an aura of earthy satire quite different from the rarefied atmosphere of wit and wildness which envelopes the amours of the earlier couples. Phaedra's guiding principle is not love but avarice. She chooses her paramours for their wealth and generosity, not for their wit and good looks. Mercury, as Sosia, is outstandingly ugly, but Phaedra agrees to accept him as lover if he will give her a gold goblet. Her avarice is satirically represented by Dryden as typical. Jupiter says of her,

> This is a very Woman:
> Her Sex is Avarice, and she, in One,
> Is all her Sex.

Mercury too is exhibited in a satirical light. Unlike the earlier gallants, he is not only temporarily embarrassed but permanently thwarted in his pursuit of Phaedra. He begins the pursuit with misgivings: "the greatest Wits," he observes, "are commonly the greatest Cullies"—a comment paralleling Jupiter's "this Love can make a Fool of *Jupiter*." His misgivings are justified. When he gives Phaedra the goblet, she refuses him the favors she had promised in exchange for it. In Act V he reveals that he is a god, and Phaedra agrees to be his mistress. In the proviso episode they stipulate the conditions of their relationship. But when Sosia points out that should the god violate any of the terms of the agreement there would be no court to which Phaedra could appeal, she once more, and this time permanently, refuses herself to Mercury.

In the low plot, additional satire is afforded by occasional allusions to England or English conditions.[21] In Judge Gripus, Dryden satirizes corrupt judges. Scott supposes that Dryden had especially in mind Lord Chief Justice Scroggs, notorious for his bullying of the accused who appeared before him during the Popish Plot trials.[22] However, I think it more likely that Dryden's target was the even more notorious Chief Justice Jeffreys. Like Scroggs, Jeffreys was a voluptuary. He presided at the notorious

Bloody Assize of September, 1685, when survivors of Monmouth's abortive rebellion were put on trial. Mercury describes Gripus as "a Voluptuous Gourmand" who "sells Justice . . . fleeces the Rich Rebells, and hangs up the Poor." Despite a fifty-year tradition that only the leaders of rebellions should be executed, some three hundred of the Somerset peasants who had joined Monmouth were sentenced to death.[23]

Furthermore, Jeffreys shared with James the proceeds of a very lucrative sale of pardons to the more prosperous accused rebels. From one man alone, Edward Prideaux, there was extracted a total of fifteen thousand pounds.[24] It is true that Jeffreys was on the side of James II and the Tories; but many of the Tories were horrified by the Bloody Assize.[25] Jeffreys seems to have been even more of a political opportunist than Scroggs was. Trevelyan presents him as a "self-seeking scoundrel" who advanced himself in the favor of James by intriguing against his Tory colleagues.[26] At the beginning of the last act of *Amphitryon* Phaedra describes Gripus as a "Seller of other People," a "Weather-cock of Government."

Trevelyan lumps Jeffreys with Father Petre and the Earl of Sunderland as "counsellors who cheered James on to his ruin."[27] I have already cited Bredvold's contention that moderate Catholics, including Dryden, were opposed to the rash measures taken by James, and I have suggested that at one point in *Don Sebastian* Dryden satirizes Petre. John Robert Moore has found satirical allusions to Sunderland in *Don Sebastian* and *Love Triumphant*.[28] It seems very likely that Dryden dealt with the third member of the trio in his representation of Gripus in *Amphitryon*. Jeffreys died in the Tower in April, 1689. In May the House of Commons called for a bill to take from Jeffreys' estate the fifteen thousand pounds he had extorted from Prideaux, and in November the House unanimously passed a resolution requesting a bill for the forfeiture of Jeffreys' honor and estate.[29] The date usually given for the first performance of *Amphitryon* is October, 1690, but there is reason to believe that the play was performed in the spring of that year.[30] Even in October, Jeffreys would have been in the news recently enough for allusion to him to have topical value.

Since the satire of *Amphitryon* is general, retrospective, or incidental, it could have had little value as a corrective influence at the time the play was performed. It is, however, moral satire, since Dryden attacks such vices and follies as illicit love, foppery, avarice, and judicial corruption. At first sight the circumstance that the victimized Amphitryon is ridiculed at least as thoroughly as the errant Jupiter seems a breach of the morality of the play. However, Amphitryon's jealous rage and suspicions, not his virtues, are Dryden's targets. Dryden emphasizes this point in one of his original additions to the play. While Amphitryon and Jupiter are disputing as to which is the genuine Amphitryon, Alcmena enters. Amphitryon bitterly repulses her as an adulteress, but Jupiter treats her kindly, so she turns to Jupiter as the true Amphitryon.

Although the play is considerably more indecent than Molière's, the difference is due not to Dryden's exceptional indecency but to Molière's exceptional decency. Dryden omits an indecent motif that Plautus made available. Plautus represents Alcmena as pregnant by Amphitryon at the time of her affair with Jupiter and occasionally makes vulgar allusions to her condition. The love-poetry of Jupiter and Alcmena becomes rather lush now and then, but Dryden and his audience probably considered it passionate, not indecent. On the other hand, it must be admitted that

Dryden's low plot contains several double meanings and two or three instances of vulgarity with no disguise at all. These vulgar and indecent remarks are appropriate to the low characters who utter them. The only other excuse for them is the possibility that Dryden and his contemporaries had rather broad standards of decency. This possibility is given weight by the fact that in his dedicatory epistle, addressed to Sir William Gower, Dryden recommends the play to that "young *Berenice*" Sir William's daughter. In so doing he says that he has reason to apprehend the "sharpness of her Judgment" and that she may discover "a Thousand Imperfections . . . which might have pass'd on Vulgar Understanding," but this is conventional modesty and flattery and moreover seems to have an aesthetic rather than a moral frame of reference.

The aim of the foregoing discussion is to show that *Amphitryon,* like *The Assignation,* is a mixture of low comedy, high comedy, and higher comedy; and that the differences between the two plays are the results of the shift in Dryden's comic theory from heightening and wit to naturalness and satire. The higher comedy of *The Assignation* is founded on artificial platonic repartee and equally artificial heroic sentiments; the higher comedy of *Amphitryon* is founded on natural passions and satire. The high comedy of *The Assignation* is founded on extravagantly sprightly amorousness and repartee; the high comedy of *Amphitryon* is founded on a more natural and satirical representation of profligate love and wit. The low comedy of *The Assignation* is founded on the farcical blundering of Benito; the low comedy of *Amphitryon* is founded on the more naturally and satirically treated behavior of Bromia and Sosia. The two plots of *Amphitryon* are much better tied together than are those of *The Assignation,* and in this respect too *Amphitryon* fits Dryden's modified theory. I must confess that despite Dryden's greater concern for decency in this last period of his activity as a comic dramatist, *Amphitryon* is not perceptibly purer than *The Assignation*; but it is reasonably decent, except for the impudicity of portions of the low plot; and even this may perhaps be explained on the grounds that it is appropriate to the characters involved and that the standards of Dryden's audience were rather tolerant.

Amphitryon is a much better play than *The Assignation*. Its superiority is partly due, I think, to haste in the composition of the earlier play and to Dryden's leaning on Molière in the later one. But Dryden did not slavishly follow either Molière or Plautus, and I believe that *Amphitryon's* superiority to *The Assignation* is due largely to the intervening development of Dryden's theory of comedy. In this myth of the amorous Jupiter, Dryden had hit upon an eminently satisfactory vehicle, both safe and suitably elevated, for a retrospectively satirical expression of his revised and disillusioned view of the "conversation" of Charles II and his courtiers. In the elevated blank-verse expressions of passion, and in the wit of his satirical spokesman Mercury, he found a solution to the fundamental problem posed by his modified theory: the problem of writing high comedy that would inspire both scornful laughter and the "nobler pleasure" of admiration for fine writing.

4.

Dryden's last play, *Love Triumphant, or Nature Will Prevail*, a tragicomedy, appeared around January, 1694, over three years after *Amphitryon* and nearly two years after his penultimate play, the tragedy *Cleomenes*, which Southerne finished for him. Probably he would not have

written *Love Triumphant* if some special need for money
had not arisen. In the prologue he informs the audience
that the play is his last, thus indicating that he no longer
felt equal to the task of writing plays even as a source of
income. And by one of his letters to Walsh we know that
during at least part of the time he was at work on *Love
Triumphant* he was "up to the Eares in law," having "been
cousend of fifty pounds, & more." It is hardly surprising
that *Love Triumphant* is not a very good play.

It seems to have failed. A contemporary letter-writer
says of it, "It is a tragi-comedy, but in my opinion, one of
the worst he [Dryden] ever writt, if not the very worst; the
comical part descends beneath the style and shew of a
Bartholomew-fair droll. It was dam'd by the universal
cry of the town, *nemine contradicente,* but the conceited
poet."[31] However, the writer's critical judgment is somewhat suspect, since he also held a poor opinion of Congreve, gloating over the recent failure of *The Double
Dealer. Love Triumphant* is a poor play, but it is not so
bad as this letter makes it out.

Oddly enough, Dryden seems to have had a high opinion of the play. He says in the dedicatory epistle, addressed
to James, Earl of Salisbury, "I must not undervalue my
present Labours, because I have presum'd to make you
my Patron. A Man may be just to himself, tho he ought
not to be partial. And I dare affirm, that the several Manners which I have given to the Persons of this *Drama,* are
truly drawn from Nature; all perfectly distinguish'd from
each other. That the Fable is not injudiciously contriv'd;
that the turns of Fortune are not manag'd unartfully; and
that the last Revolution is happily enough invented." And in
his letter to Walsh, written shortly before the play was performed, he says, "I call it [my play] Love Triumphant . . .
the two chief Characters of the Heroe & Heroine . . . not-

withstanding the Extravange [*sic*] of their passion, are neither of them faulty, either in duty, or in Honour. Your Judgment of it, if you please."

Dryden's praise of the play in the dedicatory epistle might reasonably be regarded as propaganda, but I doubt that he would have recommended it to the judgment of Walsh, whom in the postscript to the *Aeneis* he calls "the best critic of our nation," unless he really thought well of it. Although he did not relish the task of writing *Love Triumphant,* he probably did his best to make the play a good one, as, in similar circumstances, he had done with *Don Sebastian.* He was by no means in his dotage; Congreve speaks of him as "an improving writer to his last, even to near seventy years of age."[32] I do not believe that Dryden turned out *Love Triumphant* as nothing more than a potboiler, or that he had fallen into senile decay; I believe that he wrote a poor play that he thought to be a good one.

The passion to which Dryden alludes in his letter to Walsh is the love of Alphonso and Victoria. It is extravagant in that the lovers are supposedly brother and sister, the children of Veramond, King of Aragon. When the play begins, Alphonso and Garcia, King of Navarre, have just defeated in battle and captured Ramirez, King of Castile. Alphonso infuriates Veramond by opposing his desire to reward Garcia with the hand of Victoria. In Act III it is discovered that Alphonso is really the son of Ramirez; but Veramond, ill-pleased to learn that his supposed son and heir is the child of his enemy, refuses to let him marry Victoria. Assisted by Victoria's strong sense of filial obligation, Veramond stubbornly persists in his refusal even after Alphonso at the head of a revolting army has taken him prisoner. Alphonso in despair gives up the rebellion and throws himself on Veramond's mercy. Veramond is about to have him executed when he is at last persuaded by his younger daughter, Celidea, to permit the marriage. Celidea has loved Garcia all the time, and he now obligingly transfers his affections to her. In the comic plot two young colonels, Carlos and Sancho, compete for the love of Dalinda, daughter of the old courtier Lopez. They are unaware that Dalinda's love has already been sold once, to the Conde Don Alonzo, by whom she has had two illegitimate children. Sancho, a conceited fool, marries Dalinda and learns the truth too late.

In his dedicatory epistle Dryden points out that the time of the play is "much within the compass of an Astrological Day, which begins at Twelve, and ends at the same hour the Day following," and that, following the example of Corneille, he has observed the unity of place less justly than did the ancients, stretching "the Latitude to a Street and Palace, not far distant from each other in the same City." He admits that the action is double and blames the English taste for variety. The two plots are linked much less effectively than are those of *The Spanish Friar* and *Don Sebastian*. As colonels, Sancho and Carlos once in a while appear on the stage with the serious characters, and Carlos takes a perfunctory part in the rebellion.

In its love-duty conflict and the political upheavals associated with this conflict, the serious plot resembles Dryden's heroic plays. The serious plot also contains two extended passages in the rhymed heroic style. In one, Alphonso and Victoria bemoan their frustrated love; in the other, even more heroic, they debate the conflicting requirements of love and duty. Allen's theory that Dryden had written the serious plot some years earlier seems reasonable.[33] However, the incest motif is characteristic of Dryden's later plays, and portions of the serious plot are in Dryden's later Shakespearean manner. For example, the

opening lines of the play are reminiscent of the opening
lines of *Richard III:*

> Now the long Wars betwixt *Castile* and *Arragon*
> Are ended in the ruin of our Foes.
> And fierce *Ramirez,* the *Castilian* King,
> Who tugg'd for Empire, with our Warlike Son,
> In single Combat taken, adds his Lawrels
> To the young Victor's Brow.

The passionate blank verse in which Veramond and Alphonso quarrel is also Shakespearean.

Whenever they were written, the artificial heroics of
the serious plot are inconsistent with Dryden's modified
dramatic theory. Possibly he was deliberately contraven-
ing his theory in a nostalgic effort to recapture some of the
unearthly splendor of the earlier plays.

In the *Essay of Dramatic Poesy* Lisideius, following
Aristotle, objects to change-of-will denouements, and Neander makes no attempt to defend them. But in the dedicatory epistle of *Love Triumphant* Dryden says that Aristotle was condemning the clumsy denouements of Greek
dramatists who changed the minds of their protagonists
only because they were not clever enough to end the play
otherwise. He argues that "a simple change of Will might
be manag'd with so much Judgment, as to render it the
most agreeable, as well as the most surprising part of the
whole Fable." In the play Celidea persuades Veramond
to change his mind by pretending to take his part against
Alphonso and presenting his arguments in such a way
that their weakness and unjustness is obvious. Probably
Dryden actually did consider this device agreeable and
surprising; otherwise he would not have called attention to
it in the dedicatory epistle. If so, in his natural partiality

for the offspring of his mind he here reaches his point of maximum infatuation.

The comedy in the play is often low, but Dryden perhaps felt that he had not descended to the extravagance of farce. The most extravagant episode is one that Sir Walter Scott found particularly upsetting: "The absurdity of the two gallants disguising themselves, in hopes to pass for the deceased Conde upon a mistress, who had borne him two children, is too gross for a puppet-show or pantomime."[34] However, Sancho disguises himself not to deceive Dalinda, but, with her connivance, to deceive her father; Carlos does not know that Dalinda has been the Conde's mistress; and none of the three knows that the Conde is deceased until a messenger arrives at the end of the episode. The scene therefore has some claim to naturalness.

Jeremy Collier justly objects to Dryden's use of puns in the comic plot.[35] The excuse that this low form of wit is appropriate to the characters is not always applicable, for, as Collier points out, one of the punsters is Carlos, who is supposed to be a wit.

In the prologue Dryden promises that the play contains "nothing . . . of—you know what he means"— meaning, presumably, indecent sexual activities, of which the play is indeed free. However, Dryden also claims that the play contains

No double *Entendrès* . . .
To make the Ladies look they know not how;
Simply as 'twere, and knowing both together.

Actually, *Love Triumphant* contains several double meanings. Perhaps Dryden felt that they were too mild and conventional to inconvenience the ladies.

It is as satire that the comic plot best fits Dryden's

modified theory. In no other play does Dryden go so far in ridicule of the upper classes. Lopez is not merely a "gentleman," he is a courtier. Though he pretends to be wealthy, he has no source of income other than the charms of his daughter Dalinda. Without the slightest hesitation both he and she go about the business of retailing them. Sancho is foolish, conceited, ugly, and low-born (he is the bastard of a usurer), but, because he is also wealthy, she prefers him to the impoverished wit Carlos. When Sancho mistakenly sends her instead of a love-note a bill of exchange payable to bearer, she is delighted with this novel billet-doux.

Sancho also is the vehicle of satire. Unlike Dryden's earlier fools, he is a successful wencher, attracting the ladies with his wealth. Though he does not wish to marry Dalinda, she easily cajoles him into matrimony, where-upon he endures the ignominy of being saddled with her illegitimate children. In this satirical portrayal of the male profligate Dryden goes even beyond *Limberham*. In Sancho he combines the disagreeable promiscuity of Wood-all with the weak foolishness of Limberham, so that Sancho is worse than either of his predecessors.

It is true that Carlos, though hampered in practice by his poverty, is in intention as confirmed a wencher as Sancho, yet not only escapes punishment but is rewarded with the hand of the Conde's wealthy sister. However, throughout the play Carlos is represented as unlucky, Sancho as lucky, so that the final reversal of their fortunes serves to accentuate Sancho's downfall, and also edifies the audience by demonstrating that in wenching the lucky (that is, the successful) suitor is actually the unlucky one. The good fortune of the depraved Dalinda is, of course, necessary for the discomfiture of Sancho. Dalinda speaks the epilogue, in which Dryden appears to be ironically calling attention to the moral of the play for the benefit of a cynical audience, as he had done in the epilogues to *Marriage à la Mode* and *Don Sebastian*. Speculating on possible morals of the play, Dalinda decides that the poet intended to teach women

> . . . not to be too Coming before Marriage;
> For fear of my Misfortune in the Play,
> A Kid brought home upon the Wedding day!
> I fear there are few *Sancho's* in the Pit,
> So good as to forgive and to forget.

The disadvantages of wenching from the male point of view are not mentioned in the epilogue, presumably because the *"Sancho's* in the Pit" were adequately instructed by the fate of their fictional colleague.

VIII. CONCLUSION

Dryden never wrote a comprehensive, systematic, and explicit exposition of his dramatic theory. He came closest to doing so in the *Essay of Dramatic Poesy*, but even in the *Essay* he presented his theory indirectly, in the form of a debate. Characteristically his discussions of dramatic theory are fragmentary and are incidental to the discussion of some other subject: a single aspect of drama, such as plotting or characterization; the merits or faults of a particular play; or even some other branch of literature, such as epic poetry or nondramatic satire. Consequently (as the reader is by now well aware) in attempting to reconstruct Dryden's theory of comedy I have had to spend a great deal of time weighing possibilities and making inferences.

The comparison of Dryden's theory with his practice is also difficult, chiefly because of the qualitative judgments required. For example, having concluded that Dryden's theory requires naturalness in a play, we must decide whether a given play actually satisfies this requirement. We can very easily apply our own standards of naturalness to a play and thus make judgments that are no doubt valuable in determining the current worth of the play. But in attempting to determine whether or not the play satisfies Dryden's requirement of naturalness, we must try to think in terms of Dryden's standards of naturalness, not ours. And when I recall that in the first act of *All for Love*, the one play that Dryden wrote entirely for himself, the noble Antony expresses his passion by throwing himself to the

floor and soliloquizing from a horizontal position, I become somewhat hesitant about saying that a given comic
character does not satisfy Dryden's requirement of naturalness.

Despite the difficulties and the consequent possibilities
of error involved in reconstructing Dryden's theory of comedy and applying it to his plays, we must do both if we
wish to understand him either as a critic or as a writer of
comedy. For Dryden theorized as a playwright, not as a
philosopher. His ultimate aim was to find out what qualities were required to make a play delightful and instructive to the particular audience for whom he wrote. Consequently it is absurd to suppose that when he worked out
his theory he ignored the evidence of his own experience
as a playwright, or that when he wrote his plays he ignored
the theoretical principles he had evolved. His practice
throws light on his theory, and his theory throws light on
his practice; it is unsound to consider either apart from
the other.

The double illumination of his theory and his practice
displays Dryden as a comic dramatist of considerable stature, not as a comic genius but as a perspicacious and pains-
taking craftsman who almost certainly exerted considerable influence on his contemporaries. He aimed to please,
but he considered it shameful to please at too cheap a rate.
He was a royalist in his literary theory as well as in his
political theory; he considered the crowd no more fit to
judge a play than to govern a country. "The crowd cannot
be presumed to have more than a gross instinct, of what
pleases or displeases them," he wrote after some eighteen
years of writing plays.[1] The dramatist who carefully an-
alyzes his audience in order to please them is a better
judge of what is pleasing than the casual playgoer is. Furthermore, the dramatist is obliged not only to please the

public taste but also to educate it; he "is not to run down with the stream, or to please the people by their own usual methods, but rather to reform their judgments."[2] Hence we find Dryden pioneering in the composition of heroic drama and high comedy and, in much of his criticism, quite soberly calling attention to the beauties of his works for the benefit of the public, whose "gross instinct" might otherwise delude them into being displeased with what has been scientifically designed to please them.

Dryden was aware that his audience was not homogeneous. In the *Essay* he divided it into two groups, the noblesse and the populace. He represented the noblesse as more refined, more discriminating, more sympathetic to innovation than the populace. During his long career as dramatist, the complexion of the audience probably changed somewhat; there is reason to believe that respectable ladies and middle-class "cits" were attending the theaters in increasing numbers. But Dryden retained his conception of the audience as made up of two groups, the discriminating (the "better sort," as he called them towards the end of his career) and the undiscriminating. He sometimes catered to the tastes of the populace in his comedy, but throughout his career he also devoted some of his best efforts to pleasing and educating the tastes of the noblesse, the better sort. And during the first phase of his career as comic dramatist he probably conceived of the noblesse as made up of Charles II and his coterie of gay and cynical libertines.

As a craftsman rather than a comic genius, he derived his comic theory largely from analysis of the works of other dramatists, chiefly Jonson and Fletcher in the first phase of his theory, Shakespeare in the second. But he did not blindly abandon himself to any of them; he tried to isolate their characteristic defects and excellences, in order to avoid the former while imitating the latter.

From his analysis of the noblesse and of the comedies of Jonson and Fletcher, Dryden developed the conception of high comedy which we find in the first phase of his career as comic dramatist, a comedy of extravagant gaiety, wit, and profligacy. It features young lovers like those of Fletcher, but not imitated from them; instead, these wild couples are versions of the Restoration noblesse, pleasingly heightened in accord with Dryden's conception of Jonsonian humours characterization. In their heightening, these comic lovers resemble the serious lovers in the heroic drama that Dryden was writing during the same period. On the comic level, scintillating repartee; on the heroic level, the dazzling cleverness of the love-honor debates. On the comic level, extravagant profligacy and insouciance; on the heroic level, equally extravagant virtue and depth of passion. Dryden combined and contrasted the comic and the heroic in *Secret Love* and *Marriage à la Mode;* then, in *The Assignation,* he attempted something new: heroic comedy, higher than high comedy, lower than heroic drama.

But certain disillusioning experiences brought Dryden to a revised opinion of the court coterie. The Duke of Buckingham and others lampooned him and his heroic drama and his high comedy in *The Rehearsal,* and the rest of the court set no doubt laughed at this (from Dryden's point of view) gross caricature as uproariously as did the populace. Court intrigue seems to have hampered his career, frustrating his plan to write a great English epic. Rochester attacked him in print, and Charles II himself, who ought to have led the noblesse in their approval of Dryden's high comedy, manifested a depraved taste for D'Urfey's farce.

During this period of disillusionment Dryden was restudying Shakespeare and was noting the success of Wycherley's satirical *Plain Dealer*. And his concern with religion during this period—a concern attested by his two religious poems and by his conversion to Roman Catholicism—perhaps involved a stricter conception of morality and an increased interest in instruction as a function of drama. In view of these circumstances, it is not surprising that his conception of both serious drama and comic drama underwent a major change. Jonson and Fletcher gave way to Shakespeare as primary model. In the first phase of his theory he had conceived of a high comedy founded on heightening and wit. In the second phase he conceived of a high comedy founded on naturalness and satire.

But several difficulties stood in the way of Dryden's writing this natural and satirical high comedy. If the comedy was to be high, it must deal with the noblesse rather than the populace. The noblesse had certainly been amenable to Dryden's flattering representation of their follies in the high comedy of the first phase; but there might be ugly retaliation if he attempted any incisive and realistic satire. And during the latter part of his life the loss of court favor made him increasingly dependent on the income from his plays. Furthermore, Dryden had a constitutional dislike for scornful laughter. He preferred the "nobler pleasure" of admiration for fine writing. His earlier conception of a high comedy of heightening and wit was admirably suited to the production of this nobler pleasure; he could make the repartee of his comic couples as brilliant as he was able. But in his later conception, naturalness and satire stood in the way of the nobler pleasure, since excessive brilliance is unnatural, and admiration is inconsistent with scorn.

Consequently, in the second phase Dryden wrote less

about comedy and wrote proportionately fewer comedies and tragicomedies. When he did write them he tried to make them natural and satirical, but often he also made them low, and, if he did make them high, was apt to disguise or otherwise weaken the satire and to revert to the intendedly admirable repartee of the earlier couples. Only in *Amphitryon* did he come close to a complete embodiment of his conception of natural and satirical high comedy; and even in *Amphitryon* there is lowness, and the satire is veiled and retrospective.

On the whole, during the second phase of his career as comic dramatist Dryden was more inclined to run down with the stream than to reform the judgments of his audience. In the first phase too he sometimes wrote plays essentially at odds with his conception of comedy. Throughout his career, even in the plays that best conform to his theory, he sometimes included elements designed to please tastes of which he did not approve. On the other hand, he never ignored his theory entirely; we find evidence of it even in his close imitation of Tuke's play, even in the work he did for Newcastle, Davenant, and King Charles. And although he sometimes let himself be influenced by fear of failure, or the temptation of success, or economic pressures, he was by no means a venal crowd-pleaser. Despite the failure of *The Wild Gallant* and the success of *The Rival Ladies,* he returned to his theory in *Secret Love*; despite the great success of *Sir Martin,* he returned to his theory in *Marriage à la Mode.* Even in the second phase of his career, when not only external circumstances but his own tastes were against the embodiment of his revised conception of comedy, he conformed largely to his theory and, in *The Spanish Friar* and *Amphitryon,* produced comedy nearly as good as the best he had written in the palmier days of the first phase.

Dryden's comments on his own comedies reflect his fundamental artistic honesty. The stock charge is that he indiscriminately defended his own plays. Actually, he consistently spoke well of those plays or elements of plays which conformed to his theory, but just as consistently ignored or disparaged the plays or elements of plays which did not. He spoke of *The Wild Gallant* as an honest attempt at good comedy, deficient in execution but sound in conception. He contemptuously dismissed *The Rival Ladies* as a potboiler, showing critical interest only in the rhymed heroic episodes. He spoke well of *Secret Love* and *Marriage à la Mode*. *Sir Martin* was one of his most successful plays, but he said nothing in favor of it, not even after 1690, when an edition was published listing him as author; and he implicitly condemned it in condemning farce taken from the French. He apologized for the farce in *An Evening's Love,* but spoke approvingly of the wild couple in the play. He admitted that Benito in *The Assignation* was a concession to the vulgar taste for farce, but he defended the rest of the play.

In the second phase of his career he admitted the artistic faultiness of his tragicomedies, but claimed credit for his efforts to unify the double actions. Only in his commendation of *Limberham* and *Love Triumphant* is his evaluation of his own works seriously at odds with his theoretical conception of comedy. His high praise of *Limberham* may be accounted for partly as a defensive reaction against the banning of the play, partly as an indirect compliment to his royal collaborator; and he to some extent compensated for the misrepresentation by presenting in the prologue a less favorable appraisal of the play. His unjustifiably high opinion of *Love Triumphant* was apparently sincere; but his clear-sighted appraisals of his earlier plays outweigh his deluded fondness for this product of his old age.

At its best Dryden's comedy is not great comedy, because, as Margaret Sherwood has concluded and as Dryden himself was well aware, he lacked the comic spirit. "I know I am not so fitted by nature to write comedy," he said; "I want that gaiety of humour which is required to it. My conversation is slow and dull; my humour saturnine and reserved."[3] This confession carries its own proof. That Dryden should think the comic gift to be made up of such qualities as gaiety, quickness, and forwardness (qualities which, by the way, are paramount in his wild couples) demonstrates his unfitness for comedy more surely than his lack of the qualities does. His condemnation of laughter is just as revealing; so is his persistent association of the comic and ugliness: a "Lazar" was his symbol of the comic in 1667, and it was still his symbol in 1695.[4] His comedies are not spontaneous expressions of a perception of the ridiculous in life, but artificial mixtures of elements laboriously distilled from his study of audiences and of the works of other critics and dramatists.

I believe that the preference for high comedy which is basic in both phases of his theory is in part a rationalization of his desire to escape from an uncongenial genre. Certainly the high comedy that he wrote is much higher than it is comic. The emphasis is on the wit and elegance of the wild couples rather than on their follies. And when Dryden in *The Assignation* and *Amphitryon* tried to go still higher, his results were even less satisfactory as comedy. The heroical concerns of the former play and the elevated passions of the latter are even further removed from the comic than is the repartee of the wild couples. Furthermore, the wild couples are reasonably consistent, but the higher characters of *The Assigna-*

tion and *Amphitryon* are not. There is no genuine connection between Frederick as heroic lover and Frederick
as witty lover; between the Duke as heroic father and the
Duke as superannuated lecher; or between Amphitryon
and Jupiter as nobly passionate and Amphitryon and Jupiter as the ridiculous butts of Mercury's wit.

In the second phase of his theory Dryden saw comedy
as the vehicle of satire. But, although he was one of the
great masters of nondramatic satire, he never wrote a
great satirical comedy, partly because of external circumstances, chiefly because in satirical comedy the fools and
scoundrels must speak and act for themselves. And if Dryden had succeeded in writing a great dramatic satire, it
would not have been a great comedy, because Dryden's
satire is not comic. There is nothing funny about his satirical masterpiece, the character of Zimri in *Absalom and
Achitophel*. Reading it, we are moved not to laughter but
to admiration for "the fineness of a stroke that separates
the head from the body, and leaves it standing in its place,"
and to a kind of cool disdain for the victim of the execution. Even *MacFlecknoe* and the portraits of Og and Doeg
are great because of their annihilating rhetoric, not because of their comic insight. In reading a play by Molière
we forget the author, we are lost in delighted contempla-
tion of the ridiculous object itself; in reading one of Dryden's satires our eye is always on the author: What will be
the next feat of this brilliant prestidigitator? Our appreciation of *Le Malade imaginaire* depends upon our recognition of Argan as the ultimate comic distillation of all
the hypochondriacs who have ever lived; our appreciation
of the portrait of Zimri would be not a whit diminished if
there had never been a Duke of Buckingham or a person
like him.

Although the study of Dryden's work in comedy does

not reveal him as the equal of Molière, it is nonetheless worthwhile because of the light it throws on him as a man, as an artist, as a product of and an influence on his age. Despite the current reawakening of interest in and approval of Dryden, the old view that Dryden as comic dramatist was a grudging and servile hack is still widespread; his work as a critic and writer of comedy is still being belittled and even ignored. This study would be justified if it had no effect other than to dispel the notion that Dryden was a kind of artistic Dr. Jekyll who was suddenly transformed into Mr. Hyde every time he sat down to write a comedy.

Even those who would show that Dryden was an important force in the shaping of Restoration comedy usually cite only two or three of his plays, and one or two of his critical essays, instead of considering the whole pattern of his theory and practice. It is not in the province of this study to consider Dryden in relation to the development of Restoration comedy; yet I might profitably close with a few ideas on the subject. It seems to me that Dryden's comic theory, focusing as it does on the wit and gay profligacy of persons of quality, gives us the best contemporary definition of the Restoration comedy of manners; and that his idea of mixing Fletcherian and Jonsonian comedy provides us with a reasonable answer to the puzzling and much-discussed question of the pre-Restoration influences on Restoration manners comedy.

Etherege and Wycherley wrote better comedies than Dryden did, but they did not discuss the theory of comedy. Dryden did, and it is quite likely that in so doing he clarified the ends and methods of Etherege and Wycherley. Certainly Etherege's advance from the crude practical jokes of *Love in a Tub* to the polished manners of *The Man of Mode* is in line with Dryden's theory.

Congreve, who wrote the greatest Restoration comedies, also wrote critical discussions of comedy. But Congreve was Dryden's friend and literary protégé, and was
almost certainly influenced by Dryden. Compare Dryden's
earlier definition of a humour with the following by Congreve: "[A humour is] a singular and unavoidable manner of doing, or saying any thing, Peculiar and Natural to
one Man only; by which his Speech and Actions are distinguish'd from those of other Men."[5] With Dryden's condemnation of low comedy and farce, compare the following
by Congreve: "Is any thing more common, than to have
a pretended Comedy, stuff'd with . . . Grotesques, Figures,
and Farce Fools? Things, that either are not in Nature, or
if they are, are Monsters, and Births of Mischance. . . .
I am as willing to Laugh, as any body, and as easily di-
verted with an Object truly ridiculous: . . . but . . . I can
never care for seeing things, that force me to entertain
low thoughts of my Nature."[6] With Dryden's defense of
Morose as a humours character, with his associated ideas
of extravagance in degree and heightening, and with his
application of heightening to the representation of witty
characters, compare the following by Congreve:

Let us suppose *Morose* to be a Man Naturally Splenetick
and Melancholly; is there any thing more offensive to one of
such a Disposition, than Noise and Clamour? . . . We see
common Examples of this Humour in little every day. 'Tis ten
to one, but three parts in four of the Company that you dine
with, are Discompos'd and Startled at the Cutting of a Cork,
or Scratching a Plate with a Knife: It is a Proportion of the
same Humour, that makes such or any other Noise offensive
to the Person that hears it. . . . But *Morose* you will say, is so
Extravagant, he cannot bear any Discourse or Conversation,
above a Whisper. Why, It is his excess of this Humour, that
makes him become Ridiculous, and qualifies his Character for
Comedy. If the Poet had given him, but a Moderate proportion of that Humour, 'tis odds but half the Audience, would

have sided with the Character, and have Condemn'd the Author, for Exposing a Humour which was neither Remarkable nor Ridiculous. Besides, the distance of the Stage requires the Figure represented, to be something larger than the Life; and sure a Picture may have Features larger in Proportion, and yet be very like the Original. If this exactness of Quantity, were to be observed in Wit, as some would have it in Humour; what would become of those Characters that are design'd for Men of Wit? I believe if a Poet should steal a Dialogue of any length, from the *Extempore* Discourse of the two Wittiest Men upon Earth, he would find the Scene but coldly receiv'd by the Town.[7]

Congreve's development in the direction of increasing refinement is even more striking than Etherege's: he began with a comparatively crude imitation of Jonsonian folly in *The Old Bachelor* and ended with the transcendently polished *Way of the World,* and this development is in accord with Dryden's idea of high comedy. Congreve's Millamant has been traced back to Dryden's Melantha, Congreve's Millamant and Mirabel to Dryden's wild couples; but it seems to me that Dryden's influence on *The Way of the World* is more pervasive and general. In Congreve's masterpiece we find persons of quality occupied with love; we find elegant wit and equally elegant folly; we find a reflection of the manners of the age; we find heightening which is not carried to the extremes of unnatural extravagance; we find cool and subtle mockery of human foibles. In all these respects, but especially in its refinement, *The Way of the World* fits Dryden's idea of high comedy. In his preface Congreve mentions Terence, Menander, Theophrastus, Aristotle, Lelius, and Scipio. He also says this:

Those Characters which are meant to be ridicul'd in most of our Comedies, are of Fools so gross, that in my humble Opinion, they shou'd rather disturb than divert the well-natur'd and reflecting Part of an Audience; they are rather Objects of Charity than Contempt; and instead of moving our Mirth, they ought very often to excite our Compassion.

This Reflection mov'd me to design some Characters, which shou'd appear ridiculous not so much thro' a natural Folly (which is incorrigible, and therefore not proper for the Stage) as thro' an affected Wit; a Wit, which at the same time that it is affected, is also false. As there is some Difficulty in the Formation of a Character of this Nature, so there is some Hazard which attends the Progress of its Success, upon the Stage. . . . This I had Occasion lately to observe: For this Play had been acted two or three Days, before some . . . hasty Judges cou'd find the leisure to distinguish betwixt the Character of a *Witwoud* and a *Truewit*.[8]

When I read this I am reminded not of Terence, Menander, Theophrastus, Aristotle, Lelius, or Scipio, but of Dryden:

How easy is it to call rogue and villain, and that wittily! But how hard to make a man appear a fool, a blockhead, or a knave, without using any of those opprobrious terms! To spare the grossness of the names, and to do the thing yet more severely. . . . There is . . . a vast difference betwixt the slovenly butchering of a man, and the fineness of a stroke that separates the head from the body, and leaves it standing in its place.[9]

For various reasons Dryden himself did not achieve this degree of refinement in satirical comedy; but as his life drew towards a close he may have had the satisfaction of leading Congreve from Prue, Ben, and Foresight to Mirabel, Millamant, and Witwoud. *The Way of the World* is the culminating development of the Restoration comedy of manners; it may also be the final and highest product of Dryden's comic theory.

NOTES

At the time I write there is no definitive edition of Dryden's complete works. For Dryden's critical prose works, I have used *Essays of John Dryden*, ed. W. P. Ker (Oxford, 1900). For Dryden's plays, for the prologues and epilogues to the plays, and for the prefaces and dedicatory epistles of the plays (if they are not included in Ker), I have used *Dryden, The Dramatic Works*, ed. Montague Summers (London: Nonesuch Press, 1931-32). For the works of Dryden which are not included in Ker or Summers, I have used *The Works of John Dryden*, ed. Sir Walter Scott and George Saintsbury (Edinburgh, 1882-93). For Dryden's letters, I have used *The Letters of John Dryden, with Letters Addressed to Him*, ed. Charles E. Ward (Durham: Duke University Press, 1942).

I have thought it best not to encumber this book with a great many footnote references to Dryden's works, which would be of no use to readers using editions other than those which I have used. Instead, I have simply named in my text the works referred to (except in a few cases when the context made such reference too awkward). The works are not long, and I believe that anyone reasonably familiar with them can locate passages without much difficulty.

For dates and circumstances of the publication of Dryden's works, the performance of his plays, and the publication of contemporary attacks on him, my chief source has been Hugh Macdonald, *John Dryden: A Bibliography of Early Editions and of Drydeniana* (Oxford: Clarendon

Press, 1939). For the sources of Dryden's comedies I have relied for the most part on Ned Bliss Allen, *The Sources of John Dryden's Comedies* ("University of Michigan Publications in Language and Literature," Vol. XVI [Ann Arbor: University of Michigan Press, 1935]). However, I have not accepted all of Allen's theories as to sources and influences, and I have proposed a few theories of my own. I am of course generally indebted to Louis I. Bredvold, *The Intellectual Milieu of John Dryden: Studies in Some Aspects of Seventeenth-Century Thought* ("University of Michigan Publications in Language and Literature," Vol. XII [Ann Arbor: University of Michigan Press, 1934]). For biographical information on Dryden I have used Charles E. Ward, *The Life of John Dryden* (Chapel Hill: University of North Carolina Press, 1961). For historical background I have used George Macaulay Trevelyan, *England Under the Stuarts* (12th ed., rev.; New York: G. P. Putnam's Sons, 1925), and two books by David Ogg, *England in the Reign of Charles II* (Oxford: Clarendon Press, 1955), and *England in the Reigns of James II and William III* (Oxford: Clarendon Press, 1955). For bibliographical information on Dryden scholarship I am chiefly indebted to Samuel Holt Monk, *John Dryden: A List of Critical Studies Published from 1895 to 1948* (Minneapolis: University of Minnesota Press, 1950).

CHAPTER I

1. See A. W. Ward, *A History of English Dramatic Literature to the Death of Queen Anne* (London, 1875), II, 528-29; George Saintsbury, *Dryden* ("English Men of Letters Series" [London, 1881]), pp. 119-20; Frank H. Ristine, *English Tragicomedy* (New York: Columbia University Press, 1910), pp. 168-75; Bonamy Dobrée, *Restoration Comedy, 1660-1720* (Oxford: Clarendon Press, 1924), p. 106.

2. See John B. Henneman, "Dryden after Two Centuries (1700-1900)," *Sewanee Review*, IX (1901), 58; Joseph Wood Krutch, *Comedy and Conscience after the Restoration* (New York: Columbia University Press, 1924), pp. 15-17; Kathleen M. Lynch, *The Social*

Mode of Restoration Comedy ("University of Michigan Publications in Language and Literature," Vol. III [New York: Macmillan Co., 1926]), p. 136; John H. Wilson, *The Influence of Beaumont and Fletcher on Restoration Drama* ("Ohio State University Studies in Language and Literature," No. 4 [Columbus, 1928]), p. 79; John Wilcox, *The Relation of Molière to Restoration Comedy* (New York: Columbia University Press, 1938), pp. 105-7; Elisabeth Mignon, *Crabbed Age and Youth: The Old Men and Women in the Restoration Comedy of Manners* (Durham: Duke University Press, 1947), p. 61; Allardyce Nicoll, *A History of English Drama, 1660-1900* (4th ed.; Cambridge: Cambridge University Press, 1955), I, 226, 234.

3. David E. Baker, *Biographia Dramatica; or, A Companion to the Playhouse,* ed. Isaac Reed (London, 1782), I, 139-40.

4. [Francis Gentleman], *The Dramatic Censor; or Critical Companion* (London, 1770), II, 461.

5. Samuel Johnson, *Lives of the English Poets,* ed. George Birkbeck Hill (Oxford: Clarendon Press, 1905), I, 459-60.

6. William Hazlitt, "Lectures on the English Comic Writers," *The Collected Works of William Hazlitt,* ed. A. R. Waller and Arnold Glover (London: J. M. Dent and Co., 1903), VIII, 68.

7. "Dryden's Dramatic Works," *Retrospective Review,* I (1820), 160.

8. T. B. Macaulay, "Dryden," *Edinburgh Review,* XLVII (1828), 23, 26.

9. *The Poetical Works of John Dryden,* ed. W. D. Christie (London, 1890), p. xxvi.

10. John Churton Collins, *Essays and Studies* (London, 1895), pp. 23-25.

11. G. R. Noyes, "Dryden as Critic," *The Nation,* LXXI (1900), 232. Noyes subsequently formed a higher opinion of Dryden's work.

12. Dudley H. Miles, *The Influence of Molière on Restoration Comedy* (New York: Columbia University Press, 1910), p. 76.

13. A. W. Verrall, *Lectures on Dryden,* ed. Margaret de G. Verrall (Cambridge: Cambridge University Press, 1914), p. 17.

14. Percy Houston, "The Inconsistency of John Dryden," *Sewanee Review,* XXII (1914), 476-77. A few years earlier Prosser H. Frye, in "Dryden and the Critical Canons of the Eighteenth Century," *University of Nebraska Studies,* VII (1907), 26, had maintained that Dryden's criticism is fundamentally consistent, that his views did not change haphazardly, but progressively.

15. David Nichol Smith, *John Dryden* (Cambridge: Cambridge University Press, 1950), p. 26. It should be added that in this paragraph the author does, though very briefly, credit Dryden with helping to shape the comedy of manners. Perhaps a new trend of approval of Dryden's comedies has begun very recently with the publication of the first volume of plays in the new edition of Dryden's complete works (*The Works of John Dryden,* Vol. VIII, ed. John Harrington Smith, Dougald MacMillan, et al. [Berkeley and Los Angeles: University of

234 NOTES, PAGES 8-10

California Press, 1962]). The editors look with favor upon *The Wild Gallant* and *The Rival Ladies;* they "emphatically disagree" with Dryden's statement that he was constitutionally unfitted for writing comedy (p. 237), and say on the contrary that he was "an anti-romantic in grain" who "was intended by nature to write comedy and could not be at his best in romantic drama" (p. 297).

16. See Charles E. Ward, *The Life of John Dryden* (Chapel Hill: University of North Carolina Press, 1961), pp. 240-42; Leslie Hotson, *The Commonwealth and Restoration Stage* (Cambridge, Mass.: Harvard University Press, 1928), pp. 286-94.

17. Ned Bliss Allen, *The Sources of John Dryden's Comedies* ("University of Michigan Publications in Language and Literature," Vol. XVI [Ann Arbor: University of Michigan Press, 1935]), p. 246.

18. There are two hitherto unpublished studies. The first is my dissertation, "Dryden's Theory and Practice of Comedy" (University of North Carolina, 1953), of which the present book is a reworking. An abstract was published in *Research in Progress* ("The University of North Carolina Record, Graduate School Series," No. 66 [Chapel Hill, 1954]), pp. 96-99. The second is John William Grace's dissertation, "Theory and Practice in the Comedy of John Dryden" (University of Michigan, 1956). An abstract was published in *Dissertation Abstracts,* XVIII (1958), 2141. In some details his work parallels mine rather closely (for example, in the view of *The Wild Gallant* as a mixture of Fletcherian wit and Jonsonian humour), but on the whole his is very different from mine. Instead of making a chronological comparison of critical writings and plays, as I have done, Grace surveys the entire criticism in a long first chapter before moving in subsequent chapters to analysis of the plays. This arrangement, it seems to me, obscures the relation of the theory to the practice. Grace focuses his discussion of Dryden's theory on the concepts of wit and humour. There is little or no discussion of Dryden's ideas concerning plot construction, variety, and heightening—all of which, I believe, are important in Dryden's theory. Fletcher and Jonson are discussed as influences on Dryden's ideas of comedy of wit and comedy of humour, but virtually nothing is said of the influence of Shakespeare. I have tried to show that after 1675 Shakespeare was a more important influence on Dryden's theory and practice than were either Jonson or Fletcher. Although Grace holds that Dryden's critical attitude towards comedy changed from tentative to prescriptive to deprecatory, he sees Dryden's comic theory as fundamentally static. I, on the other hand, see two main stages of development of Dryden's theory and practice, and also some development within each of the stages, especially the first. Grace finds little significant relationship between Dryden's theory and practice. He sees as Dryden's central concept the idea of comedy as a mixture of wit and humour, with wit predominating. He holds that Dryden throughout his career did write such mixed comedy; but Dryden, he contends, also deviated from his theory repeatedly by providing insufficient wit and by adulterating his comedy with farce.

Grace adheres to the view that Dryden in his comedies catered to whatever tastes were current at the time he wrote them. His main point appears to be that the concepts of "comedy of wit" and "comedy of humour" afford a means of classifying Dryden's comedies and other Restoration comedies as well. I have tried to show that Dryden was not wholly the slave of his audience and that the relationship of his theory and his practice is more significant and complex than it appears to be in Grace's study.

19. Margaret Sherwood, *Dryden's Dramatic Theory and Practice* ("Yale University Studies in English," Vol. IV [Boston, 1899]), pp. 40-42, 51, 56-58.

20. *Ibid.*, pp. 33-34.

21. *Selected Dramas of Dryden with The Rehearsal,* ed. G. R. Noyes (Chicago: Scott, Foresman and Co., 1910), pp. xix, xliii, xlix.

22. *Ibid.*, p. xxiv.

23. *Ibid.*, p. xxxv.

24. Allen, *Sources of Dryden's Comedies,* pp. 240, 246.

CHAPTER II

1. Allison Gaw, "Tuke's *Adventures of Five Hours* in Relation to the 'Spanish Plot' and to John Dryden," *Studies in English Drama,* ed. Allison Gaw (1st ser.; Philadelphia: University of Pennsylvania, 1917), pp. 14-17.

2. See Alfred Harbage, "Elizabethan-Restoration Palimpsest," *MLR,* XXXV (1940), 304-9. Harbage suggests that *The Wild Gallant* is Dryden's reworking of a manuscript play by Brome.

3. See J. H. Wilson, *The Influence of Beaumont and Fletcher on Restoration Drama* ("Ohio State University Studies in Language and Literature," No. 4 [Columbus: Ohio State University, 1928]), p. 115; R. G. Noyes, *Ben Jonson on the English Stage, 1660-1776* ("Harvard Studies in English," Vol. XVII [Cambridge, Mass.: Harvard University Press, 1935]; and A. C. Sprague, *Beaumont and Fletcher on the Restoration Stage* (Cambridge, Mass.: Harvard University Press, 1926).

4. *Beaumont and Fletcher,* ed. J. St. Loe Strachey ("Mermaid" Series [New York: A. A. Wyn, 1949]), I, 196.

5. Ned Bliss Allen, *The Sources of John Dryden's Comedies* ("University of Michigan Publications in Language and Literature," Vol. XVI [Ann Arbor: University of Michigan Press, 1935]), p. 12.

6. Frank H. Moore, "Dr. Pelling, Dr. Pell, and Dryden's Lord Nonsuch," *Modern Language Review,* XLIX (1954), 348-51.

7. Sir Samuel Tuke, *The Adventures of Five Hours,* ed. B. van Thal (London: R. Holden and Co., n.d.), p. i.

8. John Harrington Smith, "The Dryden-Howard Collaboration," *Studies in Philology,* LI (1954), 54-56.

9. Smith (*ibid.,* pp. 61-63) supposes that Dryden's celebrated quarrel with Howard over the use of rhyme in drama had already begun,

"on an oral basis," when Dryden wrote the dedication of *The Rival Ladies.*

10. Strangely enough, Dryden goes on to cite "the tragedy of Queen *Gorboduc*" as a precedent for the use of rhyme in English drama, and says that the "new way" is more properly described as "an old way new revived." Actually, Gorboduc was a king, and the play that bears his name is notable as the first English drama in blank verse; the choruses between the acts are the only lines in rhyme. Did Dryden's memory fail him, or is he at this point writing with his tongue in his cheek? He also cites the use of rhyme in Spanish and Italian tragedies. In any case, rhyme was a new fashion in serious drama in England at the time he wrote.

CHAPTER III

1. My analysis of the *Essay* has been made easier by Frank Livingstone Huntley's *On Dryden's Essay of Dramatic Poesy* ("The University of Michigan Contributions in Modern Philology," No. 16 [Ann Arbor: University of Michigan Press, 1951]), particularly by his consideration of the *Essay* in the light of Dryden's requirements of "justness" and "liveliness."

2. "Defence of the Epilogue."

3. *The Poetics of Aristotle,* ed. and tr. S. H. Butcher (4th ed.; London: Macmillan and Co., 1936), p. 21.

4. *Ben Jonson,* ed. C. H. Herford, Percy and Evelyn Simpson (Oxford: Clarendon Press, 1925-52), VIII, 643-44. Montague Summers, in *Dryden, The Dramatic Works* (London: Nonesuch Press, 1931-32), I, 403-4, notes the parallel.

5. *Ben Jonson,* ed. Herford-Simpson, III, 428.

6. Stuart M. Tave, "Corbyn Morris: Falstaff, Humor, and Comic Theory in the Eighteenth Century," *Modern Philology,* L (1952), 109, with reference to the discussion of Falstaff in the *Essay* supposes that singularity of wit cannot qualify as a humour because wit is admirable, not ridiculous. But although wit in itself is admirable, its manifestations may be ridiculous. Certainly the manifestations of Falstaff's wit are often ridiculous enough; consider, for example, his preposterous story of his fight with the robbers (*Henry IV, Part One*).

7. In the 1684 edition of the *Essay,* Dryden changed "no poet can ever paint" to "no poet before them could paint." Perhaps he had in mind his own successful imitations, during the intervening period, of witty and debauched ladies and gentlemen in *Secret Love* and *Marriage à la Mode.*

8. Although Dryden uses the word "wit" several times in the *Essay,* he does not take pains to define it, as he does with "humour." But during the period when he wrote the *Essay,* or shortly afterwards, he wrote the preface to *Annus Mirabilis,* which contains a celebrated discussion of wit. Here Dryden distinguishes between *Wit writing,* which is "the faculty of imagination in the writer," and *Wit written,*

which is "the happy result of thought, or product of imagination."
Of *Wit writing* he says, "the first happiness of the poet's imagination
is properly invention, or finding of the thought; the second is fancy,
or the variation, deriving, or moulding, of that thought, as the judgment represents it proper to the subject; the third is elocution, or the
art of clothing and adorning that thought . . . in apt, significant, and
sounding words: the quickness of the imagination is seen in the invention, the fertility in the fancy, and the accuracy in the expression."
Of the wit of dialogue in plays, he says that the words must not be
too studiously chosen, for in drama "all that is said is supposed to be
the effect of sudden thought; which, though it excludes not the quickness of wit in repartees, yet admits not a too curious election of
words, too frequent allusions, or use of tropes, or, in fine, anything
that shows remoteness of thought, or labour in the writer." For a
general discussion of wit in Restoration comedy, see Thomas H.
Fujimura, *The Restoration Comedy of Wit* (Princeton: Princeton
University Press, 1952). Pages 51 and 201 are particularly relevant
to Dryden's ideas on the subject.

9. See *The Diary of Samuel Pepys,* ed. Henry B. Wheatley (London: George Bell and Sons, 1893-1909), 8 May 1668.

10. *Essays of John Dryden,* ed. W. P. Ker (Oxford, 1900), I, xlix.

11. Ned Bliss Allen, *The Sources of John Dryden's Comedies* ("University of Michigan Publications in Language and Literature," Vol.
XVI [Ann Arbor: University of Michigan Press, 1935]), pp. 78-80,
advances the theory that Dryden shelved one-plot tragicomedy because he was influenced by Etherege's two-plot tragicomedy, *Love in
a Tub.* Allen thinks it significant that the serious plot of Etherege's
play is heroic. But the successes of *The Indian Queen* and *The Indian
Emperour* are sufficient to account for Dryden's making his serious
plot heroic. And the comic plot of *Secret Love* is very unlike that of
Love in a Tub, which consists of three loosely-woven strands characterized by "mechanic" fools, a pair of sharpers, practical jokes, and
an over-all reliance on spectacular effects. It is, as a matter of fact,
very like *The Wild Gallant.* In view of this resemblance, and in view
of the fact that Etherege's heroic plot was preceded by *The Rival
Ladies* and *The Indian Queen,* it seems more likely that Etherege was
influenced by Dryden than that Dryden was influenced by Etherege.

12. See, for example, Allen, *Sources of Dryden's Comedies,* pp. 74-
75.

13. Kathleen M. Lynch, *The Social Mode of Restoration Comedy*
("University of Michigan Publications in Language and Literature,"
Vol. III [New York: Macmillan Co., 1926]), pp. 43-79.

14. John Harrington Smith, *The Gay Couple in Restoration Comedy*
(Cambridge, Mass.: Harvard University Press, 1948), pp. 31-34.

15. See Allen, *Sources of Dryden's Comedies,* pp. 97-98, and *The
Works of John Dryden,* ed. Sir Walter Scott and George Saintsbury
(Edinburgh, 1882-93), II, 416.

CHAPTER IV

1. *The Diary of Samuel Pepys,* ed. Henry B. Wheatley (London: George Bell and Sons, 1893-1909), 16 August 1667.

2. Gerard Langbaine, *An Account of the English Dramatick Poets* (Oxford, 1691), p. 170.

3. John Downes, *Roscius Anglicanus, or an Historical Review of the Stage from 1660 to 1706,* ed. Joseph Knight (London, 1886), p. 28.

4. For information concerning Newcastle, I am indebted to Henry Ten Eyck Perry, *The First Duchess of Newcastle and Her Husband as Figures in Literary History* ("Harvard Studies in English," Vol. IV [Boston: Ginn and Company, 1918]).

5. Anthony à Wood, *Athenae Oxonienses,* ed. Philip Bliss (London, 1813-20), III, 739.

6. *A Collection of Old English Plays,* ed. A. H. Bullen (London, 1882-85), II, 315-16.

7. Perry, *First Duchess of Newcastle,* pp. 156-58.

8. William Cavendish, *A Pleasante & Merrye Humor off A Roge,* ed. Francis Needham ("Welbeck Miscellany," No. 1 [Bungay, Suffolk: R. Clay and Sons, Ltd., 1933]), pp. v, vii-viii.

9. Alfred Harbage, *Cavalier Drama: An Historical and Critical Supplement to the Study of the Elizabethan and Restoration Stage* (New York: Modern Language Association of America, 1936), p. 75. It may be that Shirley, not Shadwell, "assisted" Newcastle in *The Humorous Lovers.* R. S. Forsythe has pointed out (*The Relations of Shirley's Plays to the Elizabethan Drama* [New York: Columbia University Press, 1914], p. 430) that the play is reminiscent of some of Shirley's comedies.

10. André de Mandach, *Molière et la comédie de moeurs en Angleterre, 1660-1668* (Neuchâtel: à la Baconnière, 1946), pp. 69-80, argues that *Sir Martin* is almost entirely the work of Newcastle, with only minor contributions by Dryden. Most authorities, however, attribute the play to Dryden.

11. *The Rival Ladies, The Indian Emperour,* and *Secret Love. The Indian Queen* was also successful, but although Dryden, in a prefatory note to *The Indian Emperour,* had announced his share in the play, contemporaries seem to have gone on thinking of *The Indian Queen* as Howard's. See John Harrington Smith, "The Dryden-Howard Collaboration," *SP,* LI (1954), 62.

12. John Wilcox, *The Relation of Molière to Restoration Comedy* (New York: Columbia University Press, 1938), pp. 180-83.

13. I do not know whether Dryden is here thinking of translation in a strict sense or in the broad sense which he later gave to the word in his "Preface to the Translation of Ovid's Epistles" (1680). There he speaks of three kinds of translation: metaphrase, or literal translation, "word by word, and line by line"; paraphrase, or "translation with latitude, where the author is kept in view by the translator,

so as never to be lost, but his words are not so strictly followed as his sense; and that too is admitted to be amplified, but not altered"; and imitation, "where the translator (if now he has not lost that name) assumes the liberty, not only to vary from the words and sense, but to forsake them both as he sees occasion; and taking only some general hints from the original, to run division on the groundwork, as he pleases." But even if Dryden in this statement in the *Essay* did have in mind only literal translation, the disapproval of French drama which he expresses makes it unlikely that he would at that time have chosen of his own accord to work with a French play, however much he altered it.

14. *The Humorous Lovers* (London, 1677), p. 6.

15. James M. Osborn, *John Dryden: Some Biographical Facts and Problems* (New York: Columbia University Press, 1940), pp. 184-91; Charles E. Ward, *The Life of John Dryden* (Chapel Hill: University of North Carolina Press, 1961), p. 57.

16. *The Poems of John Dryden*, ed. John Sargeaunt (London: Oxford University Press, 1948), p. 600.

17. Allardyce Nicoll, *Dryden as an Adapter of Shakespeare* ("Shakespeare Association Papers," No. 8 [London: Oxford University Press, 1922]), p. 17.

18. Hazleton Spencer, *Shakespeare Improved* (Cambridge: Harvard University Press, 1927), p. 201.

19. George C. D. Odell, *Shakespeare from Betterton to Irving* (New York: C. Scribner's Sons, 1920), I, 31.

20. Spencer, *Shakespeare Improved*, p. 198.

21. *Paradise Lost*, VIII, 481-559.

22. *Ibid.*, IV, 477-89.

23. *Ibid.*, IV, 309-11.

24. *Ibid.*, XI, 429-62.

25. *Ibid.*, VIII, 286-91.

26. *Diary of Pepys*, ed. Wheatley, 7 November 1667.

27. Ned Bliss Allen, "The Sources of Dryden's *The Mock Astrologer*," *Philological Quarterly*, XXXVI (1957), 453-64.

28. *Diary of Pepys*, ed. Wheatley, 20 June 1668.

29. *Memoirs of John Evelyn*, ed. William Bray (London, n.d.), 19 June 1668.

30. *The Complete Works of William Wycherley*, ed. Montague Summers (London, 1924), I, 74. Summers' note on this passage (I, 244) lists other references in Restoration plays to the use of Covent-Garden Church as a place of assignation.

31. *Dictionary of National Biography* (London, 1950), XVII, 1235.

32. Anti-Catholic feeling was particularly violent later, as may be seen in the Popish-Plot hysteria and the bitter controversy over the succession of James. But it seems to have been present throughout the period. Catholic France as a military threat was of course an important factor. By many the London fire of 1666 was blamed on the French and the "Papists." Mobs seized Catholics and Frenchmen

who appeared in the streets (George Macaulay Trevelyan, *England Under the Stuarts* [12th ed., rev.; New York: G. P. Putnam's Sons, 1925], pp. 360-61).

33. Dryden's success during this period was not confined to the theater. In April, 1668, he succeeded Davenant as Poet Laureate, at a salary of 200 pounds per year (which was not, however, paid very regularly). In June, 1668, through the agency of King Charles, he was awarded an honorary degree. And Ward thinks that during the period 1667-68 Dryden was pretty well off financially (*Life of Dryden*, pp. 52-58).

CHAPTER V

1. My account of Dryden's and Shadwell's literary relations follows in general those of Albert S. Borgman, *Thomas Shadwell: His Life and Comedies* (New York: New York University Press, 1928), and Russell J. Smith, "Shadwell's Impact upon Dryden," *Review of English Studies,* XX (1944), 29-44. My discussion of Shadwell's effect on Dryden's critical views is largely original.

2. *The Humourists* (dedicated to Newcastle's wife), *Epsom Wells, The Virtuoso,* and *The Libertine.*

3. *The Complete Works of Thomas Shadwell,* ed. Montague Summers (London, 1927), I, 11.

4. *Ibid.*

5. *Ibid.,* p. 10.

6. *Ibid.,* p. 100.

7. See Chapter IV, note 13.

8. See Louis I. Bredvold, *The Intellectual Milieu of John Dryden: Studies in Some Aspects of Seventeenth-Century Thought* ("University of Michigan Publications in Language and Literature," XII [Ann Arbor: University of Michigan Press, 1934]), pp. 16-53, and Mildred Hartsock, "Dryden's Plays: A Study in Ideas," *Seventeenth Century Studies,* ed. Robert Shafer (2nd ser.; Princeton: Princeton University Press, 1937), pp. 71-176.

9. John Harrington Smith, *The Gay Couple in Restoration Comedy* (Cambridge, Mass.: Harvard University Press, 1948), pp. 58, 70, 74-78, defends the morality of the sort of comedy found in *Secret Love* and *Marriage à la Mode* (he mentions both). His argument is, I believe, basically the same as mine.

10. Ned Bliss Allen, *The Sources of John Dryden's Comedies* ("University of Michigan Publications in Language and Literature," Vol. XVI [Ann Arbor: University of Michigan Press, 1935]), pp. 245-46.

11. Apparently Dryden was ready to make peace with Shadwell or the "ingenious men" mentioned in the preface to *An Evening's Love* as supporters of the idea that Jonson had wit. "I will not contest farther," he says, the idea that Jonson's accurate representations of

folly show wit. But, he continues, Jonson was deficient in "wit in the stricter sense, that is, sharpness of conceit."

12. This passage illustrates what Dryden means when, in the preface to *An Evening's Love,* he speaks of Fletcher's characters "interfering" with each other.

13. See Charles E. Ward, *The Life of John Dryden* (Chapel Hill: University of North Carolina Press, 1961), p. 83.

14. William Empson, *English Pastoral Poetry* (New York: W. W. Norton and Co., 1938), pp. 46-48.

15. Smith, *The Gay Couple,* p. 70, sees the play as demonstrating the impracticality of "the antimatrimonial mode." Bonamy Dobrée, *Restoration Comedy* (Oxford: Clarendon Press, 1924), p. 113, also sees a practical morality in the play. Speaking of the resolution of the comic plot, he remarks, "Dryden laughs morality back into its rightful place, as the scheme which ultimately makes life most comfortable."

16. Quoted by Harold Brooks, "Some Notes on Dryden, Cowley and Shadwell," *Notes and Queries,* CLXVIII (1935), 94.

17. Charles Blount, *Mr. Dreyden Vindicated* (1673), as quoted in *Dryden, The Dramatic Works,* ed. Montague Summers (London: Nonesuch Press, 1931-32), III, 273.

18. See Smith, *The Gay Couple,* pp. 29-44.

19. James U. Rundle, "The Source of Dryden's 'Comic Plot' in *The Assignation,*" *Modern Philology,* XLV (1947), 104-11.

20. Allen, *Sources of Dryden's Comedies,* pp. 172-74. Allen supposes that Dryden originally intended to make this plot wholly heroic, but for some reason (Allen gives none) weakened it by adding discordant comic elements.

21. *The Annals of Love* (London, 1672), p. 82.

22. *Ibid.,* p. 83.

23. *Ibid.,* p. 105.

24. *Ibid.,* pp. 104-5.

25. Frederick, by saying that this arrangement suits his "humour," lends a little additional support to my theory that Dryden's witty couples are Jonsonian in conception.

26. "Discours de l'utilité et des parties du poëme dramatique," *Oeuvres de P. Corneille,* ed. M. Ch. Marty-Laveaux ("Les Grands Écrivains de la France" [Paris, 1862]), I, 23-25. James Merrin, "Theory of Comedy in the Restoration" (Doctoral dissertation, University of Chicago, 1948), p. 38, n. 2, mentions Corneille's idea of "comédie héroïque" as one of several possible influences on Dryden's discussion of high comedy in the *Essay.*

27. *The Rehearsal,* in *Plays of the Restoration and Eighteenth Century,* ed. Dougald MacMillan and Howard Mumford Jones (New York: Henry Holt and Co., 1931), III, v, 69-70.

28. *Dryden, The Dramatic Works,* ed. Summers, III, 193, 280.

29. Leslie Hotson, *The Commonwealth and Restoration Stage* (Cambridge, Mass.: Harvard University Press, 1928), pp. 253-54.

CHAPTER VI

1. If I have correctly interpreted his critical opinions at this time, Dryden found himself in an uncomfortable position in trying to reply to Rymer. He wished to defend Shakespeare against Rymer's attack, but he agreed in part at least with the neo-classic standards of regularity upon which Rymer based his attack.

2. See Charles E. Ward, *The Life of John Dryden* (Chapel Hill: University of North Carolina Press, 1961), pp. 143-44.

3. Allardyce Nicoll, *A History of English Drama, 1660-1900* (4th ed.; Cambridge: Cambridge University Press, 1955), I, 7.

4. *Ibid.*, II, 8-25.

5. John Harrington Smith, *The Gay Couple in Restoration Comedy* (Cambridge, Mass.: Harvard University Press, 1948), pp. 132-37.

6. Ned Bliss Allen, *The Sources of John Dryden's Comedies* ("University of Michigan Publications in Language and Literature," Vol. XVI [Ann Arbor: University of Michigan Press, 1935]), p. 124, holds that after the failure of *The Assignation* Dryden deserted his "witty lovers" and "turned to low farcical intrigue." This change, says Allen, "was certainly in part an attempt by Dryden to please a changing, apparently more bourgeois, audience." Dryden, he continues, was now writing for the Duke's Company, whose theater was frequented by the citizens. Allen's theory seems questionable to me. In the first place, his account of the change in Dryden's comedy is oversimplified; there is more to Dryden's later comedy than "low farcical intrigue." Furthermore, the idea that Dryden was writing for a bourgeois audience does not stand on very firm ground. *Limberham,* which Allen (following Scott) cites as an example of low comedy written to please the citizens at the Duke's theater, was actually written to please no less a person than the King. And after the merging of the two companies of actors in 1682, Dryden wrote comedy for the United Company, whose audience must have included persons who had applauded the performances of his wild-couple comedy; for surely we cannot suppose that the audience of the King's Company stopped going to plays when the companies merged.

7. *Ibid.*, pp. 195-96.

8. *The Letters of John Dryden, with Letters Addressed to Him,* ed. Charles E. Ward (Durham: Duke University Press, 1942), pp. 11-12, 47.

9. Thomas D'Urfey, *A Fond Husband; or The Plotting Sisters* (London, 1677).

10. Aldo, Brainsick (grandiloquence), Limberham (complaisant gullibility), and Mrs. Saintly (puritanical lechery).

11. Gerard Langbaine, *An Account of the English Dramatick Poets* (Oxford, 1691), p. 164.

12. On the basis of his study of a great number of Restoration comedies, John Harrington Smith concludes that "the period was as

insistent on the 'double standard' as any other has been." (*Gay Couple*, p. 77).

13. Allen, *Sources of Dryden's Comedies*, pp. 125-26.

14. Scott compares Dominic to Falstaff, and Saintsbury says that Dominic is "little more than a blended reminiscence of Falstaff and Fletcher's Lopez [of *The Spanish Curate*]" (*The Works of John Dryden*, ed. Scott and Saintsbury [Edinburgh, 1882-93], VI, 396, 401). Like Allen, I doubt the influence of Fletcher's Lopez. Dryden says, in "The Grounds of Criticism in Tragedy," "The characters of Fletcher are poor and narrow, in comparison of Shakespeare's; I remember not one which is not borrowed from him; . . . and to imitate Fletcher is but to copy after him who was a copyer." Why should Dryden imitate Lopez, when the vastly superior Falstaff was available?

The passage quoted above should not, of course, be taken as representative of Dryden's view of Fletcher throughout his career. I have tried to show that in the first phase of his theory Dryden held a much higher opinion of Fletcher, and was considerably influenced by him.

15. See Louis I. Bredvold, "Political Aspects of Dryden's *Amboyna* and *The Spanish Fryar*," *Essays and Studies in English and Comparative Literature* ("University of Michigan Publications in Language and Literature," Vol. VIII [Ann Arbor: University of Michigan Press, 1932]), p. 131. In this article Bredvold disproves the traditional theory that Dryden, resentful because his pension had not been paid, temporarily turned against the King's party and expressed Whig sentiments in *The Spanish Friar*. Bredvold shows that there is much evidence in the play of the Tory point of view.

16. George W. Whiting, "Political Satire in London Stage Plays, 1680-83," *Modern Philology*, XXVIII (1930), 32.

17. See George Macaulay Trevelyan, *England Under the Stuarts* (12th ed., rev.; New York: G. P. Putnam's Sons, 1925), p. 385.

18. Bredvold ("Political Aspects," *Essays and Studies in English and Comparative Literature*, p. 130) cites this passage as evidence of Dryden's Tory point of view.

19. See David Ogg, *England in the Reign of Charles II* (Oxford: Clarendon Press, 1955), II, 597, 640.

20. Perhaps Dryden had particularly in mind the Green Ribbon Club, the Whig headquarters organization, which included well-to-do citizens among its members. See Trevelyan, *England Under the Stuarts*, pp. 393-94.

21. Jeremy Collier, *A Short View of the Immorality, and Profaneness of the English Stage, Together With the Sense of Antiquity upon This Argument* (London, 1698), pp. 99-100.

CHAPTER VII

1. See John Harold Wilson, *The Court Wits of the Restoration* (Princeton: Princeton University Press, 1948), p. 102.

2. Dryden's opinions on women in general did not keep him from friendship with and respect for individual women. See, for example, the series of letters that he wrote in his old age to his young kinswoman, Elizabeth Steward. For further evidence of his clinical conception of love, see Scott C. Osborn, "Heroical Love in Dryden's Heroic Drama," *Publications of the Modern Language Association,* LXXIII (1958), 480-90.

3. See Allardyce Nicoll, *A History of English Drama, 1660-1900* (4th ed.; Cambridge: Cambridge University Press, 1955), I, 78-79.

4. See the contemporary letter quoted in *Dryden, The Dramatic Works,* ed. Montague Summers (London: Nonesuch Press, 1931-32), V, 112-13.

5. See the preface to *The Husband his own Cuckold* in *The Works of John Dryden,* ed. Scott and Saintsbury (Edinburgh, 1882-93), XV, 411.

6. John Robert Moore, "Political Allusions in Dryden's Later Plays," *PMLA,* LXXIII (1958), 36, 42.

7. "A Parallel of Poetry and Painting."

8. Preface to *Don Sebastian;* dedication of *Love Triumphant;* letter to Walsh.

9. Preface to *Don Sebastian.*

10. Dedication of *Love Triumphant.*

11. Fujimura similarly defines the nobler pleasure as "the titillation of the mind that wit affords." (Thomas H. Fujimura, *The Restoration Comedy of Wit* [Princeton: Princeton University Press, 1952], p. 51).

12. *Coriolanus,* I, i, and II, iii; *Don Sebastian,* IV.

13. Letter to Steele, *The Critical Works of John Dennis,* ed. Edward N. Hooker (Baltimore: Johns Hopkins Press, 1943), II, 164.

14. *The Hind and the Panther,* Part I, lines 210-11. Dryden uses the same phrase in *Absalom and Achitophel,* line 227. For a discussion of Dryden's undemocratic sentiments, see Louis I. Bredvold, *The Intellectual Milieu of John Dryden: Studies in Some Aspects of Seventeenth-Century Thought* ("University of Michigan Publications in Language and Literature," Vol. XII [Ann Arbor: University of Michigan Press, 1934]), pp. 131-34.

15. *The Hind and the Panther,* Part I, lines 376-83; Part II, lines 128-32.

16. See *The Hind and the Panther,* Part I, lines 160-203. John Robert Moore ("Political Allusions," *PMLA,* pp. 40-41) supposes that in the Mufti Dryden represents certain opportunistic Anglican clergymen who, after preaching passive obedience to James, discerned the rising star of William and began to foment revolt.

17. Bredvold, *Intellectual Milieu,* pp. 164-83.

18. Ned Bliss Allen, *The Sources of John Dryden's Comedies* ("University of Michigan Publications in Language and Literature," Vol. XVI [Ann Arbor: University of Michigan Press, 1935]), pp. 148-49, attributes the use of incest in Dryden's later plays to "the strain which

Dryden was under, especially toward the end, to stimulate the flagging interest of his audiences," and gives the same reason for what he considers to be the extreme indecency of the comic plot of *Don Sebastian.*

19. Allen (*Sources of Dryden's Comedies,* p. 147 and note) implies that the mere use of the expression "piss-pot" is evidence of vulgarization. But in Dryden's time the term apparently did not have the unpleasant connotation it has now. Dryden's Hind, a model of virtue, at one point employs the word "piss" (*The Hind and the Panther,* Part III, line 159). As late as 1743 John Green, M. D., Secretary of the Gentlemen's Society at Spalding, used the expression "piss-pot" in a sober abstract of Hans Egedius' account of the natural history of Greenland (*Philosophical Transactions of the Royal Society,* XLII [1743], 614).

20. Margaret Kober Merzbach, "The Third Source of Dryden's *Amphitryon,*" *Anglia,* LXXIII (1955), 213-14, thinks that Dryden also borrowed some ideas from Thomas Heywood's play *The Silver Age.*

21. See for example Mercury's references to England and France and to city magistrates, and Bromia's reference to women of the town (II, ii).

22. *Works of Dryden,* ed. Scott-Saintsbury, VIII, 95 n.

23. George Macaulay Trevelyan, *England Under the Stuarts* (12th ed., rev.; New York: G. P. Putnam's Sons, 1925), p. 431.

24. David Ogg, *England in the Reigns of James II and William III* (Oxford: Clarendon Press, 1955), p. 153.

25. Trevelyan, *England Under the Stuarts,* p. 431.

26. *Ibid.,* p. 433.

27. *Ibid.*

28. Moore, "Political Allusions," *PMLA,* pp. 37, 39-40.

29. *Dictionary of National Biography* (London, 1950), X, 718.

30. Charles E. Ward, *The Life of John Dryden* (Chapel Hill: University of North Carolina Press, 1961), p. 246.

31. Quoted in *Dryden, The Dramatic Works,* ed. Summers, VI, 402.

32. Dedication of Congreve's edition of Dryden's dramatic works, as reprinted in *Works of Dryden,* ed. Scott-Saintsbury, II, 19.

33. Allen, *Sources of Dryden's Comedies,* pp. 150-51, n. 197.

34. *Works of Dryden,* ed. Scott-Saintsbury, VIII, 369.

35. Jeremy Collier, *A Short View of the Immorality, and Profaneness of the English Stage, Together With the Sense of Antiquity upon This Argument* (London, 1698), pp. 169-70.

CHAPTER VIII

1. Preface to *All for Love.*
2. "Heads of an Answer to Rymer."
3. "Defence of an Essay of Dramatic Poesy."
4. Preface to *Annus Mirabilis*; "A Parallel of Poetry and Painting."

5. William Congreve, "Concerning Humour in Comedy," *Comedies by William Congreve,* ed. Bonamy Dobrée (London, 1925), p. 7. James Merrin, "Theory of Comedy in the Restoration" (Doctoral dissertation, University of Chicago, 1948), p. 164, notes this parallel.

6. *Comedies by William Congreve,* ed. Dobrée, p. 3.

7. *Ibid.,* pp. 5-6.

8. *Ibid.,* pp. 336-37.

9. "The Original and Progress of Satire."

BIBLIOGRAPHY

Allen, Ned Bliss. "The Sources of Dryden's *The Mock Astrologer*," *Philological Quarterly*, XXXVI (1957), 453-64.
————. *The Sources of John Dryden's Comedies*. ("University of Michigan Publications in Language and Literature," Vol. XVI.) Ann Arbor: University of Michigan Press, 1935.

The Annals of Love. London, 1672.

Aristotle. *The Poetics of Aristotle*. Translated by S. H. Butcher. 4th ed. London: Macmillan and Co., 1936.

Baker, David E. *Biographia Dramatica; or, A Companion to the Playhouse*, ed. Isaac Reed. Vol. I. London, 1782.

Beaumont, Francis, and John Fletcher. *Beaumont and Fletcher*, ed. J. St. Loe Strachey. ("Mermaid Series.") 2 vols. New York: A. A. Wyn, 1949.

Bohn, William E. "The Development of John Dryden's Literary Criticism," *Publications of the Modern Language Association*, XXII (1907), 56-139.

Borgman, Albert S. *Thomas Shadwell: His Life and Comedies*. New York: New York University Press, 1928.

Bredvold, Louis I. *The Intellectual Milieu of John Dryden: Studies in Some Aspects of Seventeenth-Century Thought*. ("University of Michigan Publications in Language and Literature," Vol. XII.) Ann Arbor: University of Michigan Press, 1934.

————. "Political Aspects of Dryden's *Amboyna* and *The Spanish Fryar*," *Essays and Studies in English and Comparative Literature*. ("University of Michigan Publications in Language and Literature," Vol. VIII.) Ann Arbor: University of Michigan Press, 1932, pp. 119-32.

Brooks, Harold. "Some Notes on Dryden, Cowley, and Shadwell," *Notes and Queries*, CLXVIII (1935), 94-95.

Buckingham, George Villiers, Duke of. *The Rehearsal*. In *Plays of the Restoration and Eighteenth Century*, ed. Dougald MacMillan and Howard Mumford Jones. New York: Henry Holt and Co., 1931.

Bullen, Arthur Henry (ed.). *A Collection of Old English Plays*. Vol. II. London: Wyman and Sons, 1882-85.

Christie, W. D. (ed.). *The Poetical Works of John Dryden*. London, 1890.

Collier, Jeremy. *A Short View of the Immorality, and Profaneness of the English Stage, Together With the Sense of Antiquity upon this Argument*. London, 1698.

Collins, George Stuart. *Dryden's Dramatic Theory and Praxis*. Leipzig, 1892.

Collins, John Churton. *Essays and Studies*. London, 1895.

Congreve, William. *Comedies by William Congreve*, ed. Bonamy Dobrée. London: Oxford University Press, 1925.

Corneille, Pierre. *Oeuvres de P. Corneille*, ed. M. Ch. Marty-Laveaux. ("Les Grands Écrivains de la France.") Vol. I. Paris, 1862.

Cubbage, Virginia Cox. "The Reputation of John Dryden, 1700-1779." Unpublished Doctoral dissertation, Northwestern University, 1943.

Davies, Thomas. *Dramatic Miscellanies*. Vol. III. London, 1784.

Dennis, John. *The Critical Works of John Dennis*, ed. Edward N. Hooker. 2 vols. Baltimore: Johns Hopkins Press, 1943.

Dobell, Percy J. *John Dryden, Bibliographical Memoranda*. London: Privately printed, 1922.

Dobrée, Bonamy. *Restoration Comedy, 1660-1720*. Oxford: Clarendon Press, 1924.

Doran, Dr. John. *"Their Majesties' Servants": Annals of the English Stage from Thomas Betterton to Edmund Kean*, ed. Robert W. Lowe. Vol. I. London, 1888.

Downes, John. *Roscius Anglicanus; or, an Historical Review of the Stage from 1660 to 1706*, ed. Joseph Knight. ("A Fac-Simile Reprint of the Rare Original of 1708.") London, 1886.

Dryden, John. *Dryden, The Dramatic Works*, ed. Montague Summers. 6 vols. London: Nonesuch Press, 1931-32.

————. *Essays of John Dryden,* ed. W. P. Ker. 2 vols. Oxford: Clarendon Press, 1900.

————. *The Letters of John Dryden, with Letters Addressed to Him,* ed. Charles E. Ward. Durham: Duke University Press, 1942.

————. *The Works of John Dryden.* Vol. VIII, ed. John Harrington Smith, Douglas MacMillan, et al. Berkeley and Los Angeles: University of California Press, 1962.

————. *The Works of John Dryden,* ed. Sir Walter Scott, rev. and corr. George Saintsbury. 18 vols. Edinburgh, 1882-93.

"Dryden's Dramatic Works," *Retrospective Review,* I (1820), 112-61.

D'Urfey, Thomas. *A Fond Husband; or, The Plotting Sisters.* London, 1677.

Eliot, T. S. *John Dryden: The Poet, the Dramatist, the Critic.* New York: Terence and Elsa Holliday, 1932.

Ellis, Amanda M. "Horace's Influence on Dryden," *Philological Quarterly,* IV (1925), 39-60.

Elwin, Malcolm. *The Playgoer's Handbook to Restoration Drama.* London: Jonathan Cape, 1928.

Empson, William. *English Pastoral Poetry.* New York: W. W. Norton and Co., 1938.

Etherege, Sir George. *The Dramatic Works of Sir George Etherege,* ed. H. F. B. Brett-Smith. 2 vols. Oxford: B. Blackwell, 1927.

Evelyn, John. *Memoirs of John Evelyn,* ed. William Bray. London: Frederick Warne and Co., n.d.

Forsythe, Robert Stanley. *The Relations of Shirley's Plays to the Elizabethan Drama.* ("Columbia University Studies in English and Comparative Literature," No. 48.) New York: Columbia University Press, 1914.

Frye, Prosser Hall. "Dryden and the Critical Canons of the Eighteenth Century," *University of Nebraska Studies,* VII (1907), 1-39.

Fujimura, Thomas H. *The Restoration Comedy of Wit.* Princeton: Princeton University Press, 1952.

Gaw, Allison. "Tuke's *Adventures of Five Hours* in Relation to the 'Spanish Plot' and to John Dryden," *Studies in English Drama,* First series, ed. Allison Gaw. ("Publications of the University of Pennsylvania, Series in Philology and Literature," Vol. XIV.) Philadelphia: University of Pennsylvania, 1917, pp. 1-61.

[Gentleman, Francis]. *The Dramatic Censor; or Critical Companion*. Vol. II. London, 1770.

Gosse, Edmund. *A History of Eighteenth Century Literature*. London, 1889.

Grace, John William. "Theory and Practice in the Comedy of John Dryden." Unpublished Doctoral dissertation, University of Michigan, 1956.

Green, John. "An Abstract of a Natural History of Greenland, by Hans Egedius," *Philosophical Transactions of the Royal Society*, XLII (1743), 607-15.

Harbage, Alfred. *Cavalier Drama. An Historical and Critical Supplement to the Study of the Elizabethan and Restoration Stage*. New York: Modern Language Association of America, 1936.

————. "Elizabethan-Restoration Palimpsest," *Modern Language Review*, XXXV (1940), 287-319.

Hartsock, Mildred. "Dryden's Plays: A Study in Ideas," *Seventeenth Century Studies*, Second series, ed. Robert Shafer. Princeton: Princeton University Press, 1937, pp. 71-176.

Hazlitt, William. *The Collected Works of William Hazlitt*, ed. A. R. Waller and Arnold Glover. Vol. VIII. London: J. M. Dent and Co., 1903.

Henneman, John B. "Dryden after Two Centuries (1700-1900)," *Sewanee Review*, IX (1901), 57-72.

Hotson, Leslie. *The Commonwealth and Restoration Stage*. Cambridge, Mass.: Harvard University Press, 1928.

Houston, Percy. "The Inconsistency of John Dryden," *Sewanee Review*, XXII (1914), 469-82.

Huntley, Frank Livingstone. *On Dryden's Essay of Dramatic Poesy*. ("The University of Michigan Contributions in Modern Philology," No. 16.) Ann Arbor: University of Michigan Press, 1951.

Jacob, Giles. *The Poetical Register; or, The Lives and Characters of the English Dramatick Poets*. Vol. I. London, 1719.

Johnson, Samuel. *Lives of the English Poets,* ed. George Birkbeck Hill. Vol. I. Oxford: Clarendon Press, 1905.

Jonson, Ben. *Ben Jonson,* ed. C. H. Herford, Percy and Evelyn Simpson. 11 vols. Oxford: Clarendon Press, 1925-52.

Ker, W. P. (ed.). *Essays of John Dryden.* 2 vols. Oxford: Clarendon Press, 1900.

Krutch, Joseph Wood. *Comedy and Conscience after the Restoration.* New York: Columbia University Press, 1924.

Langbaine, Gerard. *An Account of the English Dramatick Poets.* Oxford, 1691.

————. *Lives and Characters of the English Dramatick Poets,* ed. Charles Gildon. London, 1699.

Lynch, Kathleen M. *The Social Mode of Restoration Comedy.* ("University of Michigan Publications in Language and Literature," Vol. III.) New York: Macmillan Co., 1926.

Macaulay, Thomas Babington. "Dryden," *Edinburgh Review,* XLVII (1828), 1-36.

Macdonald, Hugh. "The Attacks on Dryden," *Essays and Studies by Members of the English Association,* XXI (1936), 41-74.

————. *John Dryden: A Bibliography of Early Editions and of Drydeniana.* Oxford: Clarendon Press, 1939.

Malone, Edmond (ed.). *The Critical and Miscellaneous Prose Works of John Dryden.* Vol. I. London, 1800.

Mandach, André de. *Molière et la comédie de moeurs en Angleterre (1660-1668).* Neuchâtel: à la Baconnière, 1946.

Merrin, James. "Theory of Comedy in the Restoration." Unpublished Doctoral dissertation, University of Chicago, 1948.

Merzbach, Margaret Kober. "The Third Source of Dryden's *Amphitryon,*" *Anglia,* LXXIII (1955), 213-14.

Mignon, Elisabeth. *Crabbed Age and Youth: The Old Men and Women in the Restoration Comedy of Manners.* Durham: Duke University Press, 1947.

Miles, Dudley H. *The Influence of Molière on Restoration Comedy.* New York: Columbia University Press, 1910.

Molière, Jean-Baptiste Poquelin, Sieur de. *Oeuvres de Molière,* ed. Eugène Despois and Paul Mesnard. ("Les Grands

Écrivains de la France.") 13 vols. Paris: Librairie Hachette et Cie., 1873-1900.

Monk, Samuel Holt. *John Dryden: A List of Critical Studies Published from 1895 to 1948.* Minneapolis: University of Minnesota Press, 1950.

Moore, Frank H. "Dr. Pelling, Dr. Pell, and Dryden's Lord Nonsuch." *Modern Language Review,* XLIX (1954), 348-51.

————. "Dryden's Theory and Practice of Comedy." Unpublished Doctoral dissertation, University of North Carolina, 1953.

Moore, John Robert. "Political Allusions in Dryden's Later Plays," *Publications of the Modern Language Association,* LXXIII (1958), 36-42.

Nettleton, George H. *English Drama of the Restoration and Eighteenth Century, 1642-1780.* New York: Macmillan Co., 1914.

Newcastle, William Cavendish, Duke of. *The Humorous Lovers.* London, 1677.

————. *A Pleasante & Merrye Humor off A Roge,* ed. Francis Needham. ("Welbeck Miscellany," No. 1.) Bungay, Suffolk: R. Clay and Sons, Ltd., 1933.

Nicoll, Allardyce. *Dryden as an Adapter of Shakespeare.* ("Shakespeare Association Papers," No. 8.) London: Oxford University Press, 1922.

————. *A History of English Drama, 1660-1900.* 4th ed. Cambridge: Cambridge University Press, 1955.

Noyes, George R. "Dryden as Critic," *The Nation,* LXXI (1900), 231-33.

————(ed.). *The Poetical Works of John Dryden.* Boston: Houghton Mifflin Co., 1909.

————(ed.). *Selected Dramas of Dryden with The Rehearsal.* Chicago: Scott, Foresman and Co., 1910.

Noyes, Robert Gale. *Ben Jonson on the English Stage, 1660-1776.* ("Harvard Studies in English," Vol. XVII.) Cambridge, Mass.: Harvard University Press, 1935.

Odell, George C. D. *Shakespeare from Betterton to Irving.* New York: C. Scribner's Sons, 1920.

Ogg, David. *England in the Reign of Charles II.* 2 vols. Oxford: Clarendon Press, 1955.

——. *England in the Reigns of James II and William III.* Oxford: Clarendon Press, 1955.

Osborn, James M. *John Dryden: Some Biographical Facts and Problems.* New York: Columbia University Press, 1940.

Osborn, Scott C. "Heroical Love in Dryden's Heroic Drama," *Publications of the Modern Language Association,* LXXIII (1958), 480-90.

Pepys, Samuel. *The Diary of Samuel Pepys,* ed. Henry B. Wheatley. 9 vols. London: George Bell and Sons, 1893-1909.

Perry, Henry Ten Eyck. *The First Duchess of Newcastle and Her Husband as Figures in Literary History.* ("Harvard Studies in English," Vol. IV.) Boston: Ginn and Company, 1918.

Plautus, Titus Maccius. *Plautus.* Translated by Paul Nixon. ("The Loeb Classical Library.") Vol. I. New York: G. P. Putnam's Sons, 1916.

Quinault, Philippe. *L'Amant indiscret.* In *Les contemporains de Molière,* ed. Victor Fournel. Vol. I. Paris, 1863-75.

Ristine, Frank Humphrey. *English Tragicomedy, its Origin and History.* New York: Columbia University Press, 1910.

Rundle, James U. "The Source of Dryden's 'Comic Plot' in *The Assignation,*" *Modern Philology,* XLV (1947), 104-11.

Saintsbury, George. *Dryden.* ("English Men of Letters Series.") London, 1881.

Sargeaunt, John (ed.). *The Poems of John Dryden.* London: Oxford University Press, 1948.

Schelling, Felix E. *English Drama.* London: J. M. Dent and Sons, 1914.

Scott, Sir Walter, and George Saintsbury (eds.). *The Works of John Dryden.* 18 vols. Edinburgh, 1882-93.

Shadwell, Thomas. *The Complete Works of Thomas Shadwell,* ed. Montague Summers. 5 vols. London: Fortune Press, 1927.

Sherwood, Margaret. *Dryden's Dramatic Theory and Practice.* ("Yale University Studies in English," Vol. IV.) Boston, 1899.

Smith, David Nichol. *John Dryden.* Cambridge: Cambridge University Press, 1950.

Smith, John Harrington. "The Dryden-Howard Collaboration," *Studies in Philology,* LI (1954), 54-74.

———. "Dryden's Critical Temper," *Washington University Studies, Humanistic Series,* XII (1925), 201-20.

———. *The Gay Couple in Restoration Comedy.* Cambridge, Mass.: Harvard University Press, 1948.

Smith, Russell J. "Shadwell's Impact upon Dryden," *Review of English Studies,* XX (1944), 29-44.

Spencer, Hazleton. *Shakespeare Improved.* Cambridge, Mass.: Harvard University Press, 1927.

Sprague, Arthur C. *Beaumont and Fletcher on the Restoration Stage.* Cambridge, Mass.: Harvard University Press, 1926.

Summers, Montague (ed.). *Dryden, The Dramatic Works.* 6 vols. London: Nonesuch Press, 1931-32.

Tave, Stuart M. "Corbyn Morris: Falstaff, Humor, and Comic Theory in the Eighteenth Century," *Modern Philology,* L (1952), 102-15.

Trevelyan, George Macaulay. *England Under the Stuarts.* 12th ed., rev. New York: G. P. Putnam's Sons, 1925.

Tuke, Sir Samuel. *The Adventures of Five Hours,* ed. B. van Thal. London: R. Holden and Co., n.d.

Verrall, A. W. *Lectures on Dryden,* ed. Margaret de G. Verrall. Cambridge: Cambridge University Press, 1914.

Wallerstein, Ruth. "Dryden and the Analysis of Shakespeare's Techniques," *Review of English Studies,* XIX (1943), 165-85.

Walpole, Horace. *The Works of Horatio Walpole, Earl of Orford.* Vol. II. London, 1798.

Ward, A. W. *A History of English Dramatic Literature to the Death of Queen Anne.* Vol. II. London, 1875.

Ward, Charles E. "Dryden's Drama, 1662-1677: A Study in the Native Tradition." Unpublished Doctoral dissertation, Duke University, 1934.

———(ed.). *The Letters of John Dryden, with Letters Addressed to Him.* Durham: Duke University Press, 1942.

———. *The Life of John Dryden.* Chapel Hill: University of North Carolina Press, 1961.

Whiting, George W. "The Condition of the London Theaters,

1679-83: A Reflection of the Political Situation," *Modern Philology,* XXV (1927), 195-206.

————. "Political Satire in London Stage Plays, 1680-83," *Modern Philology,* XXVIII (1930), 29-43.

Wilcox, John. *The Relation of Molière to Restoration Comedy.* New York: Columbia University Press, 1938.

Wilson, John Harold. *The Court Wits of the Restoration.* Princeton: Princeton University Press, 1948.

————. *The Influence of Beaumont and Fletcher on Restoration Drama.* ("Ohio State University Studies in Language and Literature," No. 4.) Columbus: Ohio State University, 1928.

Wood, Anthony à. *Athenae Oxonienses,* ed. Philip Bliss. 4 vols. London, 1813-20.

Wycherley, William. *The Complete Works of William Wycherley,* ed. Montague Summers. 4 vols. Soho: Nonesuch Press, 1924.

INDEX